23⁹⁵

Medical power
in prisons

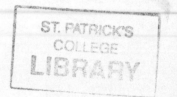

CRIME, JUSTICE AND SOCIAL POLICY
Series Editors: Phil Scraton, Joe Sim and Paula Skidmore

Titles in the series include:

Tony Jefferson: *The case against paramilitary policing*
Mick Ryan and Tony Ward: *Privatization and the penal system*
Joe Sim: *Medical power in prisons*

Medical power
in prisons

THE PRISON MEDICAL
SERVICE IN
ENGLAND 1774–1989

Joe Sim

Open University Press

MILTON KEYNES · PHILADELPHIA

Open University Press
Celtic Court
22 Ballmoor
Buckingham MK18 1XW

and

1900 Frost Road, Suite 101
Bristol, PA 19007, USA

First Published 1990

Copyright © Joe Sim

British Library Cataloguing in Publication Data

Sim, Joe
    Medical power in prisons: the prison medical service in
    England 1774 – 1988. – (Crime, justice and social policy)
    1. Great Britain. Prisons. Health Service
    I. Title   II. series
    365.66

    ISBN 0-335-15183-3   ISBN 0-335-15182-5 (pbk)

Library of Congress Cataloging-in-Publication Data

Sim, Joe
      Medical power in prisons: the prison medical service in England
    1774 – 1988 / Joe Sim.
        p. cm.—(Crime, justice, and social policy)
      ISBN 0-335-15183-3   ISBN 0-335-15182-5 (pbk.)
        1. Prisoners—Medical care—England—History.   I. Title.   II. Series.
    [DNLM. 1. Health Services—history—England. 2. Prisoners—
    psychology. 3. Prisons—history—England. 4. Public Policy—
    history—England. 5. Social Control, Formal. HV 8833 S588m
    HV8844.G7S56   1990
    365'.66—dc20   90-6926 CIP
    DNLM/DLC   for Library of Congress

Typeset by Rowland Phototypesetting Ltd
Bury St Edmunds, Suffolk
Printed in Great Britain by
St Edmundsbury Press Ltd, Bury St Edmunds, Suffolk

To Tillie and Joe for the past;
to Jamie and Richie for the future.

Contents

Preface

The nature and philosophy of regimes for the imprisoned has been the central cornerstone in debates about penology since the emergence of the modern prison at the end of the eighteenth century. The continuing resonance of this question, both within the state and in popular consciousness, and the powerful emotions which it generates, is inextricably linked to the perceived role of the prison as a bulwark against an encroaching tide of crime, deviance and disorder. The umbilical cord which ties prisons and crime together is built on a fundamental proposition: if prison regimes are 'easy' then the crime rate will rise, if they are 'hard' then criminal behaviour will be either held in check or even decline because of the visible threat of punishment that confinement poses to individual lawbreakers and the wider collective who consider themselves to be law-abiding. Since the late eighteenth century it is this latter view that has prevailed.

A number of important consequences have flowed from this view. First, and most clearly, it has resulted in double punishment for the confined. Not only are they deprived of their liberty and feel the pain which this engenders but also they endure physically decrepit and alienating regimes which for many inflict further psychological and physical distress. Second, all aspects of prison life – from letters and visits to recreation and education – have been subjugated to the disciplinary vice of retribution and punishment. They have become mechanisms not of empowerment and human development, but strategies for individual regulation and collective control. Finally, it has led to the confined reacting negatively and often violently to a system which they perceive to be relentless and impenetrable.

This book explores these themes through analysing the history and consolidation of the Prison Medical Service (PMS) in England and Wales. At one level this subject would seem to contradict the arguments outlined above. As a body of knowledge and as a profession, medical science occupies a pivotal and symbolic place in the consciousness of our culture. Medicine is positioned as the embodiment of virtue, the triumph of science over superstition where accuracy, certainty and neutrality have replaced expediency and guesswork in healing physical and psychological pain. Yet, the analysis of the PMS developed in this book reveals a more complex reality than a benevolent reading of medical history allows. It challenges the view that medical care for prisoners has been a journey from barbarism to enlightenment. It argues that prison medical workers, rather than operating from a perspective bereft of ideology and politics, have been intimately involved in reinforcing the discipline of penality, attempting to create the well-adjusted individual from the undifferentiated mass of criminals lying dangerously behind the penitentiary's walls. As the book makes clear, the will to discipline has had a profound impact on the level of medical care that prisoners have received since the end of the eighteenth century with deleterious and sometimes fatal consequences for a number of them.

The book also examines the role of medicine in maintaining the fragile order in prisons. This has operated at two levels. First it examines the relationship between prison medical workers and the physical and chemical programmes of control which have been utilized in the last two hundred years. Second, it analyses how medicine has worked at an ideological level through reinforcing individualistic explanations of deviance which dominate state policies, particularly towards those regarded as disorderly, recalcitrant and difficult. At the same time, it points to the deeply embedded and significant patterns of resistance developed by prisoners and prisoners' rights organizations and the strategies they have adopted to deny medicine a position of hegemonic domination within penal establishments. The dialectics of prisoner resistance is thus a central theme in the book's analysis.

Finally, it should be noted that this area of prison research has been a particular source of controversy in the last decade or so. There have been a number of libel actions instigated against individuals who have written and researched in the area. In the light of these actions this book has been subjected to close scrutiny by a libel lawyer and has involved a degree of self-censorship which is perhaps rare in contemporary academic work. The final text, therefore, reflects and has taken account of the current laws covering libel in this country.

Joe Sim

Acknowledgements

In the last eight years many people have contributed, in more ways than I can count, to the production of this book. Thanks, then, to the following for their support: Kristi Ballinger, Tia Ballinger, Gillian Hall, Susan O'Malley, Pete Beharrell, Tony Jefferson, David Hayden, Janet Johnson, Dave MacDonald, Tim Owen, Linda Quinn, Chris Powell, Michael Ignatieff, Victoria Greenwood, Paul Gordon, Pat Craddock, Dave Llewellyn, Dave Godwin, Mike Fitzgerald, Pete Archard, Ayesha Saleem, Sheila Scraton, Geoff Coggan, Gareth Pierce, Mick Ryan, Tony Ward, Penny Smith, Phil Thomas, Tony Bunyan, Hilary Wilson, Catherine Hall, Margaret Ward, Anne-Marie Webster, Ricky Webster, Teresa Sim, Billie Sim, Jimmy Boyle, Sarah Boyle, and Courtney Griffiths, to Phil Scraton and Paula Skidmore for their editorial comments; to Stuart Hall for his critical comments on earlier drafts, which were central to the book's development; to Paul Gilroy and Vron Ware, whose discussions, beds and food were particularly important at crucial moments; to Paddy Hillyard and Pat Carlen, whose overview provided me with the best possible basis for a final draft; to John Skelton of the Open University Press, who in his musical tastes and patient support should set the standards for book publishers.

Students I have worked with in the last five years on undergraduate courses at Liverpool Polytechnic and the postgraduate MA at Edge Hill College in Ormskirk provided critical and challenging environments for my ideas.

Despite their own commitments caused by the present outrageous educational policies colleagues at Liverpool Polytechnic gave me the time and space to discuss and develop some of the themes in this book. In particular, Marion Price, Pauline Pasker, Peter MacMyler, John Hewitt, Tim Ashplant, Sandra Walklate, Pete Gill, Mike Brogden, Stan Meredith, David Amigoni, Brenda Day, Lorraine Glover, Linda Halliwell, Peter Bailey and Paul Smith.

Staff in the following libraries were extremely helpful: Liverpool Polytechnic; Open University; Gloucester Hospital, especially Helga Perry; Prison Service Staff College, Wakefield; Institute of Criminology, Cambridge;

British Library; Liverpool University Medical Library; the Home Office; Liverpool Central, especially Mark Urbanowicz; Public Record Office, Kew; Wellcome Institute for the History of Medicine.

Bob Dylan and his 'chimes of freedom' gave me necessary musical relaxation over the years.

Finally, the book would never have been finished without the support, encouragement, technical skills and intellectual insights of Anette Ballinger. A sentence or two does not do justice to her contribution to the finished product. It shines through on every page.

CHAPTER 1

Analysing the prison medical service: the sociological context

It is a subtle, erosive process. Almost every agency of education, social welfare and mental health talks the seductive language of prevention, diagnosis and treatment; and almost every client is a hostage to an exchange which trades momentary comfort and institutional peace for an indefinite future of maintenance and control.[1]

This book is concerned with the origins, development and consolidation of medical power in English prisons. Until now, there has been no serious sociological study of the men and women who make up the medical service in the prisons of England. Indeed, it was only in 1984 that the first book dealing with the service's role and practice was published.[2] While critical of some aspects of its work, the book limited itself to a general overview of health care for the confined, rather than a specific analysis of why medicine takes the form that it does in prisons. In addressing this more specific sociological question, this chapter utilizes the recent work of a number of writers in the area of prison history, most notably Michel Foucault. It considers the different sociological dimensions arising from his work which taken together provide the theoretical context for the analysis of the Prison Medical Service (PMS) in English prisons. There are three dimensions which are particularly important. First, there is the use of a historical perspective to identify the continuities and discontinuities in the relationship between medical power and the confined. Second, there is the issue of resistance to power and domination and the theoretical questions that derive from this. Finally, there is the question of power itself and its relevance to the emergence and consolidation of a discourse articulated by those who came to see themselves as a professional body of medical workers dealing with a deviant and disorderly group.

1

PRISONS IN HISTORY

Until the late 1960s, with the notable exception of Georg Rusche and Otto Kirkhheimer's *Punishment and Social Structure*, published three decades earlier, the emergence and consolidation of prisons throughout Western Europe and North America was portrayed as a process of benevolent evolution, a movement from barbarism to enlightenment. This process was regarded as independent of wider structures of political economy, social class, ideology and power.[3] However, at the end of the 1960s and throughout the 1970s and 1980s, the idea that prison regimes and philosophies had humanely and significantly progressed was severely jolted in the aftermath of a number of major and bloody disturbances in Europe and North America.

On 24 October 1969 there was a serious disturbance at Parkhurst on the Isle of Wight in the course of which thirty-five prison officers and twenty-eight prisoners were injured.[4] In November 1970 there was a strike at Folsom Prison in California: it was the longest and best supported in that state's penal history. For nineteen days, 2,400 prisoners demonstrated their support for a thirty-one-point prison manifesto that demanded a radical overhaul of the prison system.[5] On 21 August 1971 George Jackson, the black revolutionary and author of the highly acclaimed *Soledad Brother*, was shot dead in San Quentin, California. It was said by the prison authorities that he and two other prisoners who died had been attempting to escape. Within a month, prisoners at Attica Prison in New York State, deeply affected by Jackson's death, occupied 'D' Yard, and held it for three days. On 13 September state troopers stormed the prison, retook the yard and shot dead thirty-four prisoners and nine prison officer hostages.[6] Finally, in the summer of 1972, there were strikes in over 30 British prisons, a major disturbance at Peterhead maximum security prison in Scotland and at the end of the year another at Inverness Prison in the north of the country, which resulted in one prison officer losing an eye. Four of those involved, who were serving life sentences, were given an extra six years.[7]

This is not a complete list of the confrontations and disturbances that occurred in Western Europe and North American prisons at this time. None the less, these events do illustrate the serious challenge that was emerging to the authority and legitimacy of the penal systems on both continents. It was a challenge which in North America at least was driven and fuelled by an increasing political consciousness especially among black prisoners who were making connections between struggles inside and conflict outside of the walls.[8] As Angela Davis wrote at the time:

> Prisoners – especially Blacks, Chicanos and Puerto Ricans – are increasingly advancing the proposition that they are *political* prisoners. They contend that they are political prisoners in the sense that they are largely the victims of an oppressive politico-economic order, swiftly becoming conscious of the causes underlying their victimisation.[9]

These upheavals within the prisons were related to the more general political and economic schisms that gripped Western capitalist democracies in the late

2

1960s. In Europe, these schisms crystallized around the moment of May 1968 and the demonstrations and uprisings in Paris. In North America, it was the increasing polarization brought about by American involvement in South-East Asia. Both influenced each other.[10] These events had a profound impact on criminology fracturing the dominant positivist/labelling axis and laying the foundations for the emergence of the Marxist paradigm which was to be characterized as 'the new criminology'.[11] They were also to have a significant impact on those academics interested in the development of institutions such as prisons and asylums. Their researches too were a challenge to the dominant evolutionary paradigm within which prisons up until then had been theorized.

In February 1971 the Groupe d'Information sur les Prisons (GIP) was established in France. The group was committed to creating the conditions in which prisoners could not only speak for themselves but also would be heard. In other words, the GIP challenged the traditional apparatus of secrecy that dominated the French penal system. It did this by supporting and publicizing the struggles of prisoners, particularly the thirty or so revolts that occurred in France in the winter of 1971–2. In relation to prison secrets, the group's ideas were quite clear, to break down the secrecy that was an essential element 'of its normal functioning' and to create 'the possibility for other kinds of discourse on prisons'.[12] It was interested in mounting a 'particular local attack on the social regime of truth which served to disrupt for a time the State apparatus of punishment'.[13]

Michel Foucault was involved with the GIP. In April 1972 he visited Attica. In a subsequent interview with John Simon, which was published in *Telos* in the spring of 1974, Foucault outlined the ideas that were to be developed three years later with the publication of the seminal *Discipline and Punish: The Birth of the Prison*. In the interview he described Attica as a 'machine' and took issue with the humanitarian idea that prisons were there to rehabilitate and reform the confined: rather, prisons were about discipline and elimination. Within the walls psychiatry played its part in this process:

> Attica is a machine for elimination, a form of prodigious stomach, a kidney which consumes, destroys, breaks up and then rejects, and which consumes in order to eliminate what it has already eliminated. You remember that when we visited Attica they spoke to us about the four wings of the building, the four corridors, the four large corridors A, B, C, and D. Well, I learned again through the same former prisoner, that there is a fifth corridor which they didn't talk to us about; it's the corridor E. And you know which that one is?

SIMON: No.

FOUCAULT: Ah, well, it is quite simply the machine of the machine, or rather the elimination of the elimination, elimination in the second degree; it's the psychiatric wing. That's where they send the ones who cannot even be integrated into the machine and whom the machinery cannot succeed in assimilating according to its norms, that it cannot

3

crush in accordance with its own mechanical process. Thus they need an additional mechanism.[14]

In 1978, the year after the publication of *Discipline and Punish*, Michael Ignatieff published *A Just Measure of Pain*. Again the book was a historical study and once more challenged the theory of benevolent reform as it had been applied by academics to the prison system in England in the years between 1750 and 1850. For Ignatieff, the philanthropy that reformers such as John Howard and Elizabeth Fry were expressing was not simply a humane concern for the incarcerated but the yearning for 'what they imagined to be a more stable, orderly and coherent social order . . . a new strategy of class relations'.[15] In the preface to the book, Ignatieff set his analysis within what he termed the breakdown of 'the fragile order inside prisons',[16] which was followed by 'nearly a decade of hostage-takings, demonstrations and full-scale uprisings. At first an American phenomenon, the prison revolt has spread to prisons in Spain, France, Canada, Britain and Italy'.[17] Once more, Attica loomed large in his deliberations as an example of 'the issue of the morality of state power in its starkest form'.[18]

A third strand in critical work on prisons appeared in English in 1981 under the title of *The Prison and the Factory*. Originally written in 1977 by Dario Melossi and Massimo Pavarini, the book outlined what the authors saw as the functional connection between prisons and the capitalist mode of production. Put at its starkest, their thesis was based on the idea that the capitalist organization of labour 'shapes the form of the prisons as it does all other institutions . . . the only modifications are those required by the evolving exigencies of capitalism'.[19] In the introduction to the book, the authors pointed once more to the fact that their initial interest in the history of the prison 'was aroused during the late 1960s at a time when this institution in Italy (and elsewhere) was thrown into a deep crisis'.[20]

For the purposes of the present study what was important about this body of work, despite the theoretical differences between the authors,[21] was that each emphasized a historical perspective that eschewed benevolent progression for more structural dimensions of political economy, social class, ideology and power.

Additionally, both Foucault and Ignatieff raised questions about the role of medicine and psychiatry in prisons and asylums. Once more, they moved beyond the idea that medicine had evolved as a set of benevolent practices and benign programmes which has been (and still is) the dominant view of institutional health care.[22] For Foucault, the great reform movement in the asylums in the second half of the eighteenth century was not a sign of psychiatric progress but was better conceptualized as a 'strange regression':

medicine engaged in the first instance with the subjects constituted in the space of exclusion not so much in order to differentiate crime from madness or evil from illness but rather to act as protector of those endangered by the 'permeable' walls of the houses of confinement . . . the power to cure

4

wielded by the doctor derived at root from the key structures of bourgeois society.[23]

For Ignatieff, the introduction of medical personnel into prisons revolved around the issue of disciplining the confined, making their bodies and minds pliable to the new social order and class relationships of capitalism. In that sense, health care, bathing and medical inspection were not simply benevolent innovations but were part of the wider imposition of discipline and regulation.

This book picks up on the original insights of both Foucault and Ignatieff. In particular, the question of discipline, regulation and exclusion which they see as integral to the genesis of medicine in institutions is traced from the late eighteenth century to the present. Such regulation is not simply based on the more obvious manifestations of discipline such as drugs, straitjackets or cellular confinement but also crystallizes around how medical care itself developed within the disciplinary thrust of prison regimes. Throughout the nineteenth and into the twentieth century the discipline of less-eligibility underpinned penality so that it was widely felt that prisoners could not and should not live and work in conditions superior to those outside the walls of the penitentiary. As the book illustrates, ideologically prison medical workers were not free from these wider concerns nor indeed from the concerns that arose in relation to maintaining order internally behind the walls. In that sense, the relationship between medicine and the confined was much more complex and contradictory than the evolutionary model of medical benevolence has hitherto recognized.

RESISTING DOMINATION

The question of resistance to medical power and its theoretical relationship to the wider sociological debates around class struggle, forms the second, central theme in this book. As different chapters will indicate, men and women, both young and old, have, individually and collectively, raised serious questions about the health care of the confined and the role of medicine in controlling the behaviour of the ill-disciplined and recalcitrant. These protests have been supported, particularly through the twentieth century, by outside pressure groups who have called for significant and fundamental changes to be made in the management and work of the PMS.

The importance of consciousness and resistance within concrete political and material settings has formed the basis for a series of publications which have analysed the uneven development of collective and group action in England. These studies have focused on craft-guilds, youth subcultures, black people and the past and present women's movement.[24] As John Clarke et al. point out, these studies emphasize the dynamic relations between different classes and groups:

> Negotiation, resistance, struggle; the relations between a subordinate and a dominant culture, whenever they fall within this spectrum are always

intensely active, always oppositional in a structural sense. . . . Their outcome is not given but *made*. The subordinate class brings to this 'theatre of struggle' a repertoire of strategies and responses – ways of coping as well as of resisting.[25]

Historians have been pivotal to this analysis. In particular, the question of consciousness and resistance to domination has been tied to the wider framework of understanding social reality from the point of view of the powerless through what George Lefebvre called 'history from below'. As Harvey Kaye has argued, the work of Maurice Dobb, Christopher Hill, Eric Hobsbawm, Sheila Rowbotham and Edward Thompson has forced a reconsideration of the question of social class in general and forms of struggle in particular:

> We are now asked to see class in terms of people's experiences and activities structured especially but not exclusively by their productive relations with those experiences and activities expressed in class sometimes 'fully' class-conscious ways. But to pursue such class struggle analysis we must understand the class struggle experience in its totality and its many forms of articulation.[26]

Two studies, in particular, have relevance for the perspective taken in this book. First, there is the work of Stephen Humphries and his study *Hooligans or Rebels? An Oral History of Working-Class Childhood*. The book traces the history of working-class youth subcultures between 1889 and 1939. A central theme in this history is the resistance of working-class youth to the imposition into their lives of school discipline and reformatory punishment. This resistance manifested itself in a number of different ways from subverting school syllabuses, challenging the authority of teachers, organizing strikes and finally to resisting the regimes in juvenile reformatories through escape attempts. Humphries's conclusions are worth quoting in full as they provide a lens through which seemingly pathological behaviour can be more clearly and correctly understood:

> For young people who stubbornly resisted bourgeois institutions through sabotage at school and work, persistent truancy, violent conflicts with teachers, social crime and street-gang subcultures were, as we have seen, major targets for disciplinary and corrective treatment in the reformatory. But this opposition could not be completely suppressed despite the constant resort to brutal authoritarian methods. The recollections of old people clearly reveal that this powerful undercurrent of resistance, which obstructed official aims even in institutions such as the reformatory, cannot be dismissed simply as an expression of the ignorance, immorality and immaturity that middle-class commentators have commonly attributed to working-class youth. Instead this resistance can best be understood as a discriminating response to the contradictions and inequality that were experienced in all spheres of life. Working-class people's memories of

6

childhood and youth illuminate the fundamental importance of anger, resentment, and hostility in motivating the anti-social, delinquent and undisciplined behaviour of which they stand accused in the official records.[27]

Frances Fox Piven and Richard Cloward make a similar point in *Poor People's Movements*. They see the relationship between social location, forms of defiance and resistance to domination as fundamental to poor people's social movements. They classify this resistance as structured, political behaviour which is deliberate and purposeful. It possesses a rationality and sense of direction which contradicts the functionalist accounts of Talcott Parsons and Neil Smelser, who emphasize what they see as irrationality and pathology in such behaviour. As importantly, for Piven and Cloward, this rational response is focused on specific targets within the daily experience of those involved:

> people experience deprivation and oppression within a concrete setting, not as the end product of large and abstract processes, and it is the concrete experience that moulds their discontent into specific grievances against specific targets . . . it is the daily experience of people that shapes their grievances, establishes the measure of their demands and points out the targets of their anger . . . institutional roles determine the strategic opportunities for defiance, for it is typically by rebeling against the rules and authorities associated with their everyday activities that people protest.[28]

As the book indicates, resistance to medical power has been integral to the development of the PMS. It is a history which has until now remained submerged. Close scrutiny of this history reveals a complex picture in which medical personnel have faced a series of different strategies from ridicule to murder in the attempt to consolidate their professional position within the prisons. In that sense, the power of the service has never been absolute but has been constrained and contested both by prisoners on the ground and by state servants such as prison officers who have remained unconvinced that medical power, particularly in its psychiatric and psychological manifestations, possesses the key to unlocking the door of criminality. Once more, resistance to medical power has found no part in the histories of prison medicine to which I referred above. Professional power has been seen to evolve benevolently and independently, uncontested in its work and unbiased in its orientation. It is the question of professional power itself and its theorization, which is the third dimension that underpins this book.

POWER AND PRISONS

The question of power has long been a focus of attention both in sociology and the sociology of law.[29] Within criminology, however, the marginalization of the concept has been one of a number of theoretical weaknesses in the discipline.

These theoretical gaps began to be filled only with the publication in 1973 of *The New Criminology*. While this book argued for a criminology that was both committed in practice and coherent in theory, the authors' programme for the development of a radical paradigm was not without its own weaknesses. These omissions included the schematic treatment of Marxism, the submergence of the experience of women and black people, the marginalization of resistance and the absence of any in-depth consideration of power and the state.[30] However, *The New Criminology*, and the critical work which followed it, was important in shifting the analysis of crime and crime control away from the eclectic, individualized positivism characteristic of British criminology,[31] and on to a terrain which attempted to theorize the impact that the wider dynamics of the political economy of capitalism has on individual behaviour. At the same time, the weaknesses in the theoretical base of the radical paradigm meant that concepts have been 'borrowed' and utilized from other disciplines to extend its analytical capabilities. This has led to the development of an important body of work which has included applying the insights of Nicos Poulantzas and Ralph Miliband on the state to the development of police power;[32] utilizing Gramsci's concept of hegemony to pinpoint the shift towards a more authoritarian state form;[33] analysing the construction of black criminality from the perspective of concepts derived in the field of cultural studies;[34] and critically evaluating the relationship of women to the law using the theoretical insights of feminist analysis.[35] Within these studies power and the state have played an increasingly pivotal role.

A similar argument can be applied to the sociology of the prison. It is only since the early 1970s that a critical sociological perspective has emerged to challenge the positivistic functionalism of earlier prison studies.[36] These critical studies have emphasized the rationality of prisoners' behaviour particularly during major disturbances, the resistance of prisoners to prison regimes and the role of the prison in maintaining order within capitalism.[37] This perspective stands in diametric opposition to the earlier studies, which emphasized individual pathology and psychological degeneration within the prison population. However, as with the radical paradigm in general, there are a number of theoretical gaps in these critical accounts. As Michael Ignatieff has pointed out, there are a range of areas that remain to be addressed before a full, critical and analytical account of the prison system emerges. These include the history of drug use 'as therapeutic and control devices' and the 'ascendency, of the psychiatric and social work professions within the carceral system'.[38] The work of Michel Foucault in relation to the question of power provides some of the theoretical tools necessary to fill the gap relating to the ascendency of medical and psychiatric personnel.

POWER AND MEDICINE

Foucault's analysis of power develops along a number of dimensions. First, he rejects analyses of power which place a dominant class, state or sovereign at the centre of its implementation. Rather power is dispersed through the body of society. Foucault is therefore concerned with the means through which power is exercised and the effects of this exercise. Second, he places the processes of discipline, surveillance, individualization and normalization at the centre of his analysis. These processes were key elements in the emergence of the medical profession within and without institutions at the end of the eighteenth century. Medical discourse was part of a disciplinary strategy which extended 'control over minutiae of the conditions of life and conduct'.[39] Within this discourse the doctor became 'the great advisor and expert'.[40]

These processes were particularly apparent in the prison, 'that darkest region in the apparatus of justice'.[41] The emergence of the institution and the professional groups who staffed it was built around discipline where the body of prisoners was broken down and fragmented into individual cellular spaces 'thus allowing their control and ordering through routines and time-tables'.[42] The consolidation of medical knowledge reinforced this fragmentation, constant surveillance and individualized documentation became corner-stones in penality. This body of knowledge regulated 'the exercise of penitentiary practice'.[43] The prison became a laboratory in which the advice and expertise of the medical profession, both physicians and psychiatrists, was geared to reintegrating the confined back to normality. Domination through observation objectified the prisoner as 'diagnoses began to be made of normality and abnormality and of the appropriate procedures to achieve a rehabilitation . . . to the norm'.[44] In this way probing, testing, studying and examining the body and mind of the confined was intrinsic to the development of power relationships:

> the examination is at the center of the procedures that constitute the individual as effect and object of power, as effect and object of knowledge. It is the examination which, by combining hierarchical surveillance and normalizing judgement, assures the great disciplinary functions of distribution and classification.[45]

Medical discourse was therefore part of a disciplinary project orientated to

> creating a model individual, conducting his life according to the precepts of health, and creating a medicalized society in order to bring the conditions of life and conduct in line with requirements of health.[46]

Behind the walls of the penitentiary medicine took its place alongside psychology and criminology in correcting, disciplining and normalizing the confined in a laboratory where punishment 'function[s] openly as treatment'.[47]

Finally, it is also important to note that power is resisted. Foucault points to the different forms of opposition that have emerged in western societies to challenge the imposition of power. This opposition cannot be reduced to the notion of class struggle but includes women struggling against male power, the mentally ill against psychiatric power and sections of the population against medical power.[48]

The processes described by Foucault can be applied to the development and consolidation of the PMS. Those who have staffed the service from the late eighteenth century to the present have built their position on their unique access to, and surveillance of, the confined. This applies to prisoners individually and as a collective social body. Such surveillance and the knowledge generated has been inextricably tied to the processes of less eligibility referred to above. In addition, it has also been tied to the narrow concern of managing the system internally and in a wider sense to contributing to the policing of more general social divisions. The creation of categories of deviance has been a central element in this process as prison doctors have taken an active part in the debates about the philosophy of imprisonment and the wider social problem that the criminal and the 'dangerous classes' appeared to pose to the health of the society. As I shall show, normalization of the individual criminal and of the class has been a prerogative which has governed the everyday work and research of prison medical personnel. Categorization through observation not only has contributed to the doctors' claims to be treated as professionals but also ideologically has sustained the individualized views of criminality and its restricted class-based location that have come to dominate popular and academic analyses of the problem. Prison medical workers through their researches therefore have helped to create new categories of deviance and in so doing have contributed to that very narrow understanding of criminal (and more general social) behaviour which predominates in our society.

The disciplinary web which lies at the centre of penality and in which prisoners have been positioned has thus underpinned the work of prison medical workers. At the same time, it is a web which has often proved to be fragile and brittle as prisoners and their supporters have contested the nature of the interventions made by this group into their lives. It has also proved fragile in a more general sense for even on their own terms prison medical personnel are no nearer to uncovering the roots of criminality or disorder than their eighteenth- and nineteenth-century counterparts. Taken together, both challenges raise fundamental questions about the efficacy of medical power in dealing with penal and social problems. It is the significance of this point rather than acquiescing to further medicalization that contemporary prison managers might care to ponder.

CHAPTER 2

The genesis of the prison medical service

Medical care for the confined has its origins in the profound transformation which took place in the Criminal Justice System in the second half of the eighteenth century. There were a series of interventions made by social reformers at this time who were concerned not only with changing the nature of prison regimes but also the philosophical basis of punishment itself.[1] Among the reforms was the provision of systematic health care for prisoners. This was in 1774 when the Health of Prisoners Act (14 Geo. III C. 59) was passed. This Act empowered Justices of the Peace to intervene in the administration of the prisons in order to ensure the maintenance of health standards within them. The Justices could order the scraping and white-washing of walls as well as the provision of sick-rooms, ventilation and regular washing and cleaning facilities. In addition, they were 'allowed to appoint "an experienced Surgeon or Apothecary" paying him from the rates; he was to report on the health of the prisoners'.[2] While a surgeon was appointed in Newgate in 1692 and some Houses of Correction had employed surgeons from their earliest days, the Act was the first to make statutory provision for the medical care of the confined.[3]

The Bedfordshire landowner, John Howard, was deeply involved in the reform movement. He recorded the anatomy of, and abuses in, every prison in the country. The results were published in March 1777 in his seminal work, *The State of the Prisons*. As Michael Ignatieff has pointed out, Howard's concerns extended beyond benevolent reform. He was also intent on disciplining the incarcerated. Disease in institutions had a moral as well as a physical cause:

The poor were 'bound in the chains' of addiction to riotous living, sexual indulgence and intemperance. They were susceptible to disease because they were susceptible to vice. . . . Like the hospital, the penitentiary was created to enforce a quarantine both moral and medical. Behind its walls the contagion of criminality would be isolated from the healthy, moral population outside. Within the prison itself the separate confinement of

11

each offender in a cell would prevent the bacillus of vice from spreading from the hardened to the uninitiate.[4]

Howard represented and crystallized the views of medical practitioners and social commentators of the time. The powerful voices of these organic intellectuals, speaking for the rising bourgeoisie, set the parameters within which crime and deviance was understood. The morality of the poor, the sobriety of their habits and the concern for social order provided the wider canvas on which the Prison Medical Service developed. Dr John Aikin's pamphlet on *The Character and Public Services of the Late John Howard* (published in 1792) extolled his life in the public arena and his efforts to improve the conditions of the poor by giving them 'a sober and useful education'. This included establishing schools for both sexes where girls were taught reading and needlework 'in a plain way' while boys learned reading, writing and the rudiments of arithmetic. Importantly, Aiken also clarified Howard's conception of medicine in prison and the relationship between health care inside and the demands of the new industrial order. If health care was to be provided, it had to be done in a way which did not better or indeed equal the care that those beyond the walls received. Less eligibility was a corner-stone of Howard's programme:

> he convinced himself that it was the duty of every society to pay due attention to the *health* and in some degree, even to the *comforts* of *all* who are held in a state of confinement. . . . It was, however, by no means his wish . . . to render a prison so comfortable an abode that the lowest order of society might find their condition even bettered by admission into it. On the contrary the system of discipline he desired to establish, was such as would appear extremely grievous to those of an idle and licentious disposition.[5]

The link between vice and disease was highlighted by others involved in the establishment of the early PMS. In 1795 J. M. Good, who was the physician at Coldbath Fields Prison, responded to a request from the Medical Society of London by publishing *A Dissertation on the Diseases of Prisons and Workhouses,* in which he argued that 'the greater number of all disorders in prisons and workhouses proceeded from inattention to cloathing and cleanliness'.[6] He suggested a number of reforms: prison infirmaries should be in a detached building in the most unfrequented spot in the institution, beds should be kept at a distance from each other and windows should be large, long and well-ventilated. Water closets should also be introduced, while food should never be cooked in the wards. With these medical and other changes

> the institution will flourish, the concerns of morality and religion will prevail, the grand object of this dissertation will be attained, and the poor will be cheerful and happy.[7]

Good had long boasted of his friendship with Howard as a source of 'high benefit and advantage'.[8] He argued that illnesses such as ulcers, the itch and venereal disease, which were common in prisons and poorhouses, did not originate in places of public confinement but were 'solely introduced by those who enter in consequence of prior vice, misfortune or uncleanliness'.[9] Disease derived from 'want of pure air, want of exercise and proper diet, depredations of spirit, exposure to cold and uncleanliness'. He concluded with his views on the construction of institutions:

> Prisons and poorhouses should be built on the brow of a hill so that fresh breezes could blow over it. Within the institution, if there was any room alloted for common intercourse it should be large and lofty, the night rooms should not be crowded and a bedstead and bedding should be allocated to each individual. Great advantages to health result from private and solitary cells.[10]

John Fothergill, another medical man, was Howard's closest friend 'and eventual co-adjutor on the penitentiary commission of 1779'.[11] Fothergill's protégé, John Lettsom, who was also a doctor, wrote *Memoirs of John Fothergill*, which was published in 1786. Like Good, Fothergill was interested in constructing places of confinement which would, through their regime and architectural design, relieve both the physical and psychological dangers to the individual that the old prisons brought:

> Certain it is, that the indiscriminate confinement of many persons together is productive of two unhappy inconveniences; the first as it affects the body by generating infectious diseases; and the other, as it contaminates the mind by hardening the vicious, and by their example depraving those not already abandoned . . . in attempting to prevent those injuries and diseases which human contagion produces they [Howard and Fothergill] united their labours.[12]

According to Lettsom, Howard and Fothergill recommended the building of detached or penitentiary houses 'as a mode of punishment calculated to refrain indolence and vice'.[13] Fothergill's involvement with the poor extended beyond the prisons, to the foundling hospital at Ackworth to which he left money in his will for its support in perpetuity. The hospital was described as being in a

> most flourishing state, fully answering the design of its founders; being conducted under the care of a number of chosen guardians of ability and of exemplary conduct, with an exactness of order, decency and propriety extremely striking and perfectly pleasing to all who have visited it. . . . The children are taught habits of regularity of decency and respectful subordination of their superiors . . . those habits of silence and recollection taught and practised in the ancient schools of philosophy, inculcated in the Scriptures and most emphatically called *the true door of entrance into the school of wisdom*.[14]

Lettsom was also deeply involved in the prison reform movement. He was consulted on the disinfection of Newgate after the death of Lord Gordon in the prison in 1793. He took a leading role in commissioning a statue to Howard's memory in St Paul's Cathedral. He published James Neild's critical accounts of the prisons between 1803 and 1813.[15] He also published a selection of pamphlets ranging from hints on crime and punishment, on schools for the poor, repositories for female industry and on female servants. In addition, he was president or vice-president of a number of voluntary societies such as those for the Suppression of Vice, for the Encouragement of Good Servants and for the Publication of Select Religious Tracts.

Howard's reputation reverberated into the next century. William Guy, a central figure in the development of prison medicine in the mid-nineteenth century, published *John Howard's Winter's Journey* in 1882. Guy pointed out that Howard had prepared himself for understanding disease through study and 'by intercourse with the best physicians of the day'.[16] He was particularly interested in gaol distemper which he saw originating

> among prison scenes in which it is hard to say which was most conspicuous, the disgusting filth, the reckless depravity, the lawless violence, the gross imposition or the helpless inaction of the state. One cannot think of it without horror or speak of it without disgust. Such a combination of physical and moral evils, such a seething mass of crime, misfortune, low vice and debauchery the world has never seen beyond the limits of England.[17]

At the end of the eighteenth century, then, health and illness were profoundly social processes both with regard to how they were explained and the responses that these explanations generated. Howard and the other reformers were clear about what should be done about disease in the prisons in order to preserve the health of the confined. That understanding was, however, couched in terms of morality and discipline. As Sean McConville has pointed out, Howard 'was able to blend perceptions and recommendations' on the issue of gaol fever

> with a similar interest in moral pollution and contagion. Just as prisons generated pestilence they increased depravity and crime, with equally deleterious consequences. In a small, mainly settled and rural society likely to connect death with disease and wrongdoing, this repeated association in Howard's work could not fail to have a considerable psychological impact.[18]

IN THE SHADOW OF THE PENITENTIARY: THE DEVELOPMENT OF PRISON MEDICINE

Gloucester Prison provides an important early example of many of the themes outlined above. The new prison was opened in July 1791. Under the influence of Sir George Onesiphorous Paul the old prison had been reformed but in a manner which 'would not compromise the deterrent value of punishment'.[19] Hygienic rituals and regular medical attention were among the reforms introduced. They were, however, not outside or above the more general concern with reconciling reform and deterrence. In 1784, in a report to the justices, Paul wrote about the importance of shaving the heads of prisoners 'both as a measure of hygiene and as a salutary humiliation':

14

so far as shaving the head is a mortification to the offender, it becomes a punishment directed to the mind, and is (at least so I have conceived) an allowable alternative for inflicting corporal punishment intended to be excluded from this system.[20]

As Michael Ignatieff concludes 'the medical rituals that accompanied admission to the penitentiary had a latent but explicit purpose of humiliation'.[21]

From the outset this disciplinary role was important for the medical workers in the prison. Both the prison surgeon, Dr Parker, and the physician, Dr Cheston, were involved with detecting prisoners who were feigning madness. Parker recounted the case of a prisoner who appeared to be feigning madness. He noted in his journal that he seemed

to all appearances speechless, after some time I discovered the deception, I forced down a stimulating medicine which soon brought him to his speech. He is now very abusive.[22]

When another case occurred in October 1796, Parker called in Cheston. His journal recorded the behaviour of the felon Thomas Roberts. Roberts had attempted to escape. On being recaptured he was placed in the dark cell, where he became sullen and deranged. In order to test whether he was insane, Cheston suggested that he should be plunged into the cold bath:

After 20 minutes in the bath, Roberts made several attempts to relieve himself by leaning against the sides, but he was pushed off each time.[23]

Roberts finally repented but within twenty-four hours the treatment was used again. This time the victim was a traveller named Honor Oliver. She was given three dippings on 28 October and was then strapped to her bed. There were other cases in 1798 and 1807. In 1811 Hester Harding was arrested for want of sureties. She was admitted to the infirmary with a sore throat:

When better, she affected insanity and had to be strapped down. She was given a cold bath, with a little hot water added to it, as it was December. It had little effect on her, and a straitjacket was tried and this succeeded. But when faced with Martha Jeynes' insanity an electric shock was tried instead, which the surgeon noted, 'I am pleased to say produced an immediate desired effect, she fell on her knees, confessed and promised to conduct herself properly in future'. The 'Electric Machine' was used again when she became obstinate, but without effect so the surgeon 'directed the Turnkey to drench her with Beer Caudle', and this proved effective. She was serving two months for stealing butter.

The electric shock treatment was not tried again but the cold bath was used twice more in 1816.[24]

The concern with discipline was one of a number of duties the surgeon performed. He was also responsible for the assessment of the mental and physical health of the prisoners, the administration of appropriate medicines, ensuring against the introduction of lice and contagious diseases and 'ordering such easement in discipline or supplementation of diet as might be required':

In these matters, the governor was obliged to comply with his recommendations though the surgeon's directions of individual easements in the discipline had to be reported to the justices.[25]

In addition, the surgeon was obliged to see individual prisoners at least twice a week and ensure that the governor was not abusing them. The rules and regulations governing the role of the surgeon in the new penitentiary at Millbank covered similar terrain. He was to live in the prison, attend the sick, examine new prisoners and was forbidden to have an outside practice. He was also instructed to visit every part of the prison and to see male and female prisoners in their respective infirmaries. Finally he was to

> acquaint the Governor or Matron with the necessity of suspending the discipline or varying the diet of any prisoner, and the Governor or Matron shall give direction accordingly. He shall attend on notice from the Governor or Matron, of the confinement for any offence, or the punishment by change of diet, of any offender within the prison, and shall visit every prisoner, concerning whom he shall receive such notice, once in every day as long as such confinement or change of diet shall be continued.[26]

The question of difficult prisoners, and the involvement of prison medical workers in dealing with them, was also a central concern for the regime. The prison was opened in 1817 at a cost of £450,000, an enormous sum of money for the time. From the outset prisoners rebelled against the 'regime of solitude, hard labour and meager diet'.[27] Prisoners complained about the brutality of prison staff and demonstrated their resistance by smashing cells, fighting with the guards and rioting in chapel. Even in the solitary silence of the dark cell they continued to shout encouragement in support of each other. At an individual level the collective protests were supported by prisoners pretending to be dumb. In his history of the prison, Arthur Griffiths, who was a governor in the Victorian prison system, described what happened in such cases:

> This man when brought before the governor continued obstinately dumb. The surgeon consulted was satisfied he was shamming but still the prisoner persisted in keeping silence. 'Is there any reason why he should not go to the dark?' the surgeon was asked. 'Certainly not, on the contrary I think it would be of service to him'. And to the dark he goes, where he remains for six days till he voluntarily relinquished the imposture.[28]

The dark cells were situated underground and measured nine feet by six feet. They were reached by a passage that was both pitch black and so narrow that prisoners could pass through it only by walking sideways:

> The only light for the occupant during the entire period of punishment was that brought by the turnkey when he delivered food three times a day. Evidence was given to the 1823 select committee (without provoking adverse comment) that convicts, male and female, had been kept in the cells for as long as three weeks. There was no heating and no removal for exercise; and as it is known that other parts of the prison achieved

16

afternoon temperatures of only 46 degrees Farenheit during the winter of 1822–3, the cold in the punishment cells must have been intense. Physical conditions apart, there is no doubt that the psychological damage caused by prolonged sensory deprivation made this a terrible punishment indeed. That prisoners so confined could not have escaped severe damage to their health, especially as the food was usually only bread and water, was well recognized since as a matter of course they were taken to the infirmary after this ordeal.[29]

Millbank was at the centre of a major controversy when an outbreak of scurvy occurred and thirty-one prisoners died. The PMS was deeply implicated. In particular, the physician and the surgeon had cut the prisoners' already meagre diet in response to outside pressures demanding harsher punishment for the incarcerated. At a meeting of the Superintending Committee on 19 April 1823, the committee resolved to remove Dr A. Copland Hutchinson from his position as Principal Medical Superintendent to the Penitentiary. He was removed that day. The committee's action followed a report prepared at their request by two outside doctors, Latham and Roget, who concluded that the outbreak of scurvy was principally caused by the diet in the prison. The doctors made particular reference to the diet, an issue that was to reverberate through the nineteenth and into the twentieth century:

> during the last eight months the diet was different from what it had been since its establishment. The change, which took place in July last, reduced the animal part of the diet almost to nothing. In a soup made of pease or barley, oxheads were boiled, in the proportion of one oxhead to 100 male and to 120 female prisoners: and we found upon inquiry, that the meat of one oxhead weighed, upon average, eight pounds, which, being divided among a hundred, allows only an ounce and a quarter for each prisoner. This new diet had been continued until the present time; and to it we mainly ascribe the production of the disease in question.[30]

Hutchinson had been the MO at Millbank for seven years. He maintained that the previous diet was 'rather too much' and had contributed to a 'fulness of habit' among prisoners.[31] It was in response to this 'fulness', together with an apparent rise in crime, the lack of deterrence and insubordination in the prison that the doctor recommended the reduction in food.

The events at Millbank, and the role of medical staff in them, illustrate one of the central issues regarding the work and role of the early PMS. The issue of internal prison discipline and external social discipline intertwined and over-lapped and emerged as the ground on which the doctors stood when making their judgements about prisoners. In addition, the state of medicine was such that the doctors' involvement in constructing dietary scales meant in practice they could, in the words of Dr Latham, engage in 'experiments' with the bodies and minds of the confined:

> With regard to the diet of prisoners undergoing punishment for crimes, we presume the object to be that they should have enough for nourishment

and health and nothing more. How much and what quality of food will actually suffice for this purpose can be deduced only from numerous and careful experiments. But no such experiments as far as we know have ever been made.[32]

Experimentation, attempting to quantify the last crumb of food and the final drop of liquid due to prisoners, was indeed to play an important role in the lives of the confined as the nineteenth century developed. It was underpinned by the increasing demands from, and impact of, the principle of less eligibility on the managers of the system. Frederick Hill, one of the five Inspectors of Prisons, caught the mood of this principle when he wrote:

> While it is right to give prisoners such a quantity of food as will keep up robust health, it is important to allow nothing beyond what is really necessary, both because excess of food is injurious to health as well as deficiency, and because the motives to honest industry will be weakened if anything like luxury be admitted into prisons.[33]

The early concerns around discipline and health took place in the context of a system where the benevolent side of the changes advocated by Howard and the other reformers had not been introduced to any great extent. Conditions inside remained deplorable, while abuses continued to arouse comment from politicians in particular. In the summer of 1814 Earl Stanhope raised a series of questions in the House of Lords about the treatment of prisoners in Gloucester and Bristol prisons. Stanhope presented petitions from prisoners and their relatives challenging the legality of the actions of the gaolers in opening mail to their legal representatives. They were also confined to solitary cells without writing materials, had to eat food without implements, and could speak to family and friends only through a square hole in the presence of a turnkey.[34] Stanhope read a petition from Hannah Jackson, whose husband became ill and subsequently went mad in prison:

> He was deprived in prison of all proper means of medical treatment; and after much cruel treatment, was locked up in the strong room where he was kept until the day before his death. . . . The coroner's jury who sat on the body brought in a verdict that the deceased had died in consequence of close imprisonment and want of proper advice. The doctor affirmed that if the deceased had been permitted to have a strait-jacket, he would in all probability have recovered; and it had been further stated to the petitioner, that her husband's body had been found to be covered with bruises.[35]

Henry Grey Bennett presented a similar petition on behalf of Mrs Booth, whose husband had been arrested for debt and had died in the Kings-Bench Prison. He was seriously ill at the time of his arrest. Despite this, he was transported by cart to prison and placed on a bench where 'he remained until the humanity of some of the prisoners conveyed him to a bed, in which after a short time, he died'. At the inquest, the jury found that he died from natural causes but the death had been exacerbated by his prison experience.[36] Petitions were also presented on

18

behalf of women prisoners. Bennett raised the case of Mary Ann Clarke, who suffered 'great partiality and oppression' from the Marshall of the Kings-Bench Prison. She became ill and

> was confined in a cell nine feet square, of which her bed occupied a considerable part, and which had but one small window, barricaded with iron. The approaches to her room were so obstructed that even her medical attendants found it difficult to access. . . . At ten o'clock, contrary to the ordinary regulations of the prison, her cell was locked and no one, not even a physician, was permitted to visit her. Her illness had brought on a nervous fever, by which she was so enfeebled as to be hardly able to walk.[37]

It is clear from these accounts that reform of the regimes was a slow process. It was also a process that unfolded against the background of ensuring that prison regimes did not become overtly comfortable. The reformers tried to walk a penal tightrope, on the one hand demanding changes via improved conditions, while on the other arguing that they should not undermine the disciplinary character and moral thrust of the regime. If the reformers walked the tightrope, then it was the doctors and prisoners who held the rope up. Both groups were central to their interests, doctors and surgeons because they were involved in monitoring the programmes, prisoners because they were at the end of the process, the group for whom the programmes were intended. Joseph Gurney's journey around the North of England and Scotland with his sister Elizabeth Fry in 1818 encapsulates these problems. His views (published in book form the following year) described the conditions they witnessed and the reforms they desired.[38] For Gurney, the most conspicuous problem was 'evil association accompanied with total idleness'.[39] He advocated a number of reforms involving uniforms, sleeping arrangements, cleanliness, classification and employment. He attempted to achieve a balance on the question of the diet arguing that lack of food was an evil; 'we are not justified in making inroads on the health of our prisoners'. On the other hand

> unnecessary indulgence either in the quantity or quality of food is very undesirable, and much opposed to a judicious system of prison discipline.[40]

George Holford, another leading prison reformer and chair of the committee of MPs which supervised the construction of Millbank, articulated similar views. In 1821 he published *Thoughts on the Criminal Prisons of This Country* in which he maintained 'the prisoner no longer feared disease, hunger, heavy irons and no bedding but *proper* sufferings and privations had not been substituted'.[41] Holford's desire for greater discipline was to be realized in 1834 when the New Poor Law was enacted. For particular groups, however, prisons were hard enough without the impact of the new law. Prisoners who died in custody showed quite clearly that the discipline of the regime and the medical treatment attached to it could quite literally be a matter of life and death.

DYING FOR HELP

Deaths in custody were a source of controversy from the end of the eighteenth century. Between 1795 and 1829, 376 prisoners died in Coldbath Fields Prison. Eighty-five (22.6 per cent) of the cases were women. Inquest juries returned a range of verdicts from 'visitation of God' to 'decay of nature', 'dropsy' and 'decline, debility'. In 123 cases the cause of death was not stated. As T. R. Forbes points out, a close scrutiny of the verdicts reveals

> an apparent lack of official interest in determining why prisoners died. Indeed one wonders whether the vagueness of the record represents an effort to conceal actual causes of death – a state of affairs which would not be surprising in a prison in utter disrepute. No cause was recorded for almost one-third of the deaths. Almost one-fifth were piously ascribed to a 'visitation of God', a whitewashing phrase that also was frequently used by coroners' juries of the time for deaths in prison; it was as nonspecific as it was unassailable. 'Decays of nature' referred to a decline in physical vigor and must have been nearly synonymous with 'debility'. 'Dropsy' of course we would regard as a symptom rather than a disease. These six listed causes account for 85% of the deaths; what actual diseases were responsible we can only guess.[42]

'Visitation of God' was a highly problematic yet frequently cited verdict brought in by inquest juries. In 1828 there were inquests held on fourteen prisoners and on six the following year. In all twenty cases, the verdict was death due to the 'visitation of God'.

The verdicts were not accepted without criticism. Indeed it was recognized by a number of commentators that the Coroner's Court was wholly inappropriate for determining the precise cause of death and apportioning blame. In March 1816 during the second reading of the Coroners Bill in the House of Commons Mr Swan argued that inquests were conducted as a 'matter of course' on paupers and those who had no friends or relations.[43] The Lancet, in a series of articles which continued throughout the nineteenth century, pointed to the 'imbecility and ignorance of Coroners'.[44] The journal was particularly concerned about the fact that coroners were often lawyers and therefore lacked medical knowledge:

> A lawyer in the shape of a coroner! A man who could not apply a plaster to a sore finger but who will explain to you the anatomy and physiology of the brain and the surgical treatment of its various antecendents in 3 or 4 brief sentences. Here, also let us hope for a speedy and effectual reform.[45]

Dr William Farr made a similar point. He maintained that inquests were 'very much a matter of form' and that the 'causes of death registered as the result of solemn judicial investigation, are among the most unintelligible in the register'.[46] In 1830 Colonel Blenner Lasser Fairman wrote to The Lancet complaining that when deaths occurred in prisons, the jailers, fearing that their prison could be closed did 'everything in their power to keep these calamities from knowledge of the public'.[47] He argued that juries were packed with the jailers' tradesmen, proceedings were hurried and obstructions placed in the way of those who wished to attend the court. In addition, lawyers were 'more or less' connected with the governors of prisons, were subservient to the judges and stood identified in some measure with the courts. He concluded

> 'Died by the visitation of God' is the return nine times out of ten when the verdict ought to be of 'a broken heart through persecution of the most relentless or unjust' – 'of disease brought on by a removal from a bed of sickness to a place of incarceration' – 'of abstinence and starvation through the absolute want of the comfort and necessaries of life' – or perhaps 'from excess of drinking brought on by anxiety and dejection of mind, through a long confinement'.[48]

Coldbath Fields and Millbank were not the only prisons where deaths were common. Dartmoor was also a centre of controversy, particularly in relation to the medical treatment of the confined. In January 1810 the Admiralty received a letter alleging that 'there were . . . 700 sick in the prison hospital and that medical attendance was utterly inadequate'.[49] The prison contained French prisoners, one of whom left a diary. This forerunner to more contemporary autobiographical accounts described

> with some bitterness . . . the callousness of the hospital staff. It is alleged that when the epidemic was at its worst the doctor had coffins stored in the infirmary in full view of the patients who were further 'encouraged' by hearing their medical attendant say to an assistant, 'The more deaths, the fewer enemies'.[50]

In June 1812 a similar story emerged from Lincoln Prison. A prisoner named Godfrey had a relapse after receiving medicine for a severe bowel complaint. His cries disturbed the other prisoners, who asked the turnkey to assist him. After some delay, medical assistance was called but the prisoner died. When the case was raised in Parliament it was pointed out that 'on the coroner's inquest were sworn men under the influence of the governor of the prison'.[51] On 25 June MPs heard statements made by twelve prisoners which asserted that

> Evans, the surgeon in a conversation with these persons previous to the Inquest gave a very different account of the transaction from what he thought proper to give afterwards. They also assert that the conduct of the Coroner was very improper in several instances. He told the Jurors there was no alternative between bringing in a verdict of 'Murder' or 'Died by the visitation of God' which induced the Jurors to bring in the latter verdict, through three of them afterwards said, they thought it would have been more proper to declare, that the prisoner died through the negligence of the gaoler or his servant.[52]

The confinement of the orator and activist Henry Hunt in Illchester Gaol brought the conditions inside into sharp focus. There were a number of debates both in the Commons and the Lords throughout 1822 that highlighted his plight, including being kept in solitary confinement. When he became ill he was refused permission to see his own doctor. Instead a doctor who lived five miles away was brought in. MPs argued that there was no control in the prison, 'the gaoler was not checked by the surgeon, the surgeon by the coroner nor the coroner by the magistrates'.[53] The gaoler subjected prisoners to severe punishment including the application of a blister to the head of Thomas Gardiner. Another prisoner was placed in double irons fitted to his arms and legs. The chain with which they were connected was so short that it was almost impossible to stand upright. A third prisoner named Mary Cuer was also placed in solitary confinement and held in irons for four days in a cold, damp cell. She was accompanied by her child whom she could feed only with bread and water taken from a bucket. A fourth prisoner named Treble died from the cold in the common-lodging room 'subject to all the noise and disturbance created by other prisoners'.[54] Out of 600 prisoners, 400 were ill due to the conditions. At the inquest into the death of James Bryant, the jury heard that the gaol had been flooded six times in as many weeks. Furthermore

> there was no room in which the deceased could sit with a fire in it during his illness, that was not at least six inches deep of water. The jury, upon hearing the evidence, declared that the deceased had died by the visitation of God; but added that the event had been accelerated by the damp state of the prison.[55]

In a major Parliamentary debate on the subject in April 1822, Sir Francis Burdett, who had been forceful in his claims for Hunt's release, pointed to some of the deficiencies in the gaol. He discussed the role of the doctor in relation to Hunt's demands for treatment by his own MO:

> Mr Hunt preferred trusting to nature and a good constitution rather than place himself in the hands of this humane gaol doctor. It was not enough that there were to be found in that prison, chains, stocks, handcuffs. No, this would not do. There was a doctor who did not hesitate to apply a blister to the head of a man in irons. Why? Because he was ill? No such thing. The blister was applied because the man was considered to be – 'a troublesome fellow'.[56]

Burdett discussed the case of three other prisoners who had also been blistered: the first in order to 'mend his manners'; the second because he was a 'troublesome jockey'; and the third was blistered on his side, because 'he shammed'. The MP concluded by asking

> Was it surprising that, with these facts before him, Mr Hunt should decline availing himself of the assistance of this kind and humane doctor?[57]

THE PMS AND THE NEW POOR LAW

In the 1830s the PMS was still haphazardly organized and left to the devices and discretion of local practitioners. The reports by the Inspectors of Prisons established by the recommendations of the 1835 Select Committee on Gaols

22

indicate the state of medicine in the prisons at this time. The first report contained this description of Ipswich Borough Gaol:

> The surgeon does not inspect the prisoners before they are classed. He is present at corporal punishment. The itch has been communicated from one to another within the prison. There is no infirmary. . . . The surgeon keeps no register, nor book of any sort, the Magistrate never requiring him to do so.[58]

In the second report, the Inspector made similar comments about Gloucester, pointing out that the ventilation was very defective, the cells damp and the infirmary

> not fit for the confinement of a sick prisoner. Scenes of disorder are a perpetual occurrence. The only punishment resorted to for convicts is punishment in the dark hole. The place is not in any degree ventilated and is so situated that the prisoner under punishment can talk with the prisoner outside. This constantly occurs when a female prisoner is confined in the dark hole.[59]

The disciplinary nature of the conditions was intensified with the passing of the New Poor Law in 1834. Prisoners came behind paupers and free labourers in the hierarchical access to medical treatment. As Derek Fraser has noted

> less eligibility was always the keystone of the new Poor Law; hence the medical treatment of paupers had to be inferior to that which an independent workman could provide for himself.[60]

The Lancet captured the spirit of these feelings when it compared the grant allocated to the prison at Millbank with that set aside for the sick poor of fifteen parishes. The latter whose hours and days were characterized by 'habits of industry' were to receive less medical aid than those in the prison. Through this distribution 'the sanguinary cruelty which characterises the treatment of the sick paupers in the Unions is rendered most conspicuous'.[61] The journal, however, also highlighted the impact of the New Poor Law on the lives of the confined. In an editorial (published in 1837) it maintained that prisons should be sites for reformation and not of punishment or torture. Imprisonment had been combined with

> Some injunctions of a most intolerable character. The 'silent system', the limitations of a bread and water diet and the refusal of all occupations for the mind except that which is derived from a perpetual perusal of the Bible and the Prayer Book during periods extending from six months to several years, have obtained a degree of encouragement which is equally unwise and disgusting and ought to receive an immediate check.[62]

The editorial concluded that education should be available

> to turn criminals out upon society, even a shade worse in health and ignorance than distinguished them when they entered the dungeons of a gaol is in itself a crime of the very worst description.[63]

The Lancet continued its attack the following year. The target was Edwin Chadwick, the architect of the New Poor Law. It highlighted the impact of the reduced diet on prison mortality rates and challenged Chadwick's data, which claimed that prisoners on the lowest diet were the most healthy while the full diet was the source of sickness and death. His figures were closely scrutinized and found to be 'erroneous, the data having been ingeniously collected but inaccurately interpreted'.[64] Cases of sickness were never entered in some prisons. Furthermore, while every complaint was entered at those prisons where prisoners received a full diet only those with severe diseases and sent to the infirmaries were entered 'at the gaols where the prisoners are most severely treated'.[65] The journal concluded

> It is only a perversion of words that the term 'full dietaries' has been applied to the low scale of food in any English prisons. All the dietaries are low, and the mortality of prisoners whose mean age may be taken at 20–30 is nearly double the mortality of the country population at the same age. . . . Rogues and thieves when committed to prison, rarely, if ever, labour under any serious disease. On entering they are in health. . . . The proper quantity of food for masses of men or animals is the average quantity that they eat when the supply is regular and unlimited. When subsistence is stopped or reduced much below this standard, the well-known consequences of famine ensue; and every degree below the standard has a corresponding death.[66]

In July 1840 *The Lancet* launched another assault on the reliability of the official figures for deaths in prison. The journal looked, in particular, at Millbank and was quite clear where it stood on the question of prison health. Its writers noted that 'health is impaired and life is shortened by imprisonment'.[67] It calculated that in the five years between 1826 and 1831, the death-rate in 93 prisons was 16 in 1,000. This compared with 10 or 11 in 1,000 for England in general. Once again, the journal took issue with the methods by which the statistics were collected. It had made a similar point earlier in the year when its writers criticized the Superintending Committee of the prison for not considering the full dimensions of the statistics surrounding mortality rates. It concluded that

> the situation of the Millbank Penitentiary is bad, cannot be disputed; but imprisonment in any place invariably injures the health. The Penitentiary system – involving imprisonment in cells – would produce a high rate of mortality among the prisoners. It had been shown by incontrovertible statistical facts, that imprisonment now destroys ten times as many lives as the executioner in this country.[68]

The journal continued to highlight the cases of particular doctors and their role in the prisons, especially when they failed to live up to, or indeed undermined, the good name of medical practice. Thus in the early 1830s Dr Stevens, the MO at Coldbath Fields, was charged with exaggerating the number of cholera cases in the prison in order to treat them with the method he favoured, namely saline treatment. The important point for *The Lancet* was that in using this method

24

prisoners died who ought not to have done. The journal was convinced that the epidemic had been 'most reprehensibly exaggerated' by both Dr Stevens and the magistrates. Furthermore, 'that considering the vast number of "premonitory" cases included in the cholera list, the mortality rate was greater in this prison than it has generally been elsewhere under the most opposite modes of treatment'.[69]

For particular groups of prisoners a sentence could be especially severe on their health. Chartist prisoners are a good example of this. The health of those sent to Northallerton Prison was affected by the cold and damp. Three of their number died in the prison in the early 1840s. Samuel Holberry wrote to a friend:

> They have destroyed my constitution. . . . I am reduced to such a state of debility that I can hardly crawl. . . . And dear friend, you may rest assured that I shall never serve two years more in prison; no before half that time has expired I shall be in my grave.[70]

Cells were cold, damp and below ground level, with water running down the walls. At Monmouth, Wright Beatty complained of the damp, while at York, Peter Hoey lost the use of a leg, 'which prevented him from returning to his trade as a linen weaver upon his release'. The food was particularly bad. It was meagre and coarse:

> At Fisherton Gaol, William Carrier had to eat sour bread, not even getting potatoes. He received neither soap nor towels, and wrote that 'itch, lice and filth of every description prevails in almost every part of the prison'. Many of the Chartist prisoners complained to the inspectors of indigestion and diarrhoea.[71]

Some doctors voiced their concern about the direction of penal policy and its impact on the health of the confined. Frederick Kent, the surgeon at Lincoln, complained that he was

> much inconvenienced for the want of an infirmary. There has been no epidemical disease, nor a single death. The prisoners are very subject to constipated bowels and the addition of a small quantity of vegetables to the present diet would, I think, be beneficial. After being here for a few months, I am satisfied the prisoners suffer in health, which I attribute to the want of ventilation and the monotony of the diet.[72]

The surgeon of Walshingham County House of Correction wrote that the ordinary diet was

> too low. You cannot keep a man here three months without injuring him, and rendering him incapable of that labour which is required of him to produce the means of self-support. If I did not interfere in this general way and order extra diet I should have nothing but disease; the numerous orders for extra diet in my journal are cases of prevention not of actual disease.[73]

The prison diet was thus a central focus of attention both for the managers of the penal system and medical personnel. In 1843 Sir James Graham's proposal for a table of dietaries was introduced into local prisons and adapted to fit the needs of the convict prisons. From this date dietary scales were up or down graded in relation to the wider demands for greater discipline. It was usually the latter policy that was adopted which for some prisoners meant that they 'became the subjects of deliberate experiments designed to test the limits of its meaning in terms of their bodily well being'.[74]

From the prisoners' perspective hunger and ill-health were constant features in their lives. As the Howard Association commented, 'a man goes to bed hungry and gets up hungry, in fact he is always hungry; and this lasts for not weeks, not months, but for years'.[75] Prisoners supplemented the diet with beetles, railway grease, brown paper, earth, candles, poultice, snails, slugs, frogs and earth-worms. They also resisted both through developing an 'acute sensitivity to the weight of the food they were given' and engaging in more collective forms of action in terms of disturbances. They supported hungry prisoners by redistributing 'their irrationally allocated rations on a more equitable basis'.[76]

Boils, rashes, spots, indigestion and flatulence were common ailments suffered by the confined. Loss of weight was a frequent outcome of the dietary provision. One prisoner described its ill-effects:

> When, by-and-by, he can eat the unpalatable mess provided, he acquires chronic indigestion, dimness of eye-sight, tinnitus aurum, roarings in the head, gastric spasms, shortness of breath, sickly giddiness and absence of staying power generally . . . he may (also) contract heart disease.[77]

There were also doctors who argued for an increase in provision to be made for prisoners. In October 1848 the *British and Foreign Medico-Chirurgical Review* carried a long article reviewing a book by the Revd J. Field on the separate system of confinement. Field, who was chaplain at Reading Prison, favoured a punitive diet, food that was coarse and although perfectly wholesome should 'prevent self indulgence'.[78] The *Review* rejected this perspective, citing cases of prisoners who had lost weight through a reduction in the diet. The writers also drew attention to the prison doctors whom they felt had not been vocal enough in defending the purely medical side of their duties:

> Medical men have been too much biassed by the opinions of their masters. They have feared to place prison boards in a difficulty by strong representation of evils which could only be remedied by measures entailing great expense and infinite trouble on magistrates. . . . The question of expediency and policy is for others; and had the subject been so viewed by our prison officers, the government and magistracy might have had occasion long before this to hold in high esteem and regard a branch of the prison service which now by no means commands the respect it deserves.[79]

The writers concluded that many members of the medical profession supported Field's views on prison diets. They had fallen into error 'by having taken a low

26

view, not only of the subject, but also of their own position as the high priests of Nature'.[80]

The Lancet also commented on the situation at Reading, pointing out that the local justices had stubbornly refused to 'adopt even the *minimum* of food proposed by Sir James Graham'.[81]

The issue of the prison diet was thus central to the debates about prison regimes in the mid-nineteenth century, particularly in the context of the often-reported view that prisons were more luxurious than workhouses and were therefore no deterrent to crime. *The Lancet* summed up this view perfectly in September 1858:

> let us see what are the consequences of making prisons paradises and workhouses pandaemoniums. In the first place, the prison is greatly preferred to the workhouse as a place of abode by the lower classes. Magistrates, chaplains and visitors acknowledge this to be the case, and the preference is openly allowed especially by the females. . . . The prison offers a clean and comfortable lodging, food far superior to that of some of the workhouses, and comparatively kind and attentive officers of a higher grade than those provided for the simply unfortunate and starving.[82]

This belief helped to justify the demands for greater discipline inside and for the perpetual surveillance of prisoners in order to identify malingerers, particularly those who sought to avoid the penalty of the work situation. As Sean McConville points out, this could have a profound effect on prisoners. At Parkhurst even when it was recognized that boys were unfit to work and in a poor state of health 'they were not spared outdoor labour'.[83] When the marks system was introduced, it only allowed prisoners in the infirmary to earn six per day:

> this was sufficient to allow the convict to maintain but not to improve his position with regard to progress through the stages. Medical officers claimed that this had the desired effect on the rate of malingering, as apparently had the use of separate confinement in infirmary cells. John Campbell, a convict prison surgeon for many years, used both galvanism and the cold douche as treatments. He noted in his memoirs that 'Patients suffering from the real disease gladly submit to this or any other remedy likely to benefit them, but malingerers show a great repugnance'. So strong was the determination to reduce to the minimum absences from labour that medicines were administered during meal-breaks. Faced with what was, very probably, a uniformly disbelieving attitude to the claims of all but the most obviously and gravely ill, some prisoners inflicted injuries on themselves in order to escape work.[84]

The concern with discipline and regulation was further compounded by the continuing involvement of the doctors in disciplining offenders. The governor of Bedford emphasized this in entries in his journal in March and April 1858. John Robinson, who was noisy and troublesome, refused to work and threw a stone at a warder. The governor, chaplain and surgeon thought he was feigning insanity:

> It is therefore necessary that prompt means be adopted to reduce this man to order and regularity. (Sat. 5th April) The prisoner 'Robinson' continues obstinate and does no work. He is still kept under slight restraint at the request of the surgeon to keep him out of mischief.[85]

Prisoners could be denied medical attention if they were labelled trouble-makers:

> May 4 1853: Jones, a government convict complained this evening of being unwell and wished to go to bed. I visited him in his cell and there certainly did not appear to be much (if anything) the matter with him. He requested he might have the surgeon sent for. The surgeon had seen him in the morning and had not left the prison 5 minutes before he complained. I did not grant his request, in either case, he is represented by the Chief Warder as a very troublesome character and exceedingly obstinate.[86]

The concern that prisoners should not live in luxurious conditions also meant that doctors engaged in what they termed 'experiments' in an attempt to quantify to the exact fraction of an ounce the diet most suited to the criminal. The work of Dr Edward Smith was widely reported in medical journals and discussed at conferences in the late 1850s and early 1860s. Smith attempted to identify the kind of diet different prisoners should have and its relation to the amount of labour performed. This quantification came from what the *British Medical Journal* described as 'the results of experiments by Dr Smith in the Coldbath Fields, Wandsworth, New Baily (Salford) and Canterbury prisons'.[87] Smith argued that the prison diet should not be used as a punishment and that the food supplied on the lowest dietary scale 'is so totally inadequate to the wants of the system that it can only be regarded as an instrument of punishment'.[88] None the less, he told the *British Association for the Advancement of Science*,

> the time was approaching when the whole subject of prison discipline must be reconsidered, and when a conclusion may be arrived at as to the propriety of continuing a system which, when practised, occasions a vast waste of the vital powers of the prisoners, and vast expenditure of money to provide a dietary, which although scarcely sufficient, is far beyond that provided for the poor in workhouses, and beyond that obtained by the working classes in general. Steps should be taken to secure uniformity in discipline; and the mode of carrying out sentences should be proportioned to the crime. This might be done in the dietary, and yet allow of such varieties of food as might be found relatively economical in different parts of the kingdom. Instruments may be kept in proper order, and care be taken that the speed at which they are worked shall be uniform; the amount of a day's work would thus be the same throughout the kingdom, and the surgeon must decide as to the fitness of a particular person to perform the required task. A committee of scientific men, properly authorised by the

Government, would find no difficulty in placing all this upon a proper basis.[89]

Under the banner of medical science, then, the quantification of punishment via experimentation in dietary provision and work-load allowed doctors to articulate their views and make interventions into the increasingly intense debate about the nature of the prison regime. This concern was to reach its apotheosis with the draconian recommendations of the Carnarvon Committee in 1863. For the moment it is important to note that their scientific discourse, its methodology and theoretical underpinning not only was based on scanty knowledge of human physiology but also was trapped inside an ideology that saw prisons as places of punishment. This punitive drive, the will to discipline, could have severe consequences for individual prisoners.

In 1854 *The Lancet* discussed the death of Edward Andrews, a 15-year-old boy who had died in Birmingham Prison. Andrews was imprisoned for stealing four pounds of beef and placed on the crank, which he was required to turn 10,000 times every day. This was divided into a number of periods: 2,000 turns before breakfast, 4,000 between breakfast and dinner and 4,000 between dinner and supper. If the task was incomplete, he was placed on bread and water while the shortcomings had to be made up. In addition, he was not permitted to go to bed until 1½ hours after the other prisoners. Consequently, the boy hanged himself. Two other prisoners attempted suicide at the same time. While the coroner's jury returned a verdict of 'suicide in a state of insanity', the government established a commission, which found

> the late governor, Lieutenant Austin, and the surgeon, Mr Blount, guilty of acts not only illegal but grossly cruel. As these two men are about to be publicly prosecuted, we shall forbear, for the present, making further remarks upon their conduct. We cannot help expressing our surprise, however, that no explanation seems, as yet, to have been demanded from Mr Perry, the Medical Inspector of Prisons. Was it this gentleman's duty to discover and prevent abuses in the Birmingham Gaol, or is this prison exempt from his supervision? The occurrences to which we have alluded did not take place in a day; on the contrary, they were spread over some length of time. Moreover, if we remember rightly, similar illegal practices were discovered to be taking place at one other prison at least.[90]

The commission noted that to achieve the task set on the crank, a boy would have to exert a force equal to 'one fourth of the ordinary work of a draught horse'.[91] Members found prisoners were controlled by leather collars or stocks:

> They were of various sizes, but those which appeared to have been most commonly used, were about 3½ inches deep at the deepest part in front, somewhat more than thirteen inches long, and rather less than a quarter of an inch thick, made of leather perfectly rigid. The mode of use of the collar consisted in the prisoner being first muffled in the straitjacket, having his arms tied together on his breast, the leather stocks fastened tightly round his neck, and being, moreover (where the punishment was inflicted by

29

day), in almost every case strapped to the wall of his cell, in a standing position, by means of strong leather straps passed round the upper parts of the arms, and fastened to staples or hooks in the wall, so tightly as to draw back the arms into and keep them in a constrained and necessarily painful position, at the same time compressing them. It was obvious that such a mode of restraint must necessarily, if continued for several hours, be productive of great pain – in truth it must be an engine of positive torture. So strapped to the wall, prisoners – chiefly boys – were kept for periods of four, five and six hours, and in some instances for a whole day, by way of punishment for the non performance of the crank labour, and for other prison offences, frequently of a very trivial character.[92]

Prisoners were also drenched in cold water. The commission criticized the prison surgeon, Dr Blount, for defending the practice on medical grounds:

he was, with some difficulty, brought to admit that in his judgment the man had no disease whatever, and that the water was in truth thrown over him solely by way of punishment for his supposed obstinacy and his filthiness. He saved the Commission the duty of giving him the sack by resigning.[93]

Blount had also been involved in restraining difficult prisoners. In its review of the case *The Lancet* described how the surgeon dealt with a 'very refractory, violent and dangerous' prisoner named Hunt. He was put in a straitjacket and when this failed 'it occurred to Mr Blount that pressing some salt, which lay at hand . . . into the prisoner's mouth might help to tranquilize him'.[94] The journal defended the doctor as a 'gentleman of integrity, of Christian feelings [and] of high professional attainments'.[95]

The Lancet's ambiguity was reflected in the more general debate and discussion about the role of medicine in prisons. That ambiguity revolved around the role of medical workers in being sensitive to the wider concerns of the society. John Davies, the surgeon at Hertford County Gaol, wrote in May 1843 that the power of the surgeon was

very great under the laws and regulations of prisons and the public have a right to expect that he will use it in such a manner as will best secure the health of the prisoners, without, at the same time losing sight of the interests of those who have to support these prisoners.[96]

For some doctors, the impact of imprisonment itself was an important consideration when analysing the ill-health or indeed the deaths of prisoners. In 1845 William Baly, the physician at Millbank and a lecturer in forensic medicine at St Bartholomew's Hospital, published a 159-page document in the *Medico-Chirurgical Transactions*; it was on 'mortality in prisons'. The document was a tightly argued, statistically based analysis of prison deaths and concluded that 'the high rate of mortality which prisoners suffer is really the effect of their punishment and is not owing to the unhealthiness of the class whence criminals are, for the most part derived'.[97] Baly produced a number of papers in which he elaborated this theme. He was concerned to pinpoint particular diseases and to show their impact on prisoners, rather than discussing disease in general. Thus he discussed cholera, fever, dysentery and inflammation, as distinct entities which contributed to, and caused the deaths of, prisoners in Millbank. In his report on the prison Baly outlined the impact of cholera on the confined. He rejected a number of factors which had been propounded to explain 'this severe visitation'.[98] These included

> low diet, want of cleanliness and bad sewerage within the prison. The diet of the prisoners, which was before abundant, was improved during the prevalence of the epidemic by the addition of half a pint of good porter to the daily rations of each prisoner. The sewerage of the prison is excellent, and at no period was there perceptible any bad smell from foul air arising within the prison. The causes which had, I believe, the principal share in favouring the spread of cholera within the prison were the three following: Its site, its construction and the predisposition of prisoners to disease arising from the depressed state of mental and bodily health, produced in them by confinement.[99]

Baly also felt that the mortality rate from tubercular diseases was affected by a number of factors including deficient ventilation, the cold, lack of exercise, a listless and dejected state of mind and the poor diet. In his view

> the diet of prisons, though often perhaps more abundant than the agricultural labourer usually enjoys, yet has generally been less stimulating and also less nutritious than seems to be requisite for the health under conditions so unnatural and depressing as are those almost necessarily attendant on the state of imprisonment.[100]

He was quick to point out that his results were 'not intended to authorize, and indeed do not justify, any sweeping condemnation of imprisonment as a system of secondary punishment'.[101] Baly concluded that improvements in food, heating and ventilation would contribute to the decline in the death-rate.

Other MOs also raised questions about the impact of confinement. In April 1843 R. J. Dean, the surgeon at Knutsford House of Correction, expressed his view to the visiting magistrates that it was impossible to

> keep men under long sentences of imprisonment in robust health, it is not that they actually fall sick, but that they become pallid, care-worn and enfeebled, and lose all their energy and exertion. This is not the effect of the diet, or the labour, the locality or discipline of the gaol but arises I believe solely from their being in confinement and the depressing circumstances attending that confinement.[102]

The MO at Portland objected to prisoners being placed on a reduced diet for punishment. But caught up in the system of discipline that prevailed, this objection could be rejected. As the governor noted:

31

The medical officer stated to me that he disapproved of punishing prisoners by reducing their diet but as he declined certifying that such punishment would do any injury to this prisoner, and as it seemed a suitable punishment for an idle man, I resolved in applying it in this instance. It appears to me that if this means of enforcing discipline was prohibited it would be impossible to manage the prisoners, as simple close confinement without short diet would be disregarded by most of the prisoners as a punishment.[103]

From the prisoners' perspective, the finer nuances in the debates between prison doctors, governors and an increasingly interventionist state did little to alleviate the hard, uncompromising and unpleasant nature of Victorian prison life. Death was an integral and ever-present element in their lives. There were a number of books published in the mid- to late nineteenth century which detailed the circumstances around the deaths of individual prisoners. As Philip Priestley has pointed out, 'there was no shortage of men in prison who when they heard of any sudden death in the hospital were ready to swear "his light has been put out by the doctor"'. The autobiography of the anonymous 'One Who Has Tried Them [the prisons]' described the death of a prisoner who

complained that he was subject to heart complaint: but the doctor and Old Bob [the hospital warder] had got it into their heads that he was shamming and the former certified him fit for first class labour. It was very hot summer weather; the man was placed upon the wheel, and used to puff and blow and exhibit signs of intense distress while at work; but this was looked upon as a dodge, and no notice was taken of it, and the man continued at wheel work. A few nights later the warder, going round to lock up cell-doors at bedtime, heard a strange gurgling noise in this man's cell, and looking in, saw him stretched upon his bed gasping for breath. . . . There was the usual inquest on the body, and the doctor stated the man had died from heart complaint, and the verdict was of course 'Death from natural causes'.[104]

As in life, the body of the dead prisoner was not free of the stigma of imprisonment. The spirit's escape was not reflected in the body's release from the pain of confinement. 'One Who Has Endured It' gave a moving but chilling account of the Victorian state's ability to regiment and humiliate the body of the deceased:

to die a convict, to be buried in an unknown, uncared-for grave, thrust into a prison coffin filled up with dirty sawdust, as I have seen them done at Dartmoor, so that the ragged old shirt given out to do duty for a shroud may be saved for other purposes, is but a sorry end for a man who has once lived, respected and beloved.[105]

The Deaths and Inquests Register For the Years 1848–63 lends support to the prisoner's claim. In this period 423 prisoners died in custody. The disposal of the bodies is illustrated in Table 1.

Table 1   Disposal of prisoners' bodies 1848–63[106]

Institution	No.	%
Prison Cemetery	147	35
School of Anatomy	102	24
Victoria Park Cemetery	137	33
Family/Friends	19	5
Not listed	18	4

The authorities in the majority of cases still laid claim to the body of the prisoner. Breaking the bond of incarceration was, for many, impossible even in death. The penal ties bound their bodies to the gaolers for eternity.

Philip Priestley's history of mid-Victorian prisons brings together a number of accounts by prisoners about the sick and dying. The anonymous accounts of 'A Merchant' and 'Ticket-of-leave-Man' about sickness and death were supported by Michael Davitt, who described how one prisoner

> fell out several times to see the doctor, and he was never admitted to the infirmary to my knowledge. One morning I observed him drop dead on the parade, and I believe it was from heart disease, or from bursting a blood-vessel or something of that sort. I think that when he was examined by the doctors, if they had had sufficient knowledge to have detected his disease they would have admitted him to the infirmary.[107]

For Priestley, mid-Victorian prison medicine, despite the humanity shown by some doctors, was none the less compromised by its

> appointment to fundamentally disciplinary tasks. The doctors patrolled the narrow straits that separate hunger from starvation and punishment from outright cruelty, hauling aboard the life raft of their dispensations this drowning soul or that, and repelling, with brute force if necessary, the efforts of the others to climb to safety. In so doing, they lent to the work of preserving their employers' reputations whatever dignity and authority their emerging profession possessed – and lost it. What these scenes *do* do is to reveal the suppressed humanity of the prisoners in acts that shine forth – like the unexpected forget-me-nots on the yards at Pentonville – as small beacons of affection and hope in a dark and hopeless world.[108]

TIGHTENING THE PENAL SCREW: MEDICINE, PENALITY AND THE CARNARVON COMMITTEE

Until the mid-nineteenth century prison medical workers did not speak with one voice when it came to pinpointing the cause of disease and death in the prisons. This was partly a reflection of the localized nature of the prison system itself, the introduction of the Prison Inspectorate following the 1835 Select Committee's report had done little to bring the various prisons under any kind of uniform control or to bring the doctors and surgeons closer together as a professional group.[109] It was also a reflection of the paucity of knowledge within the profession as to the causes of disease and the lack of systematic research into the relationship between the environment, the body and the mind. This lack of standardization allowed medical personnel a definite space to articulate diverse views. That space was however limited and was to become narrower in the second half of the century as the doctors increasingly articulated their views as a professional group of state servants rather than as individual MOs or surgeons. At the same time, the state increasingly intervened to regulate and rationalize, to put the prisons on a much firmer and uniform foundation. What linked the state and the doctors were the ideologies of discipline and management. These ideologies had been a central feature of prison medical practice since the late eighteenth century. In that sense, the increasing interventions made by the Victorian state, the directives issued and that state's concern with discipline, regulation and control struck a medical chord with prison doctors and surgeons. Once more, it was the confined who were to feel the full impact of the developing relationship between the state and medicine in the second half of the century.

In 1862 the Royal Commission on the Penal Servitude Acts was appointed. The commission was formed after mounting concern over a series of robberies in London, although how much of this moral panic was generated by the media is a matter of historical dispute.[110] In response to this panic the commission recommended a harsher, more uniform prison regime. When the Penal Servitude Bill was passed in July 1864, the new measures it contained were indeed harsh including lengthening the minimum sentence of penal servitude to five years for first offenders and to seven years for any subsequent offence. The Act also considerably increased the amount of state intervention and surveillance over ticket-of-leave prisoners with the use of photography which 'was to be employed as an aid to tracing second offenders'.[111]

The commission was supported by Lord Carnarvon, who chaired a Select Committee of the House of Lords into prison discipline. The committee recommended stricter uniformity in local prisons, which was to be imposed by an Act of Parliament; it also recommended a more punitive regime in the prisons. There was, as Carnarvon himself told the House of Lords in February 1863, 'an insufficiency of penal discipline'.[112] He made particular reference to dietary provision:

> in a large number of prisons meat was given to the prisoners every day of the week, either in solid form or as a soup. This was a serious question; but when they examined the subject a little further they would find that in many cases there were certain luxuries, certain comforts coupled with what might be called the more ordinary dietary which made it a very grave question whether the dietary generally given to prisoners was not in excess of what it ought to be.[113]

During the course of its meetings, the committee heard, from amongst others, Herbert Voules, who was the Inspector of Prisons for the Northern and Midland districts. He had seventy-two prisons under his jurisdiction. Voules's account

34

of how he saw the role of the prison diet once more brings out the ongoing concern with quantifying to the nearest micro-ounce a just measure of pain without compromising discipline:

[Chair] Would it be the duty of the governor and the surgeon, in your opinion, to improve that man's physical energies and powers to the highest point?
[Voules] I would not say to the highest point; I think that no indulgence should be allowed but simply what is necessary to maintain a man in health so that he can earn his livelihood when he goes out. I would forbid any indulgence; and would make the diet as simple as possible, giving the required nourishment.[114]

The committee was not prepared to make a positive recommendation to reduce the diet. Instead its members recommended that 'experiments might be conducted in order to ascertain what might safely be done in this regard'.[115] In 1864 a departmental committee was established whose chair was Dr William Guy, the medical superintendent of Millbank Prison. He was assisted by Dr Maitland of the Gosport Military Prison and Dr Clarke of Dartmoor. Guy was to become an important figure in the tortured debates around prison diets in the 1860s and beyond. As medical superintendent at Millbank his evidence to the Carnarvon Committee was heard with respect. He had been writing and lecturing on the subject of the social role of medicine since the early 1840s.[116]

In his evidence to Carnarvon, Guy warned against 'tampering with the dietary'.[117] None the less, his committee gave 'cautious approval' to a 'limited reduction in the separate prisons' dietaries'.[118] The three medical men also argued that they would not be responsible for advocating the kind of reduction that was made at Millbank in 1822 and Wakefield in 1849 and 1862 which resulted in a serious outbreak of disease. While they criticized the monotony of the diet in the public works prisons they found the monotony in the diet of the penal class 'acceptable and suggested that there might be some reduction in quantity to make it even less attractive'.[119]

In a paper in the *Journal of the Statistical Society* (published in September 1863) Guy was very clear about the implications of the high level of the prison diet and the need for change. He made a number of relevant points in the concluding part of his paper:

That the existing prison dietaries present many curious anomalies very difficult of explanation, except on the supposition that additions made for temporary reasons, such as a wish to satisfy the importunities of prisoners, or a transitory departure from health or outbreak of disease in a small section of the prisoners, have become permanent through inadvertence, or from an aversion to change. . . . That our prison dietaries have also been framed under the influence of a timid feeling, originating in misconceptions as to the true cause of the epidemic of Millbank Prison, but especially in the belief that it was due to a reduction in the quantity of food.
That some reduction in the dietaries of our convict establishments might

be made with safety and economy, and that further reductions would probably be justified by well-devised experiments.[120]

The three doctors attempted to analyse the diet scientifically. They conducted experiments with the prisoners, this time at Wakefield Prison. The results were not convincing. The MO at the prison complained that the dietary experiment had resulted in the 'failure of the health and strength of the prisoners, the greater loss of weight, and the greater mortality'.[121] Nevertheless, they recommended that meat and cocoa be removed from the diet of the local prisons. Philip Priestley argues that these changes had little to do with science but with more nebulous concepts such as the 'experience' of the doctor and a

> healthy, old-fashioned kind of moralizing and one, moreover, that harmonizes nicely with Carnarvon's own conclusion that 'The low animal natures of too many of the criminal class, and the admitted efficiency of reductions in prison food in cases of prison offences, renders plain the value of diet as one form of penal correction'.[122]

Guy's attempt to reconcile discipline and nutrition continued into the next decade. When there was discussion over the introduction of wholemeal bread in 1877, he forwarded a deposition to the Home Office, which argued that such a plan was important not only because of the nutritiousness and wholesomeness of the bread but also because the work of grinding meal by hand-mills was to be recommended on several obvious grounds. These included the fact that the work could be carried on in the prison cells and its amount could be easily measured, it was quite free from danger, was highly remunerative and 'being monotonous and requiring no instruction, it constitutes a good form of punishment'.[123]

Not everyone, however, was convinced about the new dietary scale. In a paper delivered to a special meeting of the health section of the Society for the Promotion of Social Science in July 1864, Dr Edward Smith criticized Guy's Committee for basing its report on the replies of 'visiting justices to queries which had been forwarded to them through the Home Office and not in any part whatsoever upon experimental researches, as was recommended by the House of Lords' Committee'.[124] Smith maintained the proposed scheme had been constructed without any 'scientific proof' and the committee had ignored the chemical composition of food. In addition

> the results were so erroneous that the low diets had been made lower, and the high diets higher in nutriment, whilst the Committee believed that they had made the low diets higher and the high diets lower![125]

In the discussion which followed Smith's paper a number of PMOs concurred with his views and pointed to the 'utter failure of the inquiry undertaken by Dr Guy'. They called for a new inquiry and for a commission of 'scientific men' to be established for such events.[126] Dr Foster, the surgeon at Huntingdon Prison, had expressed similar views in July 1863, arguing against a reduction in the diet and pointing out that as the influence of the prison was depressing and lowered the 'assimilative powers of the body' food and drink should be rather in excess of what would be required under other circumstances. The food should be presented in a digestible form; but everything that merely pleases the palate should be avoided. Monotony, on the other hand, inasmuch as it impairs digestion and assimilation, should be shunned. Lastly, the material should be as cheap as possible, consistently with other requirements.[127]

Medical voices from other parts of the country also intervened. The surgeon to the general prison at Perth in Scotland argued that the diets in England's county and borough prisons were so low 'as to be considered punitive and unfit to sustain health',[128] although that prison had its own problems with an outbreak of Asiatic cholera in July and October 1866. Prisoners in Irish gaols fared even worse than their English counterparts: their diets were pitched at a lower level in terms of nutritional value. Medical personnel were again involved, first in 1849 when the government was told that prison food was 'so much better than that which the lower classes were accustomed to receive, either within or without the workhouses, that offences were committed for the mere purpose of obtaining food in gaols'.[129] The dietary scale was lowered with the sanction of the judiciary and a doctor. In 1854 it was lowered again. By March 1868 it did not include meat at all. Prisoners received two meals every twenty-four hours, which comprised of stirabout or gruel, or bread and milk. Eighteen hours elapsed between the two servings. There were complaints about the quantity of the food and the fact that prisoners frequently fainted but the *BMJ* concluded:

> The prisoners are well lodged, clad and cared for; their food is somewhat scanty, but not very seriously so. The consequence of this able report will be to provide all that justice and wisdom can allow to prisoners, in a population where the dietary is generally very far from luxurious, and amongst whom any excess of liberality in the prison scale has been repeatedly found to act as an efficient inducement to crime.[130]

The diet was again directly linked to a number of deaths in custody. The Howard Association published a pamphlet in April 1868 calling attention to recent inquests on those who had died in prison or shortly after their release apparently because of lack of food. *The Lancet* made a similar point in the same month when it described the case of 18-year-old Edward Barrett, who had died in Coldbath Fields Prison. It was said that he went to prison in robust health, but when released he could hardly walk. A lodging-house keeper told the inquest that his was not the only case that she knew of but that convicts came out, after a few weeks in confinement, 'reduced to shadows and shorn of their strength'. The journal continued:

> It also appears that the medical examination of a complaining prisoner is of the most perfunctory kind. Not only is no convict's health inquired into on his coming in, even though, as appeared in Barrett's case, he be suffering from pulmonary tuberculosis, but when the labour of the mill proves more than he can bear, he is simply 'looked at' by the prison surgeon, reported as

having 'nothing the matter with him' to the warder, by whom, in turn, he is reported to the governor, who says – 'Coming off the wheel without cause. Two days' bread and water'.[131]

The number of deaths at Chatham Convict Prison rose to eleven in 1865 and 'a record 14 in 1866'.[132] Convicts had been reduced to eating candles to stave off hunger.

The dominant ideology underpinning penality was thus based on punishment and repression. In the words of the Director of Convict Prisons, regimes were designed to 'unite reformation with repression and teach convicts to hate prison, but hate crime more'.[133] In this situation, prison officials in general, and medical personnel in particular, were not immune to the wider debates about both penal treatment and how to respond to criminality. Prison officials involved in the debates ultimately sided 'with those who cried "luxury"', whilst taking what precautions they could to prevent too much damage being done to the prisoners in their charge'.[134] The prison rules allowed the doctor some discretion to alter the diet of new prisoners:

> Two things flowed from this proviso. It allowed the tables and scales to be retained intact, whilst allowing a degree of flexibility in individual cases, at the discretion of the medical officers. But the discretion thus placed in the doctor's hands raised tantalizing visions of food before the eyes of hungry prisoners. It was a discretion that helped swell the ranks of those who went 'sick' each day, and helped as well to turn the practice of medicine in prisons into a battleground between desperate and cunning convicts and suspicious and resentful surgeons.[135]

As in the twentieth century prisoners confronted the discipline and regulation of the system. Medical personnel came in for particular, sometimes fatal attention. In February 1856 the *Association Medical Journal* recorded the 'brutal murder of another Medical Man'.[136] Charles William Hope, the assistant surgeon to the Stirling Castle convict hulk at Portsmouth, was stabbed in the neck by a convict wielding a razor. The dead man had 'refused to certify the necessity for the convict's remaining on the lower deck or invalid ward'.[137] The Directors of Convict Prisons described a similar case the following year in their report on Pentonville, where one prisoner in particular gave serious cause for alarm when he 'opposed himself to the rules and murmured at the dietary, which he asserted was insufficient to maintain his strength'.[138] They described how

> he one day preferred a request to be allowed some indulgences in addition to his diet, and when this was refused as unreasonable he savagely attacked the medical officer and stabbed him with a weapon he had previously constructed for the purpose, which he had kept concealed in his coat sleeve, wounding also two of the warders who came to the rescue. When spoken to shortly afterwards on the serious nature of his offence, he expressed no contrition, but, on the contrary regretted that he had not 'killed the doctor'

as he had intended, alleging that for some time past his food had been 'powdered' or poisoned by the medical officer's orders.[139]

These events were underpinned by other, more common forms of rebellion, such as assaults against prison property, which included tearing clothes, smashing windows and the destruction of bedding.[140] Women, in particular, expressed their feelings in this manner. According to the prison visitor Felicia Mary Skene, this behaviour had a

> distinct *rationale* of its own, illogical enough, no doubt, but a well-considered method in the apparent madness. The object of it is simply one of deliberate revenge for the pains and penalities to which their imprisonment subjects them.[141]

The accounts of prisoners testified to the rationality in their behaviour:

> They have treated me like a beast and I have become one. . . . I did it for *variety*. Oh, the monotony of a prison life! I had to smash the glass of the cell and glass everywhere I could or I should have gone mad.[142]

This behaviour could result in a further round of disciplinary activity directed at controlling the prisoner. The body was the prime focus of attention as the authorities utilized a number of techniques designed to pacify and debilitate those who had been responsible for the destruction of the state's property. Through this destruction the body forfeited further its right to be treated with dignity. Shackles, handcuffs, manacles, chains and physical violence were powerful manifestations of the state's attempt to bring the physique of the recalcitrant into its own orbit of strict discipline. There was a particular technique reserved for women called hobbling. It consisted of 'binding the wrists and ankles of the prisoner and strapping them together behind her back'. The hobbles were

> Strong leather straps and wood appliances which fasten the leg and foot back behind the knees to the thigh, the arms being fastened down so that the hands could not be raised to the mouth, and the unhappy individual in the hobbles had only her knees to rest upon, and with her back to the wall had to be fed like a baby.[143]

Finally, for those who could not, or indeed would not, be controlled the straitjacket was used.

Order was fragile in the mid-Victorian prison system. It was often restored by the use of force. In 1861 there was a mutiny at Chatham Public Works Prison and another in Portland in 1864. The civil guard fired on the ring-leaders in both cases. In 1863 prisoners in Millbank were given corporal punishment on thirty-four occasions. All but one received lashes with a cat, while another was given twelve lashes with a birch for writing and drawing in his Bible. Most of the other offences were for destroying prison property such as blankets, rugs, jackets, glass, Bibles and prayer books:

For these offences the prisoners usually received either 24 or 36 lashes with the cat. Other offences included using threatening, abusive or disgusting language towards governors, chaplains, doctors or warders. For these the punishments were the same as above.[144]

A similar picture emerged at Dartmoor. In 1863, 880 punishments were awarded, including 504 for insolence, disobedience and using threatening language, 204 for disrespect and disorderly conduct, 16 for assault and 15 for escapes.[145]

It is clear that the first hundred years of the PMS's existence were controversial. Prison doctors not only were caught up in, but also contributed to the debates about the philosophy and practice of punishment. The disciplinary strategies which lay at the heart of penality were legitimized by the interventions which Medical Officers made. At the same time these practices were confronted and challenged by the confined, who resisted the imposition of medical power into their lives. The next eighty years were to see a consolidation of medical power both inside and outside the walls. They were also to witness further opposition from prisoners increasingly supported by pressure groups outside the walls, who questioned the work of medical personnel in prison and their role in managing the bodies and minds of the men and women in their charge.

CHAPTER 3

Consolidation and resistance 1865–1945

As professions, behavioral science, medicine and psychology derive so much of their authority from the service of corporations and the state that it is difficult to see how they can visualise a person scientifically except as an object to be predicted, controlled and improved.[1]

The years between 1865 and 1877 were important moments in the development of modern penology. In 1865 the Prisons Act was passed. It contained 82 clauses and 104 regulations relating to the administration of the prison system. There were a number of orders relating specifically to health care including the provision of an infirmary in every prison and instructions to the surgeon to see individual prisoners at least once a week. The role of the MO increased in the local prisons as doctors began to look for and find signs of insanity in an increasing number of prisoners. As Roger Smith has pointed out:

> Officials who met the accused before the trial increasingly influenced his or her subsequent history. Prison officers and particularly prison doctors became more sensitized to the possibility of insanity in those temporarily in their custody. . . . This [1865] Act regularised prison administration and ensured that the prison surgeon inspected every new arrival, which perhaps increased the chances of finding insanity.[2]

This development was bound up with more general medical and criminological developments around the idea of 'progressive degeneracy in which ever worsening moral and physical defects could be passed from one generation to another'.[3] The psychiatrist Henry Maudsley and the Scottish prison doctor James Thomson proposed that

> there was a class among criminals, of 'born criminals', lacking in intelligence and 'normal instinct' and often with physical deformities, or conditions such as epilepsy or insanity. Thomson's work in particular was supported by statistical observations and family studies drawn from his prison experience, and made quite an impression on his contemporaries.[4]

41

Other prison medical workers expressed similar views. John Campbell, a surgeon who served for thirty years in the convict service, talked of the physical degeneracy of criminals:

> The physiognomy of prisoners as well as the conformation of the skull, is often remarkable; and the result of many post-mortem examinations has proved that the brains of prisoners weigh less than the average, and that a large brain is an exception.[5]

These views were supported by writers such as Thomas Carlyle, who described prisoners as

> Miserable distorted blockheads, the generality: ape-faces, imp-faces, angry dog-faces, heavy sullen ox-faces; degraded underfoot perverse creatures, sons of indocility, greedy mutinous darkness, and in one word, of stupidity, which is the general mother of such.[6]

The 1865 Act which increased the power of the doctors did so at the expense of more openness. In December 1871 the *BMJ* complained that medical reports from the public works prisons were 'confusing and obscure'.[7] In 1874 central government reinforced its power still further by denying access to local medical officers of health who wanted to inspect the 'grave sanitary defects' that existed within one particular prison.[8] The passing of the 1877 Prison Act further reinforced the position of the PMO. According to Dr Quinton's autobiography of his life as a PMO, detailed physical examinations were introduced on reception and recorded. Similarly if a prisoner was sent to hospital, her/his history was written down. Periodical reports and returns were also established on a regular basis. As he pointed out 'it became necessary, therefore, to appoint to the prison service medical officers who could give all their time to the work in the large prisons'.[9] These changes did not quell the controversy around medical standards, medical care and discipline behind the walls. Again the question of diet and discipline was a central part of this controversy. Some of the doctors expressed their views on the subject quite clearly. Quinton, for example, was explicit about the relationship between dietary punishment, discipline and science:

> though it always seemed to me a more or less barbarous and senseless proceeding to apply to human beings, was nevertheless very necessary with unruly prisoners. I know of nothing approaching a scientific excuse for its use, except the principle on which a horse has his oats reduced in order to tame his spirit.[10]

In a letter to *The Lancet* in February 1873 Thomas Bogg, the former surgeon of Louth Prison, supported this position arguing that low diet was 'undoubtedly necessary as a punishment for convicted criminals, but it should bear some proportion to the work they perform, and where it does not impaired health inevitably follows'.[11]

This attitude towards discipline was underlined in 1878 when the newly appointed Prison Commissioners asked their medical officer, Dr Gover, to report on the use of the hated treadwheel. His report was enthusiastic and legitimized the erection of 'many new machines'.[12] Gover claimed that the treadwheel had the great merit of

> not only being an instrument recognised as the one best adapted for utilising the power of a man, but it is also the only simple machine in which a number of men can be made to work together with a certainty of each man doing his specified share of the work. It is a machine at which there can be no shirking, notwithstanding what is said about the ease of distinguishing 'old hands' from novices by the mode of moving the feet.[13]

This view was not wholeheartedly supported by the medical profession. Drs Guy and Hastings wrote to the Home Office arguing that the absolute uniformity in administering the punishment of hard labour (as Gover recommended) was impracticable. Discretion for MOs they felt was necessary to pinpoint 'the capacity of different prisoners for hard labour. The discretion is already exercised and as far as our experience extends, and in our belief, wisely and conscientiously'.[14]

Outside commentators were also critical about the direction of penal practice. In its editorial comment, *The Lancet* railed against the 1877 Act arguing that while it had contributed towards greater economy of administration and increased severity towards the prisoners, it had also curtailed the powers of the Visiting Justices to scrutinize what was happening inside. The journal considered that many of the provisions in the Act would debilitate prisoners still further. This included the new prison diet which for men on hard labour was 'too severe, and certainly insufficient for their physiological requirements'.[15] Its writers concluded that while they had no 'foolish sentiment towards the criminal classes' none the less it was their conviction that the system of prison discipline was 'still very defective, and that to many criminals it is most unjust'.[16] The journal made similar comments in August 1879, again calling for more openness in the administration of the system and the appointment of a superintending medical officer of high standing 'who would have the oversight of the medical arrangements in all convict prisons'.[17] The Howard Association also pointed out that prisoners sent to gaols to serve short sentences were having their health destroyed within a few weeks. They were 'virtually sentenced to death'.[18] William Tallack, the Association's Secretary, argued that this was caused by the new centralized regime in which the doctors had to fill in an elaborate set of forms and send them to the Home Office. This was not only to the detriment of the prisoners' health but also undermined the accountability of the system. In *The Lancet*'s view, centralization under the 1877 Act had 'the effect of preventing that local care, judgement and interest in prisons which was formerly given by the magistracy'.[19]

From the perspective of the confined, discipline, regulation and control continued to be maintained, sometimes with fatal consequences. They also resisted. In October 1866 women in Manchester gaol were gagged, particularly those who persisted 'in disturbing the prison by shouting and screaming'. The *BMJ* maintained that this was 'a mode of punishment unknown to the law'.[20] In

1888 Dr Barr, the surgeon at Kirkland Prison, was attacked and stabbed by a black prisoner.[21] The next year, the MO at Usk was attacked and knocked unconscious. The guilty prisoner was sentenced to thirty-six strokes of the cat.[22] Dr Quinton described the different strategies utilized by the confined: escapes and attempted escapes were 'a frequent occurrence';[23] they petitioned the Home Secretary about medical care; they engaged in 'active as well as passive resistance to the most benevolent designs'.[24] Prisoners' accounts describe a different reality. In a sense, they are similar to the doctors' accounts in that conflict was recognized as part of the prison experience. They differ, however, most clearly in the range of criticisms raised about medical treatment inside. *Six Years in the Convict Prisons of England* (published in 1869), written by the anonymous 'A Merchant', described spending two years in the hospital ward of Surrey Prison. This was due to a disease in his knee, which resulted in the amputation of his leg. He described how the two doctors in the prison began their rounds at 9 am. When they entered the hospital ward, the prisoners were called to attention:

> all the prisoners out of bed stood up, and as the doctors passed, noting down on a ticket the date and remarks on each man's complaint, they were saluted by the patients in the military fashion.[25]

After weeks of suffering there was no improvement. The knee became so sensitive that anyone passing near his bed caused excessive pain. It was finally removed by having 'the flesh cut, and the bone sawn through at the thickest part of the thigh'.[26] When recuperating 'A Merchant' reviewed the medical service inside and placed the blame for the standard of care on the malingerers who caused much of the

> apparent sourness, indifference to, and sometimes cruel neglect, if not positive aggravation of suffering, which I have noticed in the manner and treatment of most of the convict surgeons I have met with.[27]

Five Years' Penal Servitude (published in 1877) was written by the anonymous 'One Who Has Endured It' and told a similar story.[28] In 1881 the anonymous 'One Who Has Tried Them' published *Her Majesty's Prisons: Their Effects and Defects*.[29] The author catalogued cases of medical abuse and the decline in the health of a number of prisoners. When one complained about a warder

> the warders put their heads together and determined to make it hot for him. K——n was now beginning to complain of being ill, and to apply to the doctor for a little extra food, so the warders agreed amongst themselves that whoever went round with the doctor was to take good care that he did not give him anything extra, but whenever K——n applied they were to persuade the doctor that he was a lazy fellow trying to humbug him by shamming. They were perfectly successful in their scheme, for although K——n frequently applied to the doctor, the latter would never give him any extra food, and after three or four successive applications sent word to K——n by the corridor warder that he was not to ask for extra food any more, as he would not give it to him.

It was now December, and K——n had completed some ten months of his sentence, and it is a most significant fact, that he was the only man that had passed more than nine months in the prison who had not got extra diet of some kind. Early in January K——n again sent for the doctor, complaining that he was dreadfully weak and ill, and begged very hard for a little extra food, but to no avail.[30]

The prisoner eventually died. The author indicated how the death was handled by the authorities and the close interrelationship between the Home Office and the prison concerned:

While K——n's body was awaiting the inquest, a doctor was sent down from the Home Office to examine the prison, and he, I fancy, was rather surprised that K——n had not been sooner sent to hospital, for some little time after the Xshire doctor got a letter from the prison commissioners, asking why he had not sent K——n up to hospital sooner. What excuse he made I do not know, but there the matter ended. A prisoner's chance of getting over a serious illness was pretty small, when one calmly considers the odds against him – a careless doctor (under certain circumstances), a brutal, unscrupulous hospital warder, and a couple of ignorant labourers to act as nurses.

It may perhaps be thought that I have exaggerated this account, but it is not the case, I have, on the contrary, been most careful to keep well within bounds, and am prepared, if necessary, to substantiate from the lips of the officials themselves every word that I have stated above.[31]

For those on punishment, the medical consequences could also be extreme. The Irish Fenian Jeremiah O'Donovan Rossa spent four months on punishment diet of bread and water, at the end of which his body was covered with 'small pustules, like little boils. Not an inch of me was free of them, and they looked very ugly with their white heads'.[32] Irish prisoners were subjected to the strict discipline known as the Pentonville system. The prisoners were not allowed to speak to each other, nor as far as was possible to see each other. Each prisoner had her/his own cell, which was thirteen feet by seven feet. The prisoner ate and worked in this cell where

he is kept for six months at least, cut off, as far as ingenuity can do it, from all communication with his fellow-men. He has to conform minutely to a strict system of rules: if he fails in this he is liable to be flogged or sent – it may be for as much as twenty-eight days – to the 'blackhole' upon bread and water. . . . That we may know what it is, let us judge it by its fruits. There are in a considerable proportion of cases, suicide, fatuity or madness.[33]

The Lancet raised serious questions about treating Fenian prisoners as common criminals. The *BMJ* highlighted, without supporting, the accusations by Fenian prisoners, that they had been ill-treated, ill-fed and over-worked and this in particular had contributed to the death of Charles McCarthy in January 1878.[34]

The *BMJ*, while recognizing the seriousness of reducing the diet, supported its use in the hierarchy of punishment:

> The power of the stomach as an implement of education, moral and intellectual, is the subject of a familiar quotation from an observant poet, and it is a pity to surrender any power left us of improving the manners of criminals.[35]

The accounts by prisoners of the deleterious effects of prison discipline were reflected in the ongoing debates in the 1870s and 1880s around deaths in custody and prison mortality rates. Coroners' inquests were important forums for bringing the power of the institution to account. It was here that the statements of prison managers and MOs were often severely challenged. While the medical journals argued that coroners should be trained in medicine rather than in law, it is clear that the juries were sceptical of official accounts. As Dr Quinton commented, the inquests were

> frequently embarrassing, if not annoying, to the prison witnesses, especially medical officers. A fixed idea seemed to possess the minds of jurymen that prisoners were either starved, or done to death under the new management. The examination of witnesses often assumed an aggressive or offensive tone on matters relating to hospital and general treatment, the sufficiency of diets, the use of stimulants, and so on – questions which had not aroused any similar attention when prisoners were being maintained out of the rates . . . popular distrust of the system, judging from press comments, the attitude of jurors and other sources of information, seemed to exist in no uncertain degree. So captious and unreasonable were some juries that an intelligent onlooker remarked that 'medical officers were practically tried for man-slaughter at every prison inquest'.[36]

While prison doctors could publicly disagree over the precise interpretation of mortality rates, as Drs Rendle and Nicolson did in the columns of the *BMJ* between April and June 1871,[37] the medical press was increasingly concerned about the fatal effects that the prison diet was having on the confined. Margaret Girvan's death in Armagh Prison in August 1879 was one example given by *The Lancet*, where the inquest jury's verdict that the deceased had died of 'hectic fever in a shattered constitution' was supported by a rider that the 'very low scale of diet which she received in the prison from the day of her committal had a great deal to do with the result'.[38]

The previous February the Commissioners published the report of an inquiry into the death of John Nolan in Coldbath Fields. The prisoner's death caused both the medical and popular press to call for changes in the system of discipline and diet. According to the inquest jury, Nolan died in the prison infirmary from 'the mortal effects of acute inflammation of the lungs'. Furthermore, his death was

> accelerated by the repeated and excessive punishment of bread-and-water diet, which was ordered by the governor and sanctioned by the

surgeon. The jury are of [the] opinion that it is impossible for the medical officer properly or effectually to attend to his duties at the prison without being resident.[39]

One member of the jury stated that 'he did not believe a word of the doctor's evidence. It was full of contradictions'.[40] The doctor defended the discipline of the prison before the coroner. He provided a detailed account of life inside indicating that he examined between fifty and sixty prisoners each day. When he examined the deceased 'he had a slight cold and I kept him in the convalescent ward for two days'. He thought the dead prisoner was ill-disciplined; his bed-wetting was due to laziness; and a cold cell was better for sleeping prisoners than a warm one. Prisoners were

> legitimately punished if they do not do their work. I believe the deceased wilfully neglected his work and that it was not inability from weakness. If the deceased had stated that he could not do his work, and had showed sufficient reason, I should have lessened his amount of work.[41]

The official inquiry, which included William Guy, exonerated the surgeon and the governor and did not endorse the opinion of the coroner's jury 'that the duties of the medical officer cannot properly be performed without residence'.[42] The surgeon argued that the inquest had been unfairly conducted, public meetings had been held on Clerkenwell Green and in public houses 'to influence the jury', discharged prisoners were admitted 'to prompt the coroner with questions' and that he had

> distinctly stated to the coroner and jury . . . that I was responsible entirely for all the punishments being carried out and that no prisoner was ever punished without my certifying that he was fit to bear it. I do not in this case believe that the punishment had anything to do with the prisoner's illness and death. . . . The sudden change in the weather was quite sufficient to account for his illness.[43]

The Lancet was less sanguine and maintained that the jury's verdict was fully justified by the

> extraordinary facts disclosed by the inquest. It is impossible for the matter to rest here and the question of prison mortality, discipline and diet with special reference to Nolan's case must be brought for early discussion in the House of Commons.[44]

The journal linked a number of deaths in the early 1880s to the passing of the 1877 Act and the low diets inside. In February 1880 it drew attention to a 'lamentable series of deaths in Her Majesty's prisons under the working of the new Act'.[45] The article defended the prison doctors but chastised the disciplinary orientation of the system, and the commissioners' defence of it. Like the prison doctors, however, the journal did not condemn the system completely and argued against

47

undue leniency towards any criminal class; punishment should be awarded them to the utmost extent of their endurance but we must protest against a system that barely scathes the strong, but crushes the weak.[46]

In July 1880 it talked of the 'unparalleled' mortality among the short-term prisoners, pointing to the death of William Grant in Walton Gaol, Lancashire.[47] Once more, the writers argued that the prisoner's death was due to the

faulty arrangements of our prison system. A man apparently healthy is passed by the medical officer, after a single examination, as fit either to undergo a period of severe starvation of bread-and-water, or to perform severe mechanical labour. He is then taken charge of by the prison officials, and his punishment commences. If the man becomes ill, he is referred to the medical officer, but there seems no provision made for watching the effect of severe punishment on the various constitutions of prisoners till the effects manifest themselves pathologically.[48]

The writers concluded with a call for an increase in medical staff to supervise prisoners who were on bread and water or severe mechanical work such as the treadwheel:

The prison system has already caused some sensational deaths; but nothing is heard of those prisoners who are discharged with their health hopelessly ruined by the severe and ill-supervised discipline they have been subjected to. A committee of inquiry is urgently called for to settle this question, and we hope the investigation, when undertaken, will be thorough and impartial.[49]

In June 1881 it referred to the 'severe quality of the diet for short-termed prisoners'.[50] In December it commented on the higher death-rate amongst women prisoners in comparison to male prisoners. These statistics had been gleaned from the annual report of the Prison Commissioners but the medical inspector did not explain the cause of this disparity within the report. The lack of information in the medical statistics was a particular cause for concern. There was no information on the comparatively high death-rate from heart disease, nor about those deaths described as arising from 'natural causes':

The question at once arises, what were these natural causes? For with experience of recent inquests still fresh in our minds, we have considerable misgivings on this point. Even if we do the prison authorities injustice in this matter, still the fact remains that more than half our prison mortality is not fully reported. If medical statistics are published at all, they should be published fully.[51]

In January 1882 its writers pointed out that short terms of imprisonment were 'destructive to health, and consequently dangerous to life'.[52] In April 1882 there was 'another prison scandal' at Chester Gaol. When James Fry was admitted to the prison he was found to be suffering from bronchial cough and angina

48

pectoris, with disease of the mitral valve. He was not removed to the prison infirmary but confined to his cell. He was not prescribed medicine, nor was his food increased in any noticeable degree. At the inquest the jury returned a verdict of death by natural causes but considered that his death was accelerated 'by the want of a more nutritious and generous diet than that allowed the deceased while in prison; they also blamed the medical officer for not having him treated as a patient in the prison hospital'.[53] The journal repeated these allegations two weeks later and called for more comprehensive information to be made available on the health of prisoners in local gaols. Again its writers repeated the view that medical information in the official reports was

> utterly valueless for the purpose for which [it] is wanted, of really getting an insight into the practical working of our prison system . . . information respecting the health of the prisoners are as much called for as long statistics relate to brush and mat-making.[54]

The *BMJ* was more defensive of the PMS in particular and the system of discipline in general. In its comments on the Chester case, the journal argued that the MO had performed his duties conscientiously and professionally. Furthermore, the cause of death could be blamed on the prisoner himself because he was in the habit of accelerating his heart's action, which induced cardiac irritability, excitement and fainting:

> the evidence goes to the effect that he was in the habit of doing this, either to excite pity and obtain stimulants, or as a means of displaying personal irritation. These attacks of sudden faintness which . . . he seemed to have the power of bringing on at will, were no doubt extremely injurious to himself, and might obviously at any moment end in death.[55]

Two weeks after the editorial a correspondent wrote to the *BMJ* defending the PMS, particularly the role of the doctors in remitting prisoners from hard labour including those 'most abandoned criminals, if they be only the lucky possessors of such a trifling defect as a varicose saphena vein'.[56] What is interesting about this anonymous correspondent is that his remarks crystallized the views of the medical profession with regard to discipline and the criminal class. For while *The Lancet* often and the *BMJ* occasionally criticized the workings of the system, they staunchly defended PMOs and the disciplinary direction of the penal system of which those same MOs were an integral part. As the writer pointed out:

> in these days there is much maudlin sentiment abroad in reference to criminals and this pervades largely that class from which the coroners' juries are generally drawn. The popular interest, indeed, that attaches to the felon not engaged in his employment is so great, and so vastly superior to that accruing to his colleague in distress, the honest pauper, that prisons are fast becoming more comfortable homes than workhouses, and prisoners generally are likely to have, ere long, a better time of it than the officials charged with their care and keeping.[57]

Similar sentiments were expressed about another two deaths late in May 1882. Again they were short-term prisoners whose deaths *The Lancet* attributed to the harshness of the system, within which 'the severity of the discipline and the insufficiency of the dietary' were the major factors:

> We have recently commented on the unscientific characters of dietaries no. 1 and no. 2 that we need not enter upon that point again but it must be manifest to all who are not blinded by routine that bread and water, a plank bed and hard labour are likely to foster that despondency which is felt most acutely during the first weeks of incarceration. If such severity is to be practised, let it be towards the end of the sentence, when the prisoner has been under the observation of the medical officer for some time.[58]

This tension between the recognition that the regime was contributing to untimely deaths and the desire not to be lenient towards the criminal was captured by the contribution of a doctor to the journal the next month. The doctor maintained that it was the constitution of the Prison Commissioners itself which was at fault rather than the Prison Act. He argued for the creation of a Medical Commissioner with specially trained inspectorial staff to supervise the seventy-seven prisons in the system. As to the overall disciplinary thrust of the system, this was to remain intact. As he chillingly explained:

> It stands to reason that for the protection of society and the welfare of the State lawbreakers must be punished, and the punishment for short sentences must be such as to act as a deterrent on liberation. The country will not tolerate corporal punishment unless in extreme cases, so that the Commissioners can only punish offenders by means of their stomachs in combination with labour and cell discipline; this organ requires delicate manipulation, and the dietary system must be beautifully adjusted to punish the prisoner with hunger, and yet stop short of injuring his health. Hence dietetics and physiology are prominently set forth in prison management.[59]

The Lancet agreed with this suggestion in an editorial pointedly called 'Prison Management'. While arguing once more that the published statistics did not present a true picture of prison mortality, the writers thought that the introduction of scientific experts and proper medical inspectorial staff would alleviate these problems and reduce the death-rate. Discipline was not to be replaced but rather what was needed was

> a thorough knowledge of the effects of prison discipline, not on the herd of criminals but on the individual. How do bread-and-water diet, hard labour, and the plank bed affect respectively the robust, sturdy, and well-fed ruffian, and the broken-down, half-starved offender, whose crime in the majority of instances was committed to supply his natural wants? Does the prison system punish both equally? What, again, is the effect of seven days' bread and water, with hard labour, on prisoners with constitutional disorders, either acquired or inherited? Is it right that prisoners should be

50

submitted to such severe treatment when the officials must be in utter ignorance from the man's antecedents whether it can be safely applied? Ought not low fare and hard labour, if they are to be retained as a punishment, to be applied at the end, not at the beginning of the sentence, at a time when the prison officials have got to know something of the prisoner's condition and constitutional peculiarities?[60]

The scientific expert was to be the corner-stone of the system. The journal argued that the mental and bodily health of prisoners was entirely a medical question and that any inquiry into the prison system should be composed of experts as it was 'utterly impossible for any body of laymen, however able, to conduct such an inquiry'.[61]

In December 1882 another prisoner died, this time in Huntingdon Gaol. There was no MO in the prison and no arrangements had been made for emergency cover in the event of a prisoner's sudden illness. *The Lancet* thought the fault lay with the Prison Commissioners, who were trying to secure medical provision at the least possible expense. They therefore permitted the PMO to engage in general practice, which allowed them to pay the holder of the post £100 or £200 as opposed to £700 or £800 a year. It was, the writers said, 'niggard and parsimonious'.[62] In March 1887 it repeated its view that the combination of insanitary conditions, the plank bed and deficient dietary was contributing to the high death-rates of convicted prisoners:

> We have had repeatedly to comment on the deaths of prisoners in gaol from pneumonia or suicide or other causes, and we are repeatedly told that these are the exceptions – that no system was ever more perfect. We doubt it.[63]

The *BMJ* again took a more defensive line, commenting in the same month on the low death-rate inside, the low level of operative surgery opportunities for the ambitious surgeon and the lack of heavy work for convicts, which meant that the prisoner was 'not likely to fall a victim to the host of diseases to which a system lowered by improper and insufficient food, hurried meals and overwork is liable'.[64]

These issues continued into the 1890s. Once more, *The Lancet* published a long article from one of its correspondents complaining about 'two main subjects of unfavourable criticism . . . the prevalence of insanity and the death-rate'.[65] The writer maintained that the combination of the very scanty diet and the further reduction in the amount of food as a form of punishment meant that the prisoners 'are reduced to such a state of weakness that it often happens they leave prison physically unfit for work'.[66] R. F. Quinton, the MO at Wandsworth, responded by taking issue with the statistics on which the correspondent's arguments were based. Again he raised the question of the general discipline of the prison system:

> I yield to none in the desire to shield the prisoner from the consequences of his own misconduct, or it may be, misfortune; but as the Home Secretary pointed out in the circular to which your correspondent alluded, 'it must be remembered that prisons are places of penal discipline,' not places where

prisoners may retire to recruit their health with a view to fitting them for hard work on their discharge.[67]

This view was supported by another prison doctor two weeks later. Writing again in *The Lancet* Dr Thornton argued:

> It is not always remembered by writers that the inmates of a prison are largely made up of the scum of our population ready for any disturbance if the government is lax, and lax prison management is not a kindness nor is it safe.[68]

As ever, the *BMJ* was more circumspect in its analysis criticizing the 'chorus of excited voices' which arose among some sections of the community when a sudden death occurred in custody:

> so difficult and delicate must be the duties of guarding and caring for the weeds of our modern civilization, that trust must play a part in the public mind when that public is in the enjoyment of the comparative safety procured for them by the severely taxed officials whose lives are spent in constant intercourse with this scum of humanity.[69]

THE IDEOLOGICAL CONTEXT OF MEDICAL CONSOLIDATION

The debates around discipline and punishment, and the role of medicine within prisons, took place in the context of the consolidation of science as the dominant paradigm for explaining the natural world. Scientific explanations of the social world were a logical extension of this consolidation. Medical science was pivotal in this process. According to Roger Smith this medicalization refers to the way in which

> events previously the subject of moral judgement have become the object of medical practice. This change is usually linked to a sociology of professional medical interests, though it should also be correlated with secularisation, scientific naturalism and the rise of the social sciences.[70]

A number of writers have pointed to the inherent conservatism and authoritarianism of these changes. Lesley Doyal and Imogen Pennell have argued that science became 'the metaphor within which the existing social and sexual division of labour was justified and reinforced'.[71] Darwinism, in particular, rationalized competitive and individualistic struggle and at the same time used 'scientific and especially biological concepts for explaining and justifying particular forms of social and economic relationships'.[72] This point has been developed by Steven Rose *et al.* in tracing the emergence and consolidation of biological explanations of the social world. These explanations, within which criminology developed in the late nineteenth century, emphasized the quantification of behaviour, so that it could be 'distributed in relationship to a norm'.[73] That norm was tied up with notions of the natural order, the proper relationship

52

between rich and poor, scientifically and medically legitimized. As Rose *et al.* point out:

> Darwinism wrested God's final hold on human affairs from his now powerless hands and relegated the deity to, at the best, some dim primordial principle whose will no longer determined human action. The consequence was to change finally the form of the legitimating ideology of bourgeois society. No longer able to rely upon the myth of a deity who had made all things bright and beautiful and assigned each to his or her estate – the rich ruler in the castle or the poor peasant at the gate – the dominant class dethroned God and replaced him with science. The social order was still to be seen as fixed by forces outside humanity, but now these forces were natural rather than deistic. If anything, this new legitimator of the social order was more formidable than the one it replaced. It has, of course, been with us ever since.[74]

Roberta McGrath has made a similar point indicating how medical power and the ideologies that flowed from it was tied into new forms of hegemonic control in the late nineteenth century. Powerful medical metaphors that were mobilized such as 'moral leprosy' and the 'degeneracy of the species'

> reflected the fear of the bourgeois class. It would either maintain its rule or quite literally go under, hence the need to mobilise new institutions and new ideologies. . . . The repressive apparatuses (police, army) are merely the outer wall of the state's power. This allows us to make sense of the new alliance between state, law and medicine. If the mechanisms of power had shifted it was because control could not be exercised too violently nor too spasmodically for fear of resistance and disobedience. It is precisely for these reasons that 'medical control' increasingly replaced legal mechanisms.[75]

For writers such as Elliott Currie, this shift was neither a humanizing nor a liberating process. Rather the discourses which emerged around 'defective delinquency', 'psychopathy' and 'constitutional inferiority' provided a

> quasi-medical rhetoric that justified the use of the penal system as a means of sifting out and isolating the most expendable and intractable of a generally expendable stratum of the population and that glossed and mystified these essentially political and economic functions with a language of humane 'treatment' and 'social service'.[76]

Increasingly the medical expert became a pivotal figure in the debates. Interventions were based on

> expert decisions (certified by doctors, psychiatrists, social workers etc.) regarding the normality or pathology of 'characters', 'mental or moral states' and 'modes of life'. These decisions which need not be publicly explained, are based upon an expertise in the 'human sciences' that is not widely shared nor easily challenged.[77]

This process of normalization saw the extension of the doctor's forensic network into the mind as well as the body. Concern about the increase in insanity (a concern which was often initiated and articulated by the doctors themselves) allowed the profession to claim the insane as their own for medical intervention. In an editorial comment the *BMJ* maintained:

> Our highest privilege is to extend our ministrations to the mind as well as to the body, to offer to erring brothers the hand of help, to bring back to honesty and wisdom those who through misfortune and weakness have fallen far away from both.[78]

As David Garland comments, this period, particularly between 1876 and 1900, saw a

> remarkable proliferation of discourses of control which had endeavoured to break the classicist symmetry which held between legal forms and penal control. These knowledges and the techniques they proposed, though highly diverse and contradictory *inter se*, nonetheless were united by a general programme of intervention based not on a legal philosophy but upon a positive knowledge of (human) objects and the techniques which would transform them. Individually and collectively these discourses provided disciplinary resources as well as 'scientific' legitimation for a transformation and extension of the penal apparatus.[79]

These scientific developments included a discussion of the use of condemned criminals in cholera experiments in India. If they survived their lives were spared.[80] Similarly, the *New York Medical Record* reported on a condemned prisoner in Hawaii whose sentence was commuted to life imprisonment when he participated in an experiment involving leprosy.[81] Closer to home, *The Lancet* in a leading article headed 'The sterilization of the unfit' (written in February 1889) argued that the hereditary transmission of disease was now 'incontestably established', 'like produces like', 'healthy parent is likely to have healthy offspring' and 'the unhealthy parent tends to transmit his or her defective type of physique'.[82] The journal enjoined its readers to 'plead for truth' because it was their duty to

> instruct and forewarn . . . we are responsible for the diffusion of the light that is in us, and for the employment of our peculiar authority in promotion of the purification and well-being of human society.[83]

Thirteen years later, R. R. Rentoul was more explicit as to who should be the focus for sterilization programmes:

> those suffering from leprosy, cancer, epilepsy, idiots, imbeciles, cretins, weakminded under restraint, lunatics, persons with advanced organic diseases . . . prostitutes . . . mental degenerates . . . the sexual degenerate . . . confirmed tramps and vagrants, characters well known to workhouse officials and to the police . . . confirmed criminals.[84]

54

The space within which the doctors worked allowed these views to coexist with Havelock Ellis's contention that there was a direct connection between the length of the ear, criminality and sexual abnormality. Among criminals it was common to find 'projecting or . . . long and voluminous ears'.[85] There was space for Huxley's contentions that there were natural differences between individuals and races and that

> Physiology teaches us not only that the bodies of men differ naturally in size, strength, and capacity for development, but that the natural differences between human brains in size and richness of convolutions are an index to intellectual and moral differences. Any philosophy that ignores such a fundamental fact becomes thereby futile and delusive. A true philosophy must recognise and adjust the relative parts played by natural endowment and educational training, taken in the widest sense.[86]

There was also space for H. P. Hawkins to discuss the question of moral imbecility and crime deriving from the case of a young woman whom he visited in Holloway. Although falling short of the 'old-world legal standard of insanity', she was, none the less, 'suffering from the faults of defective surroundings or her ancestors'.[87]

The medical journals embraced the Darwinian explanations of criminality. In January 1873 *The Lancet* discussed Galton's theory of evolution and argued for the use of 'material' still available in society to arrange well-assorted marriages, to mate the wise with the wise, the healthy with the healthy in order to 'secure and keep up a class capable of government and legislation'. The reverse side of the evolutionist coin was the criminal class. Could Galton's ideas on 'hereditary improvements', the journal asked, 'be effectively applied to the diminution of crime?'[88] The writer went on:

> If among any body of the community hereditary transmission of physical and moral attributes is conspicuous, it is among the population which fills our gaols. Look at its general physique. Imperfect cranial development, with its concomitant of feeble cerebration, amounting almost to a retrogression in the direction of the brutes, is apparent in the mass of its members. Intellectually and morally they are imbeciles, intelligence being replaced by cunning and the will reduced to its elementary form of desire. In the struggle for existence, they herd together, deriving constant accessions from the degenerate of the classes immediately above them, and perpetuating themselves amid conditions most favourable to the reproduction of their like. This is not theory. At a late meeting of the Medico-Psychological Association evidence was adduced to show that the 'criminal classes constitute a persistent factor in the community, inheriting and transmitting peculiarities, physical and moral, which induce to crime with the force of gravitation.' Forty years' experience of the county prison at Perth enabled Dr. Bruce Thomson to confirm this observation, and to suggest means for removing, or at least modifying, the evil to which it points.[89]

The journal argued that the class should be broken up, removing its members to 'as great a distance from each other as possible'. The 'moral disease' of criminality should be treated in an atmosphere which encouraged recovery. Within this Darwinian universe, the increasing confidence and professionalization of medical practitioners was reflected in their burgeoning influence in late-nineteenth-century social life. In the prisons, medical personnel were neither unaware of nor immune to the changing status of their profession, nor to the positive endorsement that medical science was increasingly being given for its interventions into social problems. These interventions by prison medical personnel reflected and reinforced the views of the medical profession in general, particularly around questions of disorder. The threat of disorder was the umbilical cord that linked medical practice and classification to social control both inside and outside the walls of the penitentiary.

DOCTOR IN CHARGE

In June 1875 *The Lancet* described those who had been detained in police cells as 'the lowest of the low, the filthiest of the scum that society throws up'.[90] Medical opinion took the view such 'scum' could be reformed by interventions into the minds of individuals 'debauched by criminality'. This evil acquired

> a new power of mischief by concentration, just as contagious or infectious diseases gain greater virulence, by the aggregation of cases. The mischievous influences are, so to speak, focussed and, acting and reacting mutually, they develop with augmented energy, and bear bad fruit multiplied a hundredfold. We entirely agree with the opinion that a wise adoption of the separate system would protect the less criminal, and prove increasingly punitive to the more depraved.[91]

Medical Officers in prisons and workhouses were regarded as pivotal in the process of intervention. They were better qualified to 'bear testimony on these points than governors, who for the most part, know little or nothing of the inner life of the establishments under their nominal control'.[92] The doctors were in the front-line not only when it came to establishing the general health of the prisons but also in detecting malingering. *The Lancet* outlined the ideological context of the MO's work:

> The medical officers of these prisons have to deal with malingering of every shape and form. The art, in fact, is practiced amongst convicts with a refinement that baffles description, and seems attainable only by cunning thieves and lazy wretches, who prefer preying on society to earning an honest livelihood, and who for the most part occupy our prisons. All this adds considerably to the difficulties of their work, and if errors of diagnosis are made occasionally, they are generally in the prisoners' favour.[93]

This praise was part of a more general claim for the profession to be taken seriously by the state and 'to accord to medicine the status and scope of skilled service':

the science of life is an integral part of political economy, and the development of physical and moral health – by sanitary conditions affecting the whole population – should be the primary aim of government. The intimate relation of bodily weakness, infirmity, and decrepitude with poverty and crime, is beginning to be perceived. When may we hope to see the logic of facts working out practical conclusions?[94]

In November 1888 *The Lancet* argued that one method for dealing with society's outcasts was to increase the period prisoners spent in separate confinement. The journal had been led to this conclusion by a paper from Dr Gover, the medical superintendent of Millbank. It felt that such confinement and the treatment within the regime should be directed 'not less to the formation of criminals than to the repression of crime'. It concluded that since the infliction of punishment was

now placed under efficient medical vigilance and control, we shall be prepared to welcome a reformation of prison rules which will enable the system of separation to be carried out for longer periods than at present, and its effects to be more fully developed in that very numerous class of criminals to whom it may with great moral advantage be applied.[95]

Gover demanded a three-year period of separation which would allow the prisoner to have some industrial, occupational training 'without interference with the discipline of the prison'.[96] The doctors were therefore still concerned about maintaining discipline. By 1892 detecting malingerers had become so important to them that it was cited as part of their demands for better pay and conditions.[97]

Other PMOs outlined the clear connection between discipline, morality and control. R. F. Quinton's autobiography, *Crime and Criminals*, began with a discussion about the roots of criminality:

The habits and ways of the criminal class are frequently inscrutable, and invariably unlike those of normally constituted people. Some defect or weak spot in character is constantly found to accompany criminality. Want of self-restraint, lack of moral principle, callousness of temperament, selfishness, idle habits – these are formidable obstacles to reformatory effort which too often prove insurmountable.[98]

He maintained that any misery or suffering prisoners experienced depended 'much more on the temperament and antecedents of the offenders than on any cruelty inherent in the system'. Furthermore, the 'restfulness' of prison and 'the monotony of the dinner bell appeal strongly to thousands of the vagrant class'.[99] As with many social commentators of the time he was concerned with demoralization and the emergence of a criminal population whose roots lay within the organization of the society itself.[100] This, however, was no radical attack on social structure. Rather Quinton was eager to emphasize how society was largely responsible for the manufacture of the vagrant class. Our methods of dealing with them hitherto have been inept and futile, and the encouragement which has lately been given, in the form of eleemosynary doles to unemployed and unemployable indiscriminately, has tended to the demoralisation of thousands, and converted them into hopeless vagrants.[101]

Quinton carried these views into the prison, particularly in his search for malingerers. He thought that shamming was 'constantly in evidence and refusals to work were a daily occurrence'. The daily sick list amounted to 10 per cent of the population. There were usually 100 applicants who were seen in 45 minutes, of whom 'not more than a dozen needed medical treatment of any kind'.[102] He described one whose

> main object in life has been to avoid work in any shape or form. He was ignorant with the ignorance of the savage and so devoid was he of anything resembling moral sense, that the rights of property and the raison d'etre of the penal laws were to him dark mysteries and they remained so to the end.[103]

Quinton supported this view with a more general description of his first days as an Assistant Surgeon at Portsmouth Convict Prison in 1876. The prison contained 1,200 prisoners:

> The armed sentries, gates and bars, fetters and triangles, with other paraphernalia of the establishment, were sufficiently stern and gruesome features to me as a novice entering the service to relieve suffering, but they counted as nothing when compared with an actual acquaintance with the human beings for whose control and safe-keeping they were required. I felt that I had been suddenly transplanted into a veritable community of pirates capable of any, and every crime under the sun. Although penalties for misconduct were very severe at the time, they had apparently but little deterrent effect.[104]

He was also quite clear where he stood on the question of prison diet and the relationship of the diet to punishment. He described how requests for a change of diet 'came in shoals'. He started from the position that it was 'fairly liberal in quantity, and in a physiological sense should have sufficed for all but a small percentage of exceptional cases'. He supported the use of dietary punishment:

> it is often found to be the only way of appealing to the feelings of an idle or insubordinate person, short of the infliction of corporal punishment. Prisoners will light-heartedly submit to loss of remission marks, loss of stage privileges, loss of gratuity, or even to cellular confinement, if their diet is not reduced.[105]

He concluded by repeating his views about discipline:

> It is not unlikely that I may be called a stony-hearted official for taking a cold common-place view of the treatment that is most calculated both to

reclaim prisoners, and to reduce crime, but I have at all events more than an arm-chair knowledge of the subject, and more than a nodding acquaintance with the material to be experimented on. These credentials must be my excuse for denouncing a pampering system as one that is likely to cause much more harm than good. Pampering, in fact, is just as unsound in principle, and just as futile in practice, with a naughty man as it is with a naughty child. . . . If . . . our prisons offered such attractions as are here described, thousands would avail themselves forthwith of a rest-cure under conditions that would really mean to them Oriental splendour and luxury.[106]

John Campbell's account of his experience as a Medical Officer expressed similar views. Campbell was an MO for thirty years and published his autobiography in 1884. The book covered a range of areas that he had come across during his service. Again there was an important overlap between moral degeneration and criminality. He expressed this connection in forceful terms describing permanent criminals as those men who were 'so thoroughly debased and hardened as to resist any system of treatment'. Habitual criminals, he concluded,

> when not undergoing sentence in prison, depend on doles, or indulge their criminal propensities by acts of theft, mischief and outrage having an inordinate dislike to earning a livelihood by honest industry.[107]

For Campbell, crime was linked to a combination of degenerate and hereditary predispositions:

> The foregoing remarks on some of the bodily ailments to which the criminal classes are more peculiarly liable, are sufficient to show that the medical officers of prisons who discharge their duties faithfully have no sinecure. This is more especially the case in an invalid prison, where they have to contend with aggravated, chronic, and intractable diseases from hereditary predisposition, or from constitutional degeneracy, the result of intemperate and vicious habits. These remarks apply with even more force to mental affections, which occur among invalid prisoners in every form and degree, from simple weakness of intellect to well-marked lunacy. Mental deficiency is by no means uncommon among habitual criminals, and prevails in many different forms. Some display a marked degree of dulness of stupor; others sharpness and cunning more allied to the tricks of monkeys than the acts of reasonable men. The physiognomy, as well as the conformation of the skull, is often remarkable; and the result of many post-mortem examinations has proved that the brains of prisoners weigh less than the average, and that a large brain is an exception. These cases of mental deficiency or disorder are at times a source of great anxiety to the medical authorities, and this is increased by the inadequate means provided in the prison for the management of such cases.[108]

Like Quinton, he supported order, regularity and discipline in prisons as the fundamental mechanisms for dealing with criminals and, in particular, for reclaiming them from the vice and debauchery of criminal association:

Although I am in favour of a mild and encouraging system, with a view to the improvement of the moral and physical condition of convicts, I also desire to see the strictest discipline carried out, so as to suppress any tendency to insubordination or disobedience to prison rules. The system of a preparatory prison, so much advocated some years go, with a view of allowing convicts, on the eve of their discharge many indulgences in the shape of improved dietary, greater liberty, and increased remuneration for work, might be carried too far; for prisoners undergoing sentences for crimes more or less heinous have no right to expect luxuries, or anything more than kind and generous treatment, as long as they are industrious and amenable to other rules of the prison. By making the closing period of imprisonment agreeable, the deterrent effect must be greatly impaired.[109]

The Lancet continued to push the case for prison doctors as the best people to discuss the question of criminality and recommend solutions to curb its growth. In October 1890 it warned the Prison Commissioners that they should not be content with 'vague expressions of opinion by the governors but will obtain definite medical data on the authority of the medical officers of their prisons'.[110] The journal spoke confidently about what medical science could offer the authorities. In 1892 it told its readers:

science will work on the more humane view that society is responsible for its degenerative types and that it must leave no effort untried for their rehabilitation till with the establishment of sounder and healthier conditions it creates a social organism in which crime will become as preventable as disease.[111]

At a meeting of the Psychology Section of the British Medical Association in July 1892, Jules Morel called for the application of the 'medico-psychological service' to all recidivists and all the 'great criminals'. This in turn would allow doctors and psychologists 'to make up very complete reports of the mental state of the convicts' and

It would allow us to class . . . delinquents, and subsequently to begin an individual treatment, so far as their cerebral power allows it. . . . It would allow us . . . to make known the undisciplined and those who would simulate mental disease; it would allow us to take the necessary measures to repress their conduct.[112]

Morel criticized Cesare Lombroso and his followers for failing to understand 'the importance of the moralization of the criminals'.[113]

From the point of view of the medical profession, Lombroso offered only one of a number of possible explanations for the cause of crime. Many in the profession did not base their theories on the narrow notion of the born criminal. This would have restricted and constrained their influence and narrowed the scope for medical intervention. The Lancet caught this point well in October 1893:

we must not forget that, whilst we know not of any criminal constitution there is such a thing as a degenerate physical type, capable, indeed, of improvement under wholesome conditions of life, but which without these becomes the fruitful soil of moral weed-growths. It is clear, therefore, that whilst by means of police we must, and fortunately can, control the evil wrought by moral depravity, we must, in order to prevent this, associate with such control other and more purely remedial agencies.[114]

This view meant that Lombroso's criminal anthropology could be treated with 'respectful hearing' despite its 'occasional exaggerations'.[115] It allowed the journal to discuss operations such as the craniectomy performed on 'an idiot girl of four years of age' at the University of Paris. It had first been performed in Montreal in 1877, when Dr Fuller had made 'an incision in the cranium of an idiot child with the avowed aim of giving expansion to the cerebrum'.[116] By 1893 the Professor of Surgical Pathology at Paris had performed twenty-five such operations and claimed that twenty-four of the individuals involved had been 'cured'. While indicating that there had been criticisms of the method, the journal concluded:

> Such interventions practised in cerebral lesions of apparently an even less hopefull character, has often enough realised expectations to warrant not only its repetition, but its extension to all cases in which osseous obstruction of the cerebrum has been fairly diagnosed. The truth, indeed, seems to lie between the methods of both schools – the surgical and the medico-educational.[117]

The combined impact of inheritance and moral development, what Lombroso called 'diseased development',[118] allowed *The Lancet* to conceptualize the prison 'as a hospital for the remedial treatment of depraved bodies and diseased minds'.[119]

These debates were to have a major impact on the work and influence of prison doctors. They rejected the idea that criminality could be explained by mono-causal theories. As David Garland has pointed out, from the 1870s 'prison doctors such as David Nicolson and later John Baker set about redefining "the morbid psychology of criminals" so as to differentiate a range of conditions rather than a single type'.[120] In a paper in *The Lancet* in October 1895 the Medical Inspector of Prisons, Dr Gover, outlined the range of conditions he felt were conducive to criminality:

> Whether the somewhat pessimistic doctrines of the criminal anthropologist be accepted as the basis of action, or the more hopeful view of those who regard a proclivity to the commission of crime as the natural outcome, in the majority of cases, of unfavourable surroundings from infancy upwards, there can be no doubt that the criminal elements in society may be largely reduced by such social reforms as the prevention of overcrowding, by attention to the details of sanitation, by judicious education and by such training as will tend to eradicate habits of idleness.[121]

Gover's paper appeared in the year that the report by the Gladstone Committee was published. Liberal analyses of this report have consistently articulated the view that the committee's recommendations on treatment and training mark the beginning of the modern prison system's desire to reform the criminal. [122] However, a critical reading of the report and its ideological context reveal a more complex picture. Discipline remained central to prison regimes. As Peter Young has noted, Gladstone's reforms were 'yoked to the more mundane demands of prison discipline . . . reform and discipline were collapsed to mean the same thing'. [123] Prison doctors provided their own evidence to the committee built around the 'degenerate stock' from which criminals came, their moral insanity and their 'furtive eyes'. [124]

The committee extended the power of medical personnel in prisons. Their work was part of the 'scientific and progressive spirit' which *The Lancet* identified in the Prison Commissioners' report for 1897. [125] The following year, the Prison Act was passed, which enacted the proposed Gladstone reforms. In a statement in January 1898 the commissioners discussed the developments that had taken place with regard to PMOs. In eighteen paragraphs they provided an outline of the duties of the PMO to keep detailed records of her/his everyday dealings with the prisoners. It also instructed the MO to 'conform to the rules and regulations of the prison' and to 'support the governor in the maintenance of discipline and order and the safe custody of prisoners'. [126] *The Lancet* argued that the changes were designed to make the prison system 'more elastic and to bring the treatment of the criminal more in accordance with modern ideas'. [127] The 1898 Act, in the journal's view, allowed juveniles to be 'rescued' through 'moral education and industrial occupation'. [128] For prisoners, in general, it allowed for classification, differential treatment and regulation of the prison diet. It symbolized a new regime in which the old idea of deterrence

> gives place to the new principle of reformation; encouragement is held out to those who have casually strayed from the path of rectitude, and the better instincts of the wrongdoer are appealed to in the hope of speedy amendment. [129]

These changes increased the influence of the doctors still further, particularly in the areas of psychiatric examination, classification and disposal. At the same time, the pay which they received and the status which they were accorded remained low and was the subject for debate in the medical press, which the doctors used as a platform to discuss their grievances. This debate was to continue into the twentieth century. The controversy around management, control and medicine was also to continue into the next century. The *BMJ* captured both points well when its writers pointed out that not only was an assistant doctor paid less than the Chief Warder and the Clerk of Works but also

> young men recently appointed will frequently find a sort of moral pressure put on them to back the executive; let them, however, bear in mind that they must be held responsible for any results. [130]

INTO THE TWENTIETH CENTURY

The expansion in the role and influence of the prison doctors continued into the twentieth century. Not only were doctors such as Sutherland, Quinton and Devon trained in psychiatry but they also published 'most of the major scientific works on crime, written in Britain before 1935'.[131] They were also influential in the academic arena. Maurice Hamblin-Smith delivered the first university lectures in 1921/2 in Birmingham. They were given to postgraduate medical students. Furthermore, 'long before Mannheim began teaching at the London School of Economics in 1935 there were courses on "Crime and Insanity" offered at London University by senior prison medical officers such as Sullivan and East'.[132]

This consolidation structured around an 'institutionally-based, administratively-oriented criminology' was paralleled by other developments in the space occupied by prison doctors. It was particularly evident in the consolidation of their observational role with regard to prisoners on remand. Their gaze was turned to probing, testing and reporting on those whose mental state gave local magistrates cause for concern. Stephen Watson argues that this process began in the 1880s, when magistrates increasingly used the remand process for those prisoners 'whose mental state was suspect'.[133] It was enhanced by the Prison Commissioners, who in their reports from the mid-1890s noted an increase in prisoners who were ultimately found insane. This was attributed to the 'growing practice of remanding to prison for a period of medical observation, persons who have committed some offence while in an apparently unsound state of mind'.[134]

In 1907 the Home Secretary indicated that the policy of the commissioners was to place 'mentally deficient prisoners . . . under the special charge of the medical officers of the prisons'. In addition, they were to be continuously in the personal care of 'selected warders':

> The medical officers regulate their discipline and diet and allow them such employment as is suited to the condition of each individual. In addition to those so classified there are other prisoners temporarily under observation to ascertain their mental state.[135]

The doctors were to consolidate and increase their influence with these prisoners in the coming years. By 1920 they were attending conferences and publishing widely in the area of criminality and mental illness. In that year, a number of them attended a conference at Rampton Hospital. They included Dr Norwood East, then the PMO at Brixton, Dr Ahern from Liverpool and Dr Murray from Parkhurst. Apart from Murray 'everyone at the conference eventually published on moral imbecility'.[136] Observation and surveillance were key techniques in the doctor's repertoire. For Watson the observation techniques and mental testing of the 1920s were direct heirs to the strategies of isolation developed in the early nineteenth century.

In 1922 Sir Evelyn Ruggles-Brise, the Chair of the Prison Commissioners, recognized PMOs as experts in mental disease as did the commissioners and organizations such as the BMA's Parliamentary Bills Committee.[137] When the *Report of the Committee Appointed to Inquire into the Pay and Conditions of Service in the Prison System* was published in the same year the authors found the MOs at Brixton, Liverpool, Manchester, Birmingham and Leeds were being remunerated with 'considerable fees for giving evidence in court on the mental condition of prisoners'.[138] Norwood East, who was later to become Medical Inspector of Prisons, was producing 700 to 800 reports a year on the mental condition of prisoners. In Walton Maurice Ahern was producing 300 reports annually.[139] Some doctors were contending that their position 'meant . . . the courts should always consult them before sentencing offenders':

> The whole question of the correct treatment of offenders is a purely psychological matter. No prison punishment (corporal, dietary, or confinement to cell) can be inflicted without the concurrence of the medical officers. It is but a short and logical step to the position that no sentence of imprisonment should be awarded, or any order of court made, without the due attention being paid to the findings of an adequate medical examination.[140]

The Home Secretary gave added legitimacy to this development when, in February 1922, he opened a series of lectures on the subject of 'The Mind and What We Ought to Know About It'. He pointed out that 'more and more' scientific knowledge was being generated 'every day' in relation to 'temperamental cases'. In addition, 'great scientific men' were devoting their lives to the subject. For Borstals

> We want to have not men trained in the Army – soldiers – we want schoolmasters and doctors combined; we want men who can study each individual case.[141]

CONTRADICTIONS AND CHALLENGES

While the power and influence of prison doctors increased in the first four decades of the twentieth century, their position was not without its own contradictions, imposed limitations and challenges. These worked at a number of different levels. First, as a professional group they were not totally united on the terrain of a clear-cut strategic psychiatric programme. There were divisions between them as to the interpretation of the precise relationship between psychological processes and social action. There was even a residue of nineteenth-century Lombrosian theorizing in some of their pronouncements. As late as 1927, Norwood East wrote in his *Introduction to Forensic Psychiatry* that 'the measurement of the head circumference may be of value'.[142] Twenty years previously, J. F. Sutherland had written that

> the existence of a criminal physiognomy cannot be gainsaid . . . coarseness, scars, expression and look tell their own fate. They are the hallmarks of alcoholism, debauchery, ruffianism, dishonesty, lying and unchastity.[143]

Maurice Hamblin-Smith, on the other hand, described himself as a 'convinced and quite unrepentant Freudian' and that 'imprisonment must be regarded as a mode of treatment rather than one of punishment'.[144] He made a number of suggestions regarding treatment programmes including better pay and conditions for prison officers, the establishment of different kinds of prisons and the 'indefinite detention' of recidivist offenders in colonies where 'they might be accompanied by their wives and children'.[145]

> Let us regard a prison as a place of moral regeneration, and as on the same plane as any other hospital (mental or general). Both hospitals and prisons are, at present, unfortunate necessities. But we could be as proud of a well-ordered prison as we are of a modern hospital.[146]

The second contradiction lay in relation to the state. While state servants such as the Prison Commissioners and politicians like the Home Secretary welcomed the doctors' expert interventions, this was not reflected in an increase in either financial rewards or status. From the turn of the century they were locked into an ongoing debate with the Treasury about the legitimate financial rewards for their work. It was a debate which was to continue until the present.[147]

In a letter to the Home Secretary, written in January 1905, Ruggles-Brise commented it was 'to be regretted that this important body of officers should be in a state of chronic dissatisfaction with their conditions'.[148] The following November, the Home Secretary wrote to the Treasury, pointing out that changes in a range of areas had made the duties of PMOs

> more onerous than they were even ten years ago. Further, there is at present on the part of Judges and magistrates a growing tendency to regard crime from a medical standpoint. Hence the opinion of the p.m.o. comes with increasing frequency to have weight in the question of the course to be followed in the treatment of a criminal by the court in sentencing him or by this Department subsequently.[149]

The letter also indicated that judges and magistrates were increasingly recommending that a prisoner's mental and physical condition should be 'specially observed and that his release or continued detention for the full term of the sentence passed on him be made conditional on the view taken by the medical authorities'.[150] The Home Office in fact had issued a special order to Medical Officers in April 1902, urging them to attend courts to give evidence if required 'in any case where a question is likely to arise with regard to a prisoner's mental condition'.[151] From that time the doctors displayed a new-found confidence in their role as experts, especially in observing the mental condition of prisoners on remand. The deputy MO at Pentonville expressed these views clearly in January 1919:

> the work of prison m.o.s has in recent years become far more complicated and important. We may indeed claim to be the only body of men in the country whom training and experience have fitted to acquire a competent knowledge of scientific criminology. Moreover in our ordinary duties we have to be familiar with other branches of medicine, in respect of which the

general practitioner is accustomed to rely on specialists. An efficient prison m.o. must, for example, be somewhat of an expert in such widely different diseases as insanity and venereal diseases.[152]

In March Ruggles-Brise pursued this line with a letter to the Under-Secretary of State at the Home Office pointing to 'the very urgent need for the re-organization of the medical service of prisons'.[153] By February 1920 the MOs had rejected the Treasury's suggestion for reform which meant that 'a grave crisis is anticipated'.[154] His words were to prove prophetic.

The third contradiction in and limitation to the power of the doctors related to the prisoners. As Chapter 2 noted they were central to the development of disciplinary regimes in general and the control of difficult prisoners in particular. This continued into the twentieth century. In December 1904 Dr Smalley, the Medical Inspector of Prisons, advocated the retention of the loose canvas jacket to cope with disturbances. He supported this by outlining the different restraints that could be used, which were broken down into three categories. These he termed 'plenty of attendants', 'chemical' and 'mechanical'.[155] Smalley outlined the problems with each. Attendants could lead to 'desperate resistance' and to charges 'in the case of prisoners of unnecessary violence having been used'. Chemical or medicinal restraints were used to

signify the administration of narcotic drugs in order to control noisy and violent patients. This form of restraint has the disadvantage that it often depresses the vital powers, deranges digestion and is of doubtful benefit in some cases of delerium.[156]

He concluded that mechanical restraint was

[the] best form to use with certain prisoners e.g. when the violence arises, as it sometimes does, from a mixture of mental excitement and temper or when restraint is necessary in order to retain surgical dressings on a wound or ulcer . . . said mechanical [restraint] is preferable to restraint by personal attendants owing to the possibility of bruising etc. and of after charges of personal assault and injury, when it may be very difficult to elucidate if unnecessary violence has been used.[157]

Smalley's annual reports also highlighted the problems feeble-minded prisoners posed for prison discipline. This group 'who by reason of their mental defect are incapable of conforming to ordinary prison discipline' were regarded as an identifiable mass within the population at large.[158] Many of the debates around social policy and criminality in the first two decades of the century were taken up with what should be done with them. The term had first been used by Sir Charles Trevelyan, who was a member of the Council of the Charity Organization Society. He had used it in 1876 and it became institutionalized in 1904 with the appointment of the Royal Commission on the Care and Control of the Feeble-Minded. It reported in 1908 and included among its members Dr Horatio Donkin, who was the Medical Commissioner of Prisons.[159] The Mental Deficiency Act, which followed in 1913, indicated the threat that the increase in numbers of feeble-minded people posed to the society. As David Garland points out, 'from being a local difficulty faced by the managers of casual wards and prisons, the question of "the feeble-minded" had become a degenerative threat to the race and to national efficiency'.[160] The Act extended state control over a range of groups while simultaneously establishing 'yet more specialist enclosures where such defectives will be detained and treated'.[161] It meant

the extension of the role of state, which becomes the subject of wider and more penetrating forms of social regulation; promoting expertise and the accumulation of disciplinary knowledges; and the establishment of practices of individualisation, accompanied by rhetorics of reform.[162]

Smalley had pursued a similar line arguing for the permanent detention of this group in a 'suitable institution'.[163] As *The Lancet* commented in October 1908:

the characteristics of the individuals who come into this category and the difficulties which beset their treatment in prison have been pointed out again and again by Dr Smalley in his annual reports for several years past; and it is satisfactory to note that the views on this matter which he has so insistently urged have been fully confirmed by the report of the Royal Commission on the Care and Control of the Feeble-Minded.[164]

Smalley's identification of this group as problematic was an integral part of the ongoing discussion around eugenics, which itself was a central part of medical debate. While the well-organized eugenics lobby forcefully put the case for sterilization it did not achieve hegemony. There were deep divisions within the medical profession over the scientific status of the lobby's theory and methodology.[165] What is important is that its argument was part of a 'social programme' in which social questions were 'fundamentally *depoliticised*' and questions of power and its distribution were replaced by 'questions of individuals and their improvement'.[166] Medicine was increasingly at the centre of this displacement process both in society at large and within the prisons. However, as in the nineteenth century, prisoners did not acquiesce to medical power. This time they were sustained and supported by organized support groups outside the walls.

In January 1919 the Prison System Enquiry Committee was established by the executive of the Labour Research Department. The Enquiry was particularly important in the context of the centralization of the prisons in 1877 and the subsequent suppression of information to the outside world. The Enquiry's report was published in 1922 under the title of *English Prisons Today*. It was a major 728-page analysis of the state of English prisons between 1914 and 1919. It provided a range of material on the PMS and its relationship to prison management. The Enquiry found that medical care for the confined and the treatment of the sick was inadequate; prison hospitals were used for the purposes of solitary confinement; there was an absence of hospital treatment in small prisons; and that there were questions to be asked about deaths in custody. Finally, the increasing role the doctors were playing in classifying mental illness and lunacy was based on little training or qualifications:

We believe we are correct in stating that none of the medical officers even at Brixton or Holloway prison, to which hundreds of cases are sent for mental observation or at Parkhurst prison, the prison to which physically and mentally weak convicts are sent have any special qualification for the diagnosis and treatment of mental cases. Sir E. Ruggles-Brise states that all medical officers are required to have 'a practical knowledge of insanity'; but the phrase appears to signify little.[167]

This lack of knowledge was compounded by the involvement of the medical staff in investigating 'shamming'. The MO on the authority of the Visiting Committee or a Commissioner could apply a 'painful test' to the prisoner. At Dartmoor the prisoner could be placed in a shower bath:

Suppose a telephone box constructed of iron bars, and enclosed in a huge glass coffin. Within the bars is just room for a man standing upright, who can be easily viewed from all directions through the bars and glass. A warder's explanation of this apparatus is as follows: A convict apparently becomes insane and is suspected of shamming. He is removed to hospital, stripped and placed in the cage which is guarded by a warder and inspected by the doctor. Above the convict's (supposed lunatic's) head is an ordinary shower bath apparatus which is turned on and left on if need be for 15 minutes (but not for more).[168]

The temperature of the water plus the iron bars were designed to make the individual 'confess to the doctor that he is shamming and so escape further treatment'.[169] The report raised further questions about insanity in prisons, particularly the ways in which the prison regime contributed to the prisoners' mental demise. It concluded that 'prison discipline generally, and the "observation cell" in particular, are calculated to drive some persons to insanity'.[170]

These conclusions were reflected in the accounts by prisoners about life inside. The regime behind the prison walls in the 1920s and 1930s was still hard, uncompromising and underpinned by violence when order was threatened. Wilfred MacCartney's account of his experience in Parkhurst described in grim detail the standard of medical care, the superficial nature of the medical examination and the involvement of the doctors in a number of disciplinary duties. For MacCartney 'the medical officer is the most important, powerful and the best-paid official in the gaol. His word overrules everybody. What he says goes, and he has a large staff'.[171] The MO's duties involved being present at floggings. Furthermore, if a prisoner continually rebelled against the regime he was put on a landing in the infirmary 'so that the doctors can keep him under observation':[172]

In many cases men were kept upon the 'barmy' landing, punished frequently, lost remission, and then a few weeks before their sentence expired were certified and whisked off to Broadmoor or some institution for the weak-minded. . . . Men are for years treated as normal for the purpose of punishment, and then deemed insane or weak-minded as their day of freedom approaches. Once an accident, twice a coincidence but three times a certainty.[173]

He maintained that during his eight years in Parkhurst he came into contact with approximately nine doctors and 'with one or two exceptions they impressed the prisoner as a heartless and indolent and incompetent crew'.[174] He described their involvement in food rationing:

This starving and feeding-down of the convict are done to render him more amenable to the brutal discipline. I once heard a medical officer say, 'Well, a little starvation makes 'em wonderfully reasonable.' I remember asking Dr. Norwood-East the Prison Commissioner, if it were a scientific fact that a monotonous diet was injurious to the metabolism. He said, 'Yes.' Then I asked if 2,550 consecutive meals of margarine, cocoa, and cheese constituted monotony. He said, 'Get out before I put you on report for insolence.'[175]

For some prisoners the effects were disastrous:

In many cases, prison doctors are wretchedly incompetent. The treatment of a man called Jones who was doing three years for false pretences is evidence of this incompetency. After sentence he was examined and reported fit at two prisons. Two days after the second of these examinations he arrived at Dartmoor, and was there examined by Dr. Battiscombe. Battiscombe has the name among the convicts of being the most careful doctor in the service. He put all convicts sent to Dartmoor through a very thorough examination. . . . on examining Jones, who had been passed by gaol-doctors as fit to work in the hardest prison in England, Battiscombe found that the poor fellow was in an advanced stage of T.B., with one lung completely gone. Jones was put to bed immediately, and never left it again except to come to Parkhurst. He died almost in my arms a few days after Christmas 1933.[176]

Red Collar Man's autobiography (published in 1937) told a similar story. For him, the doctors 'with few exceptions are very callous in jail'.[177] He discussed their involvement in disciplinary activities including flogging, where the man's back was 'covered with long red weals and the skin is broken and bloody. These marks never fade right out, but remain for life'.[178] Like MacCartney, he saw the insane label being used against troublesome prisoners. As he pointed out, 'sane in jail and take your punishment come what may, but insane when freedom beckons and so be locked up again'.[179] Order and security were maintained through the use of escape lists, locating potential escapees in particular cells and keeping a dim light burning in the cell throughout the night. Clothes were left outside the cell door in the evening. Strip searches and cell turnovers were carried out at least once a month. Recalcitrants were placed in one of the seven silent cells which were like a 'ghastly Chinese puzzle box'.[180] The cells were made of concrete and heavily fortified; there was no heating in winter:

These black holes were completely devoid of any furniture whatever. For a bed there were three boards set in a concrete border about 4 inches off the floor. At one side of the cell there was a sawn off trunk of a tree clamped to the wall and embedded in the concrete floor. The only ventilation was a small iron grill about eight inches by four, high up in the wall. In the ceiling was a window of frosted glass, inches thick. Outside each cell door, to the left, was a ladder let into the wall, leading to the roof of the cell. This was used by the warders to climb to the roof to spy on the lag confined inside by means of a small spy hole which gave a complete view of the interior of the cell. A lag confined in these cells on punishment was only allowed out for one hour in the twenty-four for exercise. From 7.30 a.m. his bedding and mattress were removed from the cell and not returned until 7 p.m. each evening.[181]

Body-belts, steel bracelets and straitjackets were also used. If these techniques failed then violence was a possibility. Such beatings were described not only by prisoners at this time. In his autobiography, *The Wall is Strong*, Gerald Fancourt Clayton, the ex-governor of Wandsworth, described in frank detail an incident at the prison in the late 1930s. Two prisoners who escaped were recaptured, taken to the punishment cells and in his words given 'a good hiding':[182]

When I went to see the men in the punishment cells I noticed that the first man had bruises on his face, and I asked him how he got them. He replied that he had fallen from the boundary wall on his face on to a heap of stones. I then passed on to the other, the nastiest type of Jew and a well-known mischief-maker. However, at that time he made no reference to what had happened although he was marked. In reporting the escapes to the Prison Commissioners I did not mention the fact that the men's faces were marked. The next day, however, the mischief-maker complained that he had been assaulted, and I reported the whole circumstances to the Prison Commissioners. . . . Four officers were then suspended, placed under report and their defences heard by Mr Paterson. He ordered them to be dismissed and later I received a reprimand for not at once reporting all the circumstances to the Prison Commissioners. The sad thing is that those four officers were among the best officers in the prison, and I was very much upset by the way they had been treated. The only consolation was that I was able to find them all good jobs with a firm outside the service.[183]

Challenges to the role of medicine in prisons continued into the 1940s with the establishment of the Prison Medical Reform Council (PMRC) on whose committee sat Fenner Brockway, the co-author of *English Prisons Today*. The PMRC published a series of reports between 1943 and 1962, which provided an alternative account of prison life and the work of the PMS. In 1943 Roger Page, an ex-prisoner and the council's secretary, published *Prison Medical Service*. This pamphlet was the first account of the council's research to appear in written form. The report identified 'grave defects in the Prison Medical "Service"'.[184] As the evidence of these defects grew

[and] came in from all quarters it became increasingly plain that here was a scandal to which public attention should be drawn. So there came into being the Prison Medical Reform Council, an organisation formed by a group of people who have a concern for the well-being of their fellow-citizens and who by calling this Council into being, exercised their democratic right to criticize public administration.[185]

The PMRC's object was to press for what it called the 'proper working of the Prison Medical Service (which shall be interpreted as being responsible also for the hygiene and mental health) and for extensions and improvements therein'.[186]

In prison, Page discovered a submerged world where the authorities assumed that every prisoner was a malingerer. In discussing the PMS, Page argued that the word service should be in inverted commas as

day-to-day medical care was of the most perfunctory and casual kind imaginable; and that the regulation medical examinations were the merest matter of form, often only a glance or a question. I discovered that provision for dental care was callously inadequate. I discovered other things . . .[187]

Among the 'other things' were the conditions in which medical treatment was given. In Wandsworth there was one recess for forty-five men to empty their overnight 'slops'. This led to a 'vile stench' and further blocking of the one sink and WC which the men used. Prisoners also had to pay for medical services. Teeth were extracted by a dentist who visited the prison. He received half-a-crown (12½p) per tooth. If prisoners were not in credit then they were ignored. Those who had money could not provide assistance. Page's initial research was supported by evidence which he obtained from a questionnaire that was given to conscientious objectors. The answers were overwhelmingly critical of the medical services. As he maintained, 'I have declared the Prison Medical Service to be shamefully inadequate. Here is the evidence to support the statement'.[188] This conclusion was supported by a number of other pamphlets. In 1943 the PMRC published *Prisons for Women: Some Accounts of Life in Holloway*. Again much of the content concerned medical treatment inside, in this case in relation to women. Barbara Roads, one of the contributors, described her experience:

The medical examination is so superficial that it is a wonder that any disease is ever diagnosed. . . . [Pregnant women] have ordinary prison diet until 6 months pregnant and then have extra only 2 slices of bread and half-a-pint of milk each day. They spend 23 hours of each 24 sitting or lying down. . . . They are locked in their cells each night in solitary confinement right up to the time the baby is due. The ruling on this matter is that the expectant women are to be moved to hospital when 8 months pregnant but this was not done while I was at Holloway; the hospital was full.[189]

In 1944 Page wrote a Prisoners' Medical Charter, which was a ten-point plan to improve medical provision inside. The pamphlet pointed to the treatment pregnant prisoners received in comparison with those on the outside, who were given cod-liver oil, extra milk and orange juice provided by state-subsidized schemes. Women in prison had none of these advantages. Neither did they attend antenatal classes. In addition

> Until far advanced in pregnancy, women, usually, are subject to the normal prison routine which involves being locked up in solitary confinement for long periods including the hours of darkness. Because of the bad psychological effect and the difficulty of getting emergency attention, this state of things should be altered.[190]

The PMRC also highlighted the experiences of individual prisoners. In October 1945 it published *The Case of Prisoner Alpha*, a pamphlet which dissected the prison life of a 24-year-old prisoner who suffered 'from severe, permanent, incurable epilepsy'.[191] He had no teeth and his spectacles had been lost inside. He petitioned the Home Secretary, for which he was victimized. A hospital officer told him that if he came to hospital he would 'know all about it' – he would 'be unlucky!' When Alpha said he had already been there once as a patient the reply came: 'Yes but we didn't know all about you then'.[192]

The critical tradition established by the Prison Medical Reform Council was to be continued in the following decades by other prisoners' rights organizations. At the same time the influence of the medical profession continued to increase, particularly after the Second World War. This was legitimized by the social reconstructionist ideology of the period. Medical intervention into the social body was increasingly formulated, implemented and legitimized by the state, particularly in its role as welfare protector of the nation's physical and psychological health. Prison doctors and psychologists were beneficiaries of this ideology as they expanded their influence through formal means such as the 1948 Criminal Justice Act and through informal mechanisms such as conferences and research papers in which they claimed expert status in the search for the causes of crime. However, that expansion again was not without its own contradictions, limitations, challenges and rejections. Not only was medical hegemony incomplete but these challenges were also integral to the sense of crisis in the PMS in the late 1950s and early 1960s, which led to the establishment of, and report by, the Gwynn Inquiry in 1964. The next chapter explores these events in the crucial years between 1945 and 1966.

CHAPTER 4

Disciplining the body, reconstructing the mind: medical power and the criminal 1945–64

During the following week a doctor at Strangeways took a look at him, 'formed certain opinions about him', and asked for a fort-night in which to make further observations. This was granted, and Harry had his first taste of psychiatric investigation.

He asked me how many times did I like to go with a woman. I said, 'As many times as I can.'

'How many times do you go in a night?'

'What's that got to do with you?'

'I'm trying to judge your character.'

'Well,' I said, 'you can't judge my character by asking me how many times I go with women. How many times do you go with your wife?'

This was outside the scope of the inquiry, which was switched to a different but adjacent track.

He asked me how often I played with myself. 'It depends where I am,' I said. 'If I'm here in the nick I play about with myself a lot, because I can't go with all these women you keep talking about. And anyway, I can't see what all this has to do with my case.'

'It's got to go to court, for a Borstal report.'

'What's sex got to do with Borstal?' I said.

'Do you think I'm a sex maniac or something?'[1]

In return for prestige and limited powers, psychiatry has been assimilated by modern penality and medical jurisprudence, and, within the prisons, it has been refashioned as one more weapon in the prison's never-ending quest for ideological justification of its power to punish.[2]

The PMS was in a strong position at the end of the Second World War. The service derived its legitimacy from the reconstructionist ideology that domi-nated political debate between 1945 and 1964. This ideology rested on the belief that the state, through its employees and other professional groups, should increasingly intervene into English society in general and the lives of the deviant and criminal in particular. The doctor, psychologist and criminologist became expert figures in the debates about crime and social policy. They articulated theories about criminality which clustered around a number of themes and images: the impact of the war, the question of the environment, family disorganization, individual psychopathology and in the case of black people sexuality and miscegenation.[3] These explanations were given different emphases by different professional groups. However, each justified interventions either at an individual, family or community level to deal with the problem of crime, which according to the official statistics was inexorably rising year by year. Lurking behind this increase was the spectre of social breakdown. If crime could not be controlled then the social order, despite the advances made by the Welfare State, was in danger of collapsing. What should be done about the problem taxed the collective minds of professionals and intellectuals of the time. Their interventions were seen as a bulwark against encroaching disaster. Thus while environmental and biological explanations of criminality could lead to different policy interventions they were united on an ideological terrain which saw therapeutic intervention as the key to removing the stain of deviance from the landscape of English society. That therapy built on professional expertise, legitimized by criminological research and propelled by the philosophy of state intervention was underpinned by medical and psychiatric explanations of human behaviour. For the confined it was to play a central role in the discourse of prison medicine throughout the post-war period.

THE POST-WAR PMS

At the end of the war, responsibility for the organization of the PMS lay with the Prison Commissioners, based in London. The commissioners were responsible for the appointment of prison doctors. Medical journals such as *The Lancet* carried advertisements for doctors and at the same time provided information about the service and the kind of work successful candidates would pursue. The yearly reports by the commissioners carried similar information. The report for 1945 indicated that the PMS offered a career of 'great interest and importance'. It went on to note that psychiatric techniques had greatly added to

the interest of medicine practised in prison. . . . Further research into the causes of crime whether psychological or social will have to be undertaken in the near future and this offers an opportunity to medical men with the necessary qualifications to undertake this research either independently or in conjunction with specialists in other fields.[4]

According to Lionel Fox, the Chair of the Commissioners, the doctors had 'considerable autonomous powers and responsibilities'. These included examining new prisoners; visiting sick prisoners each day; altering the diet; alerting the governor to prisoners who were physically or mentally suffering or who were suicidal; recommending separate confinement; and introducing special observation for 'every prisoner whose mental condition appears to require it who could be segregated and if necessary certified'.[5] The doctor was also responsible for prisoners undergoing 'certain forms of punishment or under mechanical restraint' and for the general areas of hygiene, sanitation, food, work and exercise.[6] Finally, the doctor examined prisoners before release and recorded individual deaths.

The doctors were supported by Hospital Officers in male prisons, who were recruited mainly from men who had nursing experience in the Navy, Army and Air Force, or worked as attendants in mental hospitals. In women's prisons, they were supported by Nursing Sisters, who were recruited from fully trained State Registered Nurses, with assistant nurses in the larger hospitals. There were one or more Sisters at every women's prison, and in the large hospital at Holloway 'there would be 30 or more if the staff were at full strength'.[7]

The role of the doctors in the management of physical illness was complemented by their involvement in psychiatric work, which, as noted above, was an important general feature of post-war social reconstruction and from the point of view of the commissioners something to be encouraged. In 1932 the Departmental Committee on Persistent Offenders recommended that 'a medical psychologist should be attached to one or more penal establishments to carry out psychological treatment in selected cases'.[8] By 1943 a psychiatric unit had opened in Wormwood Scrubs. It dealt with sixty-six prisoners during the year. In 1946 the unit began using electric shock treatment 'for certain psychiatric cases. This treatment has been combined with psychotherapy in all cases. So far the results have been satisfactory'.[9] Altogether eighty-four cases were 'investigated' by the unit that year. Its work was supported by a new temporary ward with ten beds, which was used 'for a selected number of cases undergoing psychiatric treatment'.[10] There was another psychological unit at Holloway, which among other things classified and allocated young women to their appropriate Borstal institution. This system of classification was augmented in July 1946 with the appointment of a woman psychiatric social worker. In the same year another unit was opened in Wakefield to deal with cases in the North of England.

The reports by the commissioners outlined the importance of the psychiatric component in the work of the doctors and other medical staff. Page after page was devoted to detailing the kind of work in which they were engaged in the search for isolating the causes of crime and treating the individual offender. Classification and categorization were the corner-stones in this search as the body of the prison population was broken down into individual units and placed into categories for psychiatric examination. The report for 1949 provides a good example of not only the centrality of psychiatric work in the everyday practice of the medical profession but also the interventions they were making.

Under the title *Special Researches and Investigations*, the commissioners listed the work that the doctors were engaged in including research into the clinical histories and electroencephalographic readings of sixty-four murderers in Brixton. This research concluded that a 'significant correlation existed between apparently motiveless crime and electroencephalographic abnormality'.[11] Similar research was in progress in Wormwood Scrubs under John Mackwood. At Camp Hill Borstal, the medical and discipline staff were conducting surveys of prisoners received into the institution. The boys were classified either into those who were psychologically abnormal or into one of ten categories, including 'hysterical swindler', 'shiftless', 'unethical', 'emotionally unstable', 'submissive' and 'unclassified'.[12]

The *British Medical Journal* outlined the work Mackwood and his colleagues were pursuing. Once more, they made the claim for forms of treatment which examined the individual characteristics of prisoners. They also highlighted other methods which would support the psychiatric orientation. What linked both was the focus on the individual:

> The psychiatric methods of treatment which have been used so far . . . are by no means the only ones that may in future be considered. Recent research – for instance the electro-encephalographic studies of prisoners by Stafford-Clark and Taylor – indicates that some crimes of violence, especially those in which the motive is obscure, are related to physiological dysfunctions of the brain, and may be preventable by medical measures. It is hoped that it will eventually be possible to establish a special institute of treatment and research within the frame of the prison administration and that its function will be much wider than merely a concern with the psychodynamic aspects of crime.[13]

Dr Roper, the MO at Wakefield, argued that half the population in the prison were inadequates 'and this term represents fairly well their rather vague and ineffectual personality'.[14] From the point of view of the new Labour government these interventions through medical classification were an important part of the drive to find the causes of crime. In February 1946 the Home Secretary noted the importance of the Medical Officer with regard to psychiatric treatment. He pointed out that any prisoner at any prison could receive psychiatric treatment 'if the Medical Officer thinks it desirable'.[15]

EXTENDING THE PSYCHIATRIC NETWORK

In the light of these developments, the organization of the PMS was rationalized and the number of psychiatric personnel increased. In December 1946 the Home Office announced that 'a newly created post with the title Director of Prison Medical Services' was to be established.[16] This post was created to allow Dr Methven, the Medical Commissioner of Prisons, 'to devote a substantial part of his time to medical questions arising in the Children's Branch and the Probation Service'.[17] A large part of the day-to-day work within the prisons was to be done by the new Director, Dr Young. Young held the post until the end of 1950, when he retired. He was succeeded by Harvie Snell, the Principal Medical Officer at Wormwood Scrubs.[18] Snell, in turn, retired in April 1963 and was succeeded by Dr I. G. W. Pickering, formerly SMO at Durham. Pickering joined the PMS in August 1947 and was one of the first students to take the advanced course at the Institute of Criminology in Cambridge. He was also awarded a Nuffield Travelling Fellowship for Home Civil Servants to study the medical and psychiatric aspects of European penal systems.[19]

The changes at the top of the PMS were complemented by other developments further down the hierarchy. The passing of the Criminal Justice Act in 1948 brought with it a further increase in the number of psychological staff. The Act was an important moment in the post-war reconstruction of the criminal justice system. From the government's perspective it represented a new beginning in the state's response to offenders, a 'synthesis of deterrence and reform [that] has become known as the system of training'.[20] Harsh punishments were abolished including sentences of corporal punishment, penal servitude and hard labour. Prison regimes were to be oriented to the constructive training of prisoners to establish in them 'the will to lead a good and useful life on discharge and fit them to do so'.[21] The Act included more powers for the courts to obtain medical reports on offenders. As the *British Medical Journal* pointed out:

> It has been difficult for a court of summary jurisdiction to obtain a report unless the offender was remanded to prison; now it will be possible to remand him on bail on condition that he submits himself to medical examination. . . . Power is now to be given to the court when it appears from medical evidence that the offender may be susceptible to treatment for his mental condition to require him to submit to such treatment for a period not exceeding twelve months.[22]

The influence of medical personnel in the determination of the offender's path through the criminal justice system was substantially increased. This applied both to the pre- and post-sentence stages. The Act required the courts to consider 'the prison authorities' "suitability" reports on mental and physical health'.[23] It also introduced two new 'psychiatric sentences': a probation order with the condition of mental treatment attached and a magistrates' court order for those offenders who fell within the orbit of the Lunacy Act. They could now be given a hospital reception order. The changes meant

> an increased demand for pre-sentence psychiatric examinations and reports. In addition, the internal requirements of the prison system with its growing emphasis on classification, involved the medical staff in further diagnostic work.[24]

A number of support services were introduced including the psychiatric training of hospital officers, the appointment of psychiatric social workers and prison psychologists, who sat on the boards which determined whether a prisoner was to be sent to an open or closed institution.[25] In the remand and trial prisons, the psychologists were to work with the Medical Officers, assist them in the preparation of reports and help them fulfil the 'increasing demands by the courts for reports on the psychological condition of untried prisoners'.[26] They were also to write reports on convicted or Borstal prisoners. This was to include

the ascertainment of intelligence, the application of performance tests, education attainment tests, mechanical and other aptitude tests and general attainment tests and an opinion on the personality and character of the offender. The medical officer will take these data into account when submitting his report to the Court on the mental and physical condition of the accused.[27]

In October 1953 the Home Office announced that Mr A. Staker had been appointed Chief Psychologist in the Prison Commission. This was the first appointment to the post. His duties, to be carried out under the Director of the Prison Medical Service, were to 'direct and supervise . . . the work of psychologists and psychological testers in the prison service and to advertise generally on psychological work within the service'.[28]

From reports written by the doctors it is clear that the passing of the 1948 Act increased both their workload and influence. The examination of prisoners for psychiatric reports was a matter for particular comment. In welcoming this increased contact one pointed out that 'the mental examination of prisoners now consumes more time than any other part of my work . . . it is gratifying to find that our advice is almost always accepted'.[29] The doctor also indicated that contacts with the NHS had become more frequent and that he had been co-opted on to the Regional Psychiatric Advisory Committee. This link was important not only for meeting leading psychiatrists in the region but also for putting the prison '"on the map" in the general psychiatric framework'.[30]

Other doctors made similar points, as did the commissioners, who pointed out that while the practice of prison medicine afforded 'considerable opportunity for experience in physical medicine it is recognized that the greater part of its work lies in the psychiatric field'.[31] This increasing influence was reflected in the attitude of the courts and other areas of the criminal justice system which provided the overarching therapeutic umbrella within which the doctors worked. As one commented:

The number of observation cases at 103 remains high and the number of mental reports to court rose from 40 to 71. I found that all the courts in our area, Norfolk, Suffolk and the Isle of Ely are becoming rapidly more alert to the medical and mental aspects of crime and quite rightly refer many more cases for report under Section 26 of the Criminal Justice Act 1948. The Probation Officers and the Police give me the greatest help by their reports which continue to improve in their scope and discretion upon the antecedents of these men. This in turn calls for more investigation and larger and fuller reports on my part. I have, however, felt rewarded by the appreciation of these reports shown by the Courts, and by the number of occasions when my recommendations have been accepted in every detail and acted upon.[32]

INTO THE 1950s: DEFINING THE DEVIANT

Many of the themes identified above relating to criminality and deviance persisted into the 1950s. Heredity and environment, usually in combination, were the corner-stones of the debates over how crime should be understood. These arguments were given an air of greater subtlety through the development of what appeared to be scientific methods for measuring and predicting criminal behaviour. There was a proliferation of research projects, overwhelmingly forensically based, which continued the search for the elusive golden fleece of criminological endeavour, the cause of crime. Once more, those who spoke for society saw the rise in crime as a more general threat to the social order itself. If the cause was not found and a cure implemented, then that order was in danger of collapsing under the sheer weight of criminal practices.

In October 1953 the Nuffield Foundation invited Lord Pakenham to 'undertake a critical appraisal of current views of the causes of crime'.[33] The purpose of the inquiry was to look at the diverse opinions which were held about the causes of crime and to reveal subjects 'which would repay further close examination'.[34] The make-up of the inquiry team provided an indication of what the subjects would be. First, the Home Office, Scottish Office and Ministry of Education were to help with advice and information. Second, Pakenham was to be assisted by a small group of assessors, including the psychiatrist Dr Desmond Curran, the forensic psychiatrist T. C. N. Gibbens, the Metropolitan magistrate Frank Milton, and Max Grunhut, the criminologist from Oxford University. The forensic basis of the inquiry was supported by conferences which like those in the 1940s were attended by groups of experts eager to discuss their views on crime causation. In March 1954 the International Society of Criminology, the British Council and UNESCO organized a two-week course in London. The theme was 'Recent Advances in the Study and Treatment of Offenders'. It was directed by Dr Dennis Carroll, the President of the International Society, and by Hermann Mannheim, Reader in Criminology at London University. Among the medical contributions was a paper on electroencephalographic studies by Dr Dennis Hill, a senior lecturer in clinical neurophysiology. He claimed that with the exceptions of possible birth trauma and other forms of brain disease 'all evidence at present indicated that EEG patterns were primarily determined by heredity'.[35] In 1962 Hill was to sit as a member of the government-sponsored Gwynn Inquiry, which looked at the work of the PMS. This is discussed on pp. 100–102. Other papers included a contribution from Dr Sessions-Hodge, a consultant psychiatrist to the South Western Regional Board, who discussed the hormone treatment of sex offenders, including homosexuals. Sexual offences, he explained, were due to a

> lack of balance between primitive drives, probably originating in the hypothalamus and other lower brain centres, and the inhibitory effect of the cerebral cortex which normally inhibited them and ensured that they received only socially and ethically acceptable outlets.[36]

79

PMOs also presented papers. The Director of the PMS, Harvie Snell, discussed psychotherapy in prison while Dr Ogden, the MO in Portland Borstal, spoke about 'Typological Research on Adolescent Offenders'.[37]

Inquiries such as Pakenham's and conferences such as that organized by Carroll and Mannheim were important meeting-places for intellectuals and practitioners to discuss, debate and disseminate ideas concerning the latest forensic research. These ideas extended beyond the narrow confines of the conference hall to the pages of prestigious medical journals such as *The Lancet* and the *British Medical Journal*, as doctors and psychiatrists used their columns as platforms to reinforce further the positivistic view of criminality. In addition, official permission was given to particular individuals to conduct research in the institutions. The commissioners acted as gatekeepers, sanctioned these projects and provided facilities for the researchers. In 1952 two researchers from the Institute of Education in London conducted 'intellectual tests on young prisoners at Lewes to enable them to complete the experimental stage of a research scheme on the deterioration of mental alertness and flexibility among adolescents and young adults'.[38] In the same year T. C. N. Gibbens of the Institute of Psychiatry pursued research on prediction techniques.

> to determine on the basis of these tests whether a number of Borstal lads fall into particular groups and then, by comparison, if possible, with a control series of non-delinquents to decide whether the factors present in the groups can be regarded as causative of delinquency.[39]

In December 1953 the Institute for the Scientific Treatment of Delinquency (ISTD) published its annual report. The report listed the research projects that it was sponsoring including a statistical study of 250 delinquent boys aged 7–17 and a study of the effect of oestrogen on sex offenders. It was conducting a short investigation with the Howard League for Penal Reform into cruelty to children. The commissioners provided facilities for the psychiatric examination of those sentenced the previous year. There was also a concurrent study being carried out on the social, economic and cultural background of families in which cruelty occurred. Finally, it publicized the different courses with which the ISTD was associated. These included lectures in the new diploma in sociology at London University, arranging weekend courses on delinquent and criminal behaviour for psychiatrists, offering study courses for magistrates, assisting with the Home Office courses for probation officers in training and arranging lectures for prison officers.[40] In 1956 the study by Hermann Mannheim and Leslie Wilkins on prediction techniques was thought to be of sufficient importance to 'justify continuous validation and development'.[41] Wilkins addressed the annual conference of the PMS held at the Home Office in May 1956, directing his remarks particularly to the psychologists.[42]

Mannheim was involved in a number of other projects including a study of the use of imprisonment by magistrates' courts and two studies of group relationships in prison.[43] Finally, in 1958 it was reported that the Institute of Psychiatry at Maudsley Hospital was studying the application of 'personality tests to prisoners at Wandsworth prison with a view to investigating the use of these tests in the prediction of recidivism'.[44]

Prediction techniques and the use of scales were seen as key strategies for identifying the criminal. *The Lancet* praised the work of Mannheim and Wilkins in this area:

Those with clinical leanings may be repelled by this apparently mechanistic technique, but the firmly scientific attitude preserved throughout the book is vindicated by the prognostic success achieved. A chapter giving full case-histories will gild the pill for the intuitive psychologist and make more acceptable a text which should serve as a useful work of guidance and reference to doctors or laymen interested in the prediction of human behaviour.[45]

The *British Medical Journal* expressed similar views. In November 1958 under the title of 'Disordered Society', the journal discussed the major increase in crime that had occurred since the war.

A 'disturbingly high number' were committed by 16–21-year-olds.[46] The Home Secretary noted the lack of research which was hampering the police and courts. The *BMJ* praised the work of the ISTD as a good example of clinical research. The institute argued that crime was a form of behaviour disorder to be correlated with other social and psychological disorders. It was

logical therefore for the Institute to press for the establishment of 'obser-vation centres' where selected offenders could be diagnosed and treated. By encouraging research on these and other lines the Home Secretary might not in the future have to give such a depressing account of what he called 'a deep disorder in society'.[47]

There was a similar message in the Queen's Speech to Parliament in the same month. The Home Secretary wanted research to improve classification tech-niques 'remove the jumbled grouping together of prisoners of all kinds [and] secure more adequate treatment of the offender as an individual'.[48]

The nature of the research which the Home Secretary was proposing involved criminology and criminologists. The expansion of the discipline was supported by the medical establishment. In August 1961 in a long leading article entitled 'Aims of criminology', the *BMJ* maintained that criminology had a 'genuine contribution to make to the behavioural sciences though as a field of study rather than a science in its own right'.[49] It pointed out that 'the medical man and especially the psychiatrist has an important part to play in criminological research'.[50] The journal felt that such 'men' were able to draw attention to the differences in temperament, physique and mental health which made some individuals

particularly susceptible to inimical social influences; and may guide his more arithmetically minded colleagues away from exclusive preoccupation with easily measurable factors, like housing and income, towards the more subtle and perplexing questions of emotional life.[51]

Much of the research was to be conducted through the newly established Institute of Criminology at Cambridge, which could not 'fail to exert a considerable influence on research in Great Britain'.[52] The *BMJ* was encouraged to see that its research staff included a psychiatrist and psychologist.[53]

The research interests of prison medical workers reflected the concerns outlined above. Doctors and psychologists inhabited a universe where explanations of criminality overlapped with notions of underdevelopment, personality inadequacy and lack of adjustment to the wider society's norms. In 1951 R. S. Taylor, the psychologist at Reading Gaol and a member of the prison's Allocation Board, while acknowledging that he had little experience of prison work, was none the less very precise about the causes of crime: truancy, bad time-keeping, a poor work record and the home environment:

> So often in the home there had been death or separation of one or both parents. Homes had been situated in poor overcrowded areas and frequently the men came from a large family of four or more children of whom they were, as far as could be ascertained, the only ones to be in trouble. Quite often the father was disabled or periodically out of work and the mother harassed and overburdened had to go out to work and was unable to deal effectively with the problem created by a large family.[54]

Again the commissioners' reports contained the views of their medical employees. All the contributors were anonymous. In 1952 a doctor wrote that one of his goals was to 'make deficient men able and willing to come up to requirements'. He maintained that this would be accomplished through integrating medical and psychological work with discipline and training to form 'part of one balanced whole':

> We do not conceive of medical or psychological work as being a thing apart or as even as simply running in parallel with the other work of the prison, we conceive of it as a necessary complement to discipline and training which becomes the more necessary as the quality of the population falls.[55]

In 1954 another unnamed doctor made a similar point. He argued that severe manifestations of behavioural misconduct were the result of conflict between unstable prisoners and discipline. His prison had managed to avoid this conflict despite the 'number of potentially unstable men here. One contribution is the skill and patience of the discipline staff; the other is the pains taken by the medico-psychological staff to adjust prisoners to the requirements of discipline'.[56] Harvie Snell, the Director of the PMS, also outlined his views on the role of the MO. The successful doctor not only was a member of a team but also should 'identify himself with the aims of the service of which he forms a part, which emphasize the welfare and rehabilitation of those committed to its charge'.[57] This identification involved considerations over and above the well-being of the prisoners in terms of their physical health. The doctors were encouraged to seek out and where possible to remedy physical disabilities and maladjustments of personality which may hinder vocational fitness or social relationships and make it more difficult for them to regain a place in law-abiding society.[58]

Similar views were expressed in the 1955 report where one psychologist talked about the criminal's failure 'in the acquisition of basic adjustive techniques'. Once again this manifested itself at the level of immorality. Therefore it was 'not poverty but the failure to spend wisely; not lack of moral discipline but the failure to regard this as just and reasonable and necessary to social welfare'.[59] The commissioners repeated these views in 1957 in their summary of the reports from the governors of the training prisons who had commented on a 'falling off in the quality of men' who had come from the local prisons during the year. This manifested itself through 'irresponsibility and a passive acceptance of benefits without efforts towards self-improvement [which] are characteristic of an increasing number'.[60] Harvie Snell caught the essence of the relationship between discipline and medicine in an article for the *Howard Journal* in 1959:

> Discipline is essential, not only for the proper administration of the prison and indeed, for the general well-being of those detained therein, but also to provide a realistic background against which general training and character development can be undertaken. This discipline, plus the individual help which the prisoner must feel is available to him, not only from medical and psychological staff but also from his assistant governor and officers, will compare with the discipline of a well-managed home in which there is a sense of security plus a knowledge of disinterested but genuine help.[61]

Prison doctors and psychologists therefore did not stand outside or above the debates about crime and punishment in the 1950s. As professionals they were deeply concerned to provide solutions to a problem that was undermining the harmonious development of society's institutions. Along with psychiatrists, psychiatric social workers and the medical profession in general they brought their own perspective to bear on the problem. It was a perspective which, despite differences between the professions, was united on an ideological terrain where therapeutic intervention into the lives of individuals and families was the key to criminological success. Throughout the decade they continued to propound the view that classification, research and medical intervention were the basic elements in the search for the key. Prisons (and other institutions) were critical sites in this search which was increasingly propelled by questions of individual discipline and morality. In that sense, treatment and discipline were two sides of the same penal coin.

As in the nineteenth and early twentieth century medical hegemony in the 1940s and 1950s remained incomplete. There were challenges to the power of the doctors and psychologists and the definitions of reality which they propounded. These challenges came from both inside and outside the walls. In addition, the issue of the relationship between doctors and discipline remained an ongoing one as prisoners again raised questions about their role in managing the fragile order inside. Finally, the legitimacy of the PMS was also challenged by those who asked about the kind of medical treatment the confined were receiving particularly in conditions which were becoming increasingly dilapidated and overcrowded in the face of the inexorable rise in the prison population throughout the 1950s.

PRISONER SCEPTICISM

Prisoners were sceptical about the usefulness of prison psychology from its earliest days. In 1949 one prison doctor complained about the 'gradual unwillingness on the part of prospective recruits to join [therapy] groups and some signs of strain on the part of those who were already in groups'.[62] The doctor went on to note that prisoners

> as a whole made fun of them and called them the loony party; some of them were willing to see it through but so much difficulty was gathering that the groups were discontinued.[63]

In the psychiatric unit at Wormwood Scrubs there was also resistance to the methods employed particularly ECT. Jonathan Gould pointed to the tendency of 'patients' to break off treatment:

> In prison . . . the general attitude of the population is far less friendly to the idea of treatment: not infrequently the patient is adversely influenced by another prisoner and this, coupled with latent anxiety and hostility, far from uncommon in prison patients, crystallizes as one of fear of the treatment. Since commencing the method of electroplexy under anaesthesia, there have been no refusals to continue the course.[64]

When treatment failed, officials blamed the offender rather than the theory and methods of psychiatry. As the commissioners explained:

> The largest single factor in contra-indicating treatment is intellectual inferiority. . . . Six cases were transferred to a mental hospital for insulin shock treatment (IST). The results, as a whole, have not been good. This is probably due to the fact that although the psychotic manifestation was of recent origin, the personality had been unsatisfactory for a number of years.[65]

In December 1953 speakers at a meeting held by the Royal Society of Medicine complained about the lack of participation by prisoners in the psychotherapy programmes doctors were introducing. W. F. Roper, the PMO at Wakefield, identified the prisoners' attitude as one of the main problems confronting psychotherapy:

> The prisoner group as a whole tends to have a low opinion of psychiatric patients particularly those who are sexual offenders, there may, therefore, be a reluctance to accept treatment in order to avoid odium.[66]

Dr Peter Scott of Maudsley Hospital, who was to be involved in the Gwynn Inquiry in 1962 (see pp. 100–102), made a similar point, arguing that 'the majority of prisoners are unwilling to become patients'.[67] Prisoners' accounts also indicate the strain in the relationship between themselves and prison medical workers at this time. Their hostility is underpinned by a deep scepticism concerning the ability of psychiatry to rehabilitate them:

> I've done these tests of theirs, often, all this nonsense of bricks and blocks, fitting coloured shapes of paper into squares, picking out the odd one from lists like 'Fish-and-chips, steak-and-kidney pie, staircase'. All that sort of rubbish. I always do them wrong deliberately, but of course these people know you do it and pay no attention. I don't know why, but for some reason, when I do them wrong, I still give something away because they carry on with me despite that. . . . They ask, but they don't tell. Perhaps this is because they don't know – but in that case why probe around in me? What are they hoping to come up with in the end – a recommendation I ought to be put away somewhere in a worse nick than the one I'm in? I read once than even a good psychiatrist can get no place without co-operation from the subject he's working on. So O.K., I don't co-operate.[68]

Similar stories were told by homosexual prisoners who were a particular concern for prison medical personnel. That concern was legitimized by remarks such as those made by the Chief Constable of Nottingham, who maintained that homosexuality was 'beginning to cut into the very vitals of the nation like a cancer'.[69] Prison doctors discussed the homosexual prisoner at their annual conference in May 1953 and in June 1954 at a weekend course for psychiatrists organized by the ISTD. Dr Calder, the Principal Medical Officer at one of the London prisons, told participants that 'perversion, particularly homosexuality is . . . a matter for doctors entirely' and that it was the doctor's duty, among other things, 'to undertake radical curative treatment if possible'.[70] Prisoners were again less than forthcoming. In the commissioners' report for 1953, one PMO described the efforts he had made during the year to interview all homosexuals who were potential cases for psychological assessment or treatment. What is interesting to note is that these cases had previously refused the opportunity for treatment before their reception into the prison. The doctor also had no luck in his present establishment for as he pointed out 'in spite of numerous interviews, so far no prisoner was found who appeared to have a genuine desire for such treatment'.[71] Again the autobiographies of prisoners also present a different reality to the sanguine nature of official discourse. In March 1954 Peter Wildeblood was sentenced to eighteen months for homosexual offences. In his autobiography *Against the Law* (published in 1955) he discussed his interview with a PMO:

> The Medical Officer was a hard-bitten little Scot with grey hair brushed into a schoolboyish bang. He had been a prison doctor at Brixton for many years. He asked me how I was feeling, listened to my heartbeats, told me to sit down and began firing off the usual psychiatrist's questions, writing down my replies. Since my private life was now public property, I spoke

frankly of my childhood and adolescence, while he grunted occasionally and his pen raced over the paper.

'You say you know a lot of other homosexuals. Tell me, do you frequent the orgies in which they indulge?

'Orgies?'

'Yes, I believe in Chelsea and places there are houses where male and female homosexuals congregate to carry out unnatural practices together.'

'Do they? It sounds most unlikely to me.'

'So I am told.' . . .

'And what,' he asked, 'do you do on your free evenings? Go out importuning?'

I could have hit him.

'Certainly not. I don't do that sort of thing. In any case, I haven't got the time. I only have one free evening a week, and I usually spend that with friends.'

'Other homosexuals, of course?'

And so on.[72]

MEDICINE AND DISCIPLINE

Despite the increasing use made of medical and therapeutic discourses, prison medical workers as noted above were still tied to the yoke of discipline. There were a number of dimensions to this. First, insulin shock treatment (IST) and electroconvulsive therapy (ECT) were not the benevolent practices described in official reports. Both were violent and humiliating for individuals subjected to them. Two psychiatrists, William Sargent and Russell Fraser, had introduced IST to Britain in November 1938 when they induced deep comas in patients in Maudsley Hospital. The majority were women. It had

> emotional connotations of infantilization. After receiving her injection, the patient was put to bed to wait for the coma. For some, the worst part was waiting for the several days it initially took for the insulin level to produce a reaction, listening to the hoarse animal cries of the other comatose women, knowing they too would slobber or grunt, wet the bed, and become ugly and grotesque. . . . There were other aspects of insulin therapy, however, such as the daily hot baths, the personal attention, the diet of sugar and starch, that suggested surrogate mothering; and the infantile regression that Mary Cecil found so degrading was seen by some doctors as part of the cure. William Sargent reports that one hospital unit recommended that nurses with big breasts should have charge of the treatment so that when the patient came out of the coma, 'he or she was greeted on rebirth with this invitingly maternal sight'.[73]

ECT was developed by an Italian, Ugo Cerletti, who had initially experimented with it on pigs in the slaughterhouse in Rome. It was used for the first time on humans in 1938 and introduced in Britain early in 1940 by two neurologists working in Bristol. Its use soon became widespread in different institutions, especially for women who were diagnosed as schizophrenic and depressed. Before the introduction of muscle-relaxant drugs

> the spasms produced by the current were so powerful that nurses had to hold the patient down, and fractures of the spine, arm, pelvis or leg were not uncommon. At Colney Hatch, the occurrence of fractures among patients doubled in the late 1940s with the introduction of electro-convulsive treatment.[74]

As late as 1960 the Prison Commissioners reported that twelve prisoners at Wormwood Scrubs were given ECT on forty-nine occasions, while one was given aversion therapy.[75]

The leucotomy was a third strategy utilized to treat particular groups within (and without) the prison population. The operation was developed in 1935 by Egas Moniz, a Portuguese neurosurgeon. Moniz, who won a Nobel prize in 1949, believed that his procedure worked particularly well on individuals with 'anxiety-tension states' and 'obsessive syndromes'. It was simplified in the USA by Walter Freeman, whose 'transorbital lobotomy' could be performed in a few minutes using local anaesthetics. The patient's brain was entered 'under the eyelid with an icepick-like instrument, severing the nerves connecting the cortex with the thalamus'.[76] The majority of those lobotomized were women. Freeman lobotomized thirteen in one afternoon in 1948.[77]

In England William Sargent performed lobotomies and leucotomies at St George's Hospital, London. Sargent had visited Freeman in 1939 with a colleague, Russell Fraser. At St George's they and a third psychiatrist, Eliot Slater, performed several leucotomies and conducted experiments with different forms of the operation. Sargent also took a sabbatical in the USA where he was 'outraged when he was prevented by the Veterans' Hospital Administration in Washington from lobotomising fifty black schizophrenic patients at the Tuskegee Hospital in Alabama as part of another experiment'.[78] Again women were the main targets:

> Sargent and Slater's widely used English psychiatric textbook published in 1972 recommends psychosurgery for a depressed woman who 'may owe her illness to a psychopathic husband who cannot change and will not accept treatment'. When separation is ruled out by the patient's religious convictions or by her 'financial or emotional dependence' and when anti-depressant drugs do not work, the authors suggest that a lobotomy will enable the woman to cope with her marriage.[79]

Prisoners categorized as psychopaths experienced this operation. Harry Howard's account of his imprisonment in Borstal in the mid-1940s illustrates the impact of the categorization process and the interwoven network of control that flowed from it. After escaping from Feltham Borstal he was recaptured and put in the hospital block, where he began to 'smash up'. He was then put in a straitjacket. In 1949 he was still in and out of trouble and appeared once more before the courts. A medical report described his behaviour for which he must be deemed responsible, [as] one of rebellion against authority. He had shown a grudging and surly obedience to orders while in custody.[80]

The Chair of the Court, in the light of the report, postponed sentence to allow Howard time to undergo a pre-frontal leucotomy. The operation involved having two holes bored in his skull. A blade was then pushed through the holes and the fibres that connected the frontal lobe of the brain to the thalamus were severed. It was thought that the fibres were concerned in some way 'with the intellectual and emotional aspects of mental activity, and it was believed that cutting them prevented pathological ideas from generating emotion'.[81] Howard described the operation in the following way:

> I had all the hair shaved off my head till it was like a billiard ball. I was wheeled to the theatre and strapped down, because the sister said I might kick out.
> 'But you put me to sleep, don't you?'
> 'No, we just numb you. Your mind has to be clear for this operation.'
> They marked a blue cross on either side of my head, and the surgeon took his electric drill and started to bore the holes. As soon as he touched me I kicked like hell, and smashed the table, even though I was strapped. 'Sister,' I said, 'give me something to put me to sleep, it's terrible, I can feel it.' She said they couldn't and the surgeon carried on boring, while four male nurses held me down as best they could. I couldn't see, because they'd covered my eyes, but I could feel him shove an instrument through the hole and cut something.[82]

This method of behaviour modification was supported by other mechanisms of control including the use of violence. Wally Probyn's account of institutional life in Wormwood Scrubs, Wakefield and Rampton in the late 1940s and early 1950s contains vivid descriptions of beatings. For the Borstal boys in Wormwood Scrubs, 'kickings by groups of warders' were a frequent and painful part of their lives.[83] In Wakefield he was often in solitary confinement and on dietary punishment. He was transferred to Rampton Special Hospital when he was categorized as a moron under the Mental Deficiency Act. After escaping he was recaptured and placed in darkness for two weeks. He was also required to polish the stone floor of a corridor using sand and water. This was done on his hands and knees for twelve hours a day and lasted for two weeks:

> Kneeling down for so many hours eventually made one's knees swell up to huge proportions, but one was not allowed to report sick or receive treatment. One was not allowed to stop or rest in any way, to attempt to do so would be to risk confrontation, and any confrontation always resulted in the prisoner getting a kicking from the screws. Sometimes the beatings were so severe that the victim's face would literally be unrecognizable for many days. One of the techniques of brutality used, especially on the female side of the institution, was to twist a wet towel round the victim's neck as with a tourniquet until the victim became unconscious. The female

screws used this more frequently because they were frightened of getting faces marked if the victim struggled or retaliated. Thus an unconscious victim could be beaten and kicked at leisure.[84]

Psychotropic drugs were also used to control behaviour. Harry Howard's transfer to a padded cell was supported by a dose of Paraldehyde 'to knock me out. I've had so many of these drugs in my time that if I hadn't given them up myself in later life I'd have become an addict'.[85] In Probyn's case the prison officers who were to escort him to Rampton visited his police cell and

> tried by coercion and threats to make me drink a potion referred to at Rampton as a 'sleeping draught'. The substance was used to drug particularly difficult cases. The subsequent doses were administered before the previous one had worn off and people had been kept drugged in this way for many months. A man who had been subjected to this treatment for a long period who was said once to have had an outstanding physique was, by the time I first saw him, like a fugitive from Belsen. His legs would hardly support his weight and he staggered about like a perpetually drunk man.[86]

By the late 1950s prison medical workers had a range of psychotropic drugs available to them for use in the prisons. The long, unsigned statements which appeared in the commissioners' yearly reports indicated the impact that these drugs had on the doctors' relationship with the difficult and damaged inside. In the report for 1958 a doctor described how he had conducted a pilot trial with Hydroxyzine aimed at 'the irritable suspicious dullard who flies into violent rages on imaginary or trifling provocation'.[87] The prisoners he said felt better, but prison staff did not find it an overwhelming success although they did notice 'that the boys under genuine treatment incurred as many reports as before but did not resent punishment or reprimand as they had been accustomed to do'.[88] Another doctor discussed the problem of chronic schizophrenics:

> The chronic schizophrenics are our biggest problem, of whom there are always a number of cases in the prison. These men are usually unable to adapt themselves satisfactorily to the discipline of the main prison. In hospital where their condition is thoroughly understood, and where allowance is made for their eccentricities, they frequently remain for long periods without causing any trouble, and often do regular and useful work. It is not always possible to certify these men as being of unsound mind, but fortunately the introduction of the phenothiazine drugs has enabled us to control the aggressiveness and grosser eccentricities of our schizophrenic patients, so that they can lead more active and useful lives, as well as being much more contented. We have paid special attention to the treatment of the various mental disorders by drugs, as we did in 1958.[89]

A third doctor discussed drugs used in his local prison including Tofranil, Mepavalon and Epanutan used with 'epileptoid psychopaths'. It gave variable results with this group but with young people 'there was a very marked improvement in behaviour generally'. The drug Pacatal was also given in doses up to 100mgs., three times a day. This drug has its main use in the major mental disorders e.g. in the schizophrenics, in chronic senile dementia and in the occasional agitated and disturbed psychopathic personality.[90]

Chlorpromazine, which operated under the trade name of Largactil, was a particularly useful drug for the doctors in dealing both with those prisoners diagnosed as suffering from mental illness and those who were agitated and difficult to control. The drug had been developed by French scientists in 1952. By the late 1950s the commissioners and doctors were quite open about its use. The official report for 1958 described prisoners who were suffering from early schizophrenia

> who were treated with a combination of E.C.T., modified with Pentothal and Scoline, with Chlorpromazine in increasing doses up to over 100mgs. per day.[91]

Another doctor noted that

> We have given special attention this year to the treatment of psychiatric cases with drugs. Several mild cases of depression have responded particularly well to 'Ritalin' and Meprobamate has given excellent results in a number of cases showing prolonged tension. Chlorpromazine has been used on a fairly large scale with agitated patients and also in several chronic schizophrenics who were not sufficiently ill to justify certification.[92]

Similar views were expressed in 1962:

> During the year an increasing use has been made of the psychotropic drugs. Largactil has been used, mainly due to personal experience of it and as a standard to compare the effect of others. It has been used in fluid form, 25mgs. being contained in a fluid oz. and the usual dosage being one fluid oz. three times a day. It has been found useful in controlling prisoners who were always at odds with authority and spent much of their time in 'E Hall'. Many of these cases appeared to be suffering from emotional tension and instability exacerbated by interpersonal irritations in their dealings with the staff and other prisoners. The climate situation and inaccessibility for visits are further causes of resentment against authority. . . . Some of them have taken advantage of advice from the medical staff to report sick when they feel themselves becoming tense or more than usually 'fed up'. They can then be given further help from Largactil before they resort to acts of indiscipline to relieve their feelings.[93]

For the doctors then, the emergence and development of the drug industry was an important new element in their medical armoury. The distinction between treatment and control, became increasingly blurred as they saw the benefits that could be derived from these technological developments. Writing in *The Lancet* in December 1961, two PMOs argued that drugs could replace traditional methods of control:

it may well be possible and it would certainly be desirable to abolish them although that is not to say that some modified form of restraint may have to be retained for use as a temporary measure with violent patients until the drug of choice has begun to take effect.[94]

This development took place in the context of a wider debate about the discipline and control of the prison population. While the prisons did not experience the thunder of prisoner protest that was to rock them in the following two decades, it is equally true to say that they did not progress through the 1950s with equanimity and harmony. While on the surface there often appeared to be a calm acceptance of the legitimacy of the prison regime, as in the 1940s this calmness could be shattered by individual and collective acts of concerted indiscipline.

The reports of the commissioners for the 1950s reflect the tension between, on the one hand, arguing that the prison system was quieter than in the immediate post-war period, while on the other attempting to explain the acts of ill-discipline and disturbances that did take place. In the latter case, the mobilization of psychiatric images which were attached to the minority of prisoners labelled as recalcitrant, was an important weapon in the managers' armoury when struggles over the order and legitimacy of the system did occur.

In 1954 an unnamed doctor pointed out that it had not been necessary to place any prisoner in the loose canvas restraint jacket during the year: 'one does not see the violent psychopathic behaviour in prison today that existed 20 years ago. The pattern of the prisoner appears to have changed in this respect'.[95]

Despite this optimism, the vision of progressive harmony could be shattered. In November 1954 there were two disturbances at Parkhurst on the Isle of Wight. One lasted for a week during which 'a substantial proportion of the men dining in association consistently refused to eat their dinner'. In May more serious disturbances occurred at Wandsworth when five prisoners attacked prison officers in a workshop and barricaded themselves into a store-room. Twenty-one prison officers were injured in the incident. Altogether ten prisoners took part in what was described as an 'isolated outbreak by a handful of violent men'. The commissioners argued that such incidents were 'happily rare' and the fact that they had not led to any widespread mutiny or disorder in the prisons was 'a tribute to the firm, rational and humane control exercised by their Governors and staff'.[96]

The commissioners' report for 1955 continued in a similar vein, arguing that the great majority of prisoners at Parkhurst had adjusted to their long sentences but there remained

a definite though small minority of prisoners who seem quite unable to comprehend that Preventive Detention is the logical outcome of their many previous offences and that all their outbursts of indiscipline, all their threats contained in letters and petitions and all their haunting of the hospital with trivial or non-existent complaints will do nothing to shorten their time.[97]

91

Prisoners expressed their frustrations in other ways. An unsigned letter from an MO in the same year pointed out that there had been a 'considerable rise in the number of petitions' since his last tour of duty in the prison. In addition there were numerous letters to MPs as well as the frequent threats to 'commence litigation for alleged negligence in medical or surgical treatment':

> [This] must breed an attitude of excessive caution in the medical officer; and he will begin to see the prisoner, not so much in the light of a patient but as a possible plaintiff in an action for negligence. I need hardly say that such an attitude does not necessarily conduce to the best medical practice, and will impair that improved relationship between medical officer and prisoner which has been so laboriously built up over the past five years. [98]

He made a similar point the following year when he discussed the 'constant allegations of negligence and threats of litigation. Negligence is imputed almost daily to the MO whether verbally or in letters to friends, or Members of Parliament or in petitions'. [99] In 1959 these themes recurred when sit-down strikes happened at Cardiff and Birmingham prisons. Once again the commissioners discussed how these strikes had been well-organized 'under the leadership of a small group of malcontents'. [100] They discussed the instructions given to governors to control violent or potentially violent prisoners who were to

> select special staff to deal with them and the attention of the medical staff has been specially directed towards their care. The object of these special instructions is simultaneously to contain violence and to seek ways in which the causes may be removed. [101]

Other prisons also had problems with discipline and control. In 1957 there were two disturbances in Dartmoor, the second of which lasted for several days when there was a mass refusal of food. Once again, the commissioners argued that the majority of men in the prison were acting

> at the dictation of a small group, who used this method to try to assert their authority in the prison. Suspected members of this group were dispersed to other prisons. [102]

There were also disturbances at Camp Hill Prison and at Wormwood Scrubs.

The reports from the commissioners never addressed the complexity of these disturbances. In addition, they were rarely challenged. When alternative accounts did emerge (as Chapter 3 noted with the activities of the Prison Medical Reform Council), they indicated that the roots of the conflict were more complicated than the individualized explanations propagated by prison managers and medical personnel. They also showed the state's response to be more repressive and violent than the official reports acknowledged.

In August 1958 Sir Geoffrey Vicks published his report into allegations of ill-treatment made by prisoners in Walton. He substantiated a number of them, including assaults by hospital officers:

I am satisfied that there is a *prime facie* case that assaults accompanied by varying degrees of violence were made upon prisoners by prison officers. Similarly that practical jokes in the worst possible taste were perpetrated, in particular squirting water through the apertures of cell doors on to the occupant within, taking him by surprise and giving him a good wetting. This was done in the hospital and the instruments used were medical syringes which were produced and demonstrated before me.[103]

In May 1959 there was a serious disturbance in Pentonville when prisoners demonstrated in solidarity with an executed prisoner. Prison officers responded with a series of random attacks on prisoners. A black prisoner was held upside down over the prison landing. After the disturbances a number of prisoners were charged with offences against discipline, including assaults on prison officers. Prisoners complained they were assaulted. One had

quite serious injuries, and had been interviewed in the punishment cells. Nevertheless, although in bandages, the senior doctor had marked his Report Sheet on 8 May 'Fit all punishment' and no mention was made of his injuries, either on his record or at the subsequent hearing of the V.C. [Visiting Committee].[104]

QUESTIONING MEDICAL CARE

It was not only the relationship between medicine and discipline which was a cause for concern in the post-war period; the conditions in which prisoners received medical treatment remained a contentious issue. Charles Carter's *Snail's Progress* (published in 1948) highlighted the experience of Quaker prisoners between 1939 and 1948. Carter was particularly concerned about the standard of medical care, the level of hygiene and the poor diet which all contributed to the ill-health of the confined.[105] Peter Baker's account of his sentence which he started in 1954 was also highly critical of the PMS whose 'reputation . . . throughout the prison could hardly have been lower'.[106] The doctors, with one notable exception, appeared to 'regard their task as the promulgation of discipline rather than of medicine'.[107] The hospital wing was used to discipline troublesome boys who were

nearly always shut in a padded cell and then given a severe and scientific beating-up. Although their cries and screams of pain could be heard throughout the hospital, this was always excused on the basis that the process was the best medical remedy for hysteria.[108]

These criticisms continued into the 1960s. In August 1962 the Prison Reform Council (a group which had grown out of the Prison Medical Reform Council discussed in Chapter 3) published *Inside Story*. The report contained fifteen proposals for changing the PMS. These proposals centred on questions of recruitment, the 'don't care' attitude of prison staff, the perfunctory nature of medical examinations on admission and the diet for pregnant women, which was 'not up to the standards generally recommended outside'.[109] It called for an inquiry into

> the practice of young girls . . . slashing themselves in the arms when in a state of frustration and rebellion. This is clearly a symptom of mental disorder but because it is so general inside it seems to be regarded with surprising complacency at lay level.[110]

The prison diet also continued to be a source of controversy. In August 1945 *The Lancet* pointed to a deficiency of vitamins in prison food which particularly affected long-term prisoners. This was compounded when the diet was restricted for punishment.[111] The journal returned to the subject in February 1947 citing research carried out during the war by Magnus Pike, which showed that the commissioners set the nutritional needs of prisoners 'at a lower level than set by ordinary rationing'.[112] In January 1948 the Home Secretary told the Commons that the diet for individual prisoners 'was less than the value of the diet of an ordinary worker'.[113] In December 1947 105 prisoners protested at the level of food provision by engaging in a demonstration at Parkhurst.

The standard of medical care was also affected by overcrowding, which was a perennial problem throughout the 1950s and 1960s. Between 1956 and 1961 the prison and Borstal population rose from 20,500 to 28,500. At the end of 1960 over 7,000 men were confined three to a cell.[114] The commissioners commented on the problem throughout the 1950s and the 'potential risk to health consequent upon overcrowding in certain prisons'.[115] However, when the sickness rate did rise, they, along with unnamed prison doctors, blamed the prisoners and their 'greater tendency to complain of trivialities'.[116] They discussed the changes in the sick treatment rate at Wakefield which rose from 6.4 per cent in 1946 to 12.2 per cent in 1951. The Principal Medical Officer linked the rise to 'a decline in morale consequent upon the departure to open prisons of the better type of prisoner who rarely complains sick without due reason'.[117] In 1954 similar views were expressed. The commissioners talked of prisoners having immature personalities, exhibiting hysterical traits and exaggerating symptoms. They were sometimes propelled by ulterior motives or tended to lose a sense of perspective. These factors 'have to be taken into consideration in the investigation and treatment of their ailments and complaints and may increase the complexities of the task'.[118] One unnamed doctor maintained that

> The more defiant types received in later years seek medical treatment much more frequently because of their greater immaturity of personality which impels them to seek some kind of substitute maternal care and protection when they are in any difficulty. The sick rate in prisons is not necessarily, or even mainly, an index of physical health; it is more an index of morale and the management of morale is as important as the giving of ordinary medical treatment.[119]

This line of argument continued into the early 1960s. In 1961 the Director of Medical Services discussed the discomfort brought about by overcrowding, which in his view had not resulted in increased ill-health. The number of 'trivial sick complaints' remained high but this 'may be no more than a reflection of an attitude present in the outside world. However, this must be qualified by the observation that trivial sickness complaints tend to decrease when morale is high'.[120] Others were less sanguine in their comments about the health care of prisoners and the impact that conditions had on their physical and mental welfare. In 1954 the annual report of the Howard League suggested that to cope with its increased work-load and 'to secure some uniformity of procedure and a broadening of experience a closer relation between the Prison Medical Service and the National Heath Service should be encouraged'.[121]

In April of the same year Frank Allaun MP raised the question of medical treatment in Strangeways. Allaun was concerned that prisoners with tuberculosis and confined to bed for long periods were kept in ordinary prison cells. In addition, while the prison held 1,100 prisoners, there were only four one-bed rooms for men who had to be isolated either for physical or mental reasons. Allaun asked:

> Would the minister agree that, whatever a man's prison sentence, his health should not be damaged by it? Will the minister therefore ensure that sufficient hospital beds are made available at Strangeways, for tuberculosis patients and others with serious illness, particularly since, as I saw last week, it is extremely difficult for prison officers to carry sick prisoners into the four single bedrooms, two of them padded cells, because of the narrowness of these archaic corridors.[122]

From the government's point of view, the hospital was 'admittedly inadequate'. It proposed building a new hospital which would involve 'substantial reconstruction of other parts of the prison'. This was to be done when funds became available.[123]

There were further questions in the following months. Victor Yates expressed concern about the medical treatment and welfare arrangements for discharged prisoners. In Parkhurst, the facilities for tubercular prisoners were 'totally inadequate'. A government minister defended the PMS, arguing that individuals who were dissatisfied with treatment could ask to see the Director of the PMS, petition the Home Secretary or write to an MP:

> He had no wish to be complacent; he knew that there was a deficiency of medical officers and the present overcrowding in prisons was a very grave menace. But last year there were no serious outbreaks of infectious disease, and prisoners generally were in better health on leaving prison than when they came in.[124]

The qualifications of the doctors regarding the psychological treatment of prisoners was also a cause for concern. In March 1957 Dr Barnett Stross raised the issue in Parliament by asking how many full-time doctors employed in the PMS had a Diploma in Psychological Medicine (DPM). Of the forty-nine full-timers, six held the diploma. Stross then asked:

Would it be unreasonable to ask that when any improvements are made in the service a special point should be made of ensuring that as many medical men as possible who serve full-time in the prisons should have the diploma and that outsiders coming in to assist should also, where possible, be skilled in psychological medicine?[125]

Leo Abse raised similar questions concerning the regularity with which PMOs were submitting court reports on the sanity of accused people. Many were doing so without a recognized psychiatric diploma. This was particularly relevant for individuals charged with murder and remanded in custody. They were 'being compelled to submit to psychiatric examinations by Prison Medical Officers and the facts so obtained were supplied to the Director of Public Prosecutions'.[126] In February 1961 he maintained that nearly all the PMOs 'lamentably lacked any psychiatric diploma'. Despite this, a doctor could examine a prisoner and submit a report to the Director of Public Prosecutions on her/his sanity. This could lead to the accused being convicted of murder rather than manslaughter:

if the existing malpractices continued, we were in danger of verdicts of murder being given as a consequence of a clandestine investigation conducted in a prison cell between a doctor and a patient he had compulsorily acquired, and not as a result of evidence which would otherwise have been placed before an open court. The position now being adopted by the Prison Commissioners required their medical employees to be flagrantly in breach of the Hippocratic oath.[127]

Abse was supported by Allen Bartholomew, who in a letter to the *BMJ* argued that 'many medical officers reporting on the mental state of prisoners not only lacked a diploma but also lack (at least initially) experience'. Bartholomew maintained that as it took only two years working in an approved hospital to sit for the DPM, many of the MOs in the prisons must either be failed DPMs or have worked in the psychiatric field for less than two years. He concluded that the way forward was to have fully trained personnel who were knowledgeable in psychiatry, law and penology and who were not asked to be general practitioners, public health experts or nurses.[128]

In November 1962 Abse again asked questions about the inadequate numbers and sparse psychiatric qualifications of the doctors. He was also concerned about the use of straitjackets, a point he reiterated in February 1963. He pointed out that in 1961 straitjackets were used on more than 100 occasions, some for 'incredibly long periods of time'. There was also a gap between 'the practice and judgement of those with psychiatric experience and qualifications inside the National Health Service and doctors in the Prison Medical Service'. He called for an 'intelligent ebb and flow' between the services.[129]

The doctors themselves were unhappy about their status and position. This was debated both in the national and medical press.[130] In April 1959 a correspondent wrote to *The Lancet* outlining his anxiety about the kind of work he was asked to perform. Signing the letter 'White Slave' he argued that a prison doctor was a 'jack of all trades and a master of none' who performed both as a specialist psychiatrist and a general practitioner and 'as a side-line' was 'expected to approve or condemn food, as well as other public health duties'.[131] Prison doctors feared that as more specialist work became available it was likely to be done by specialists from outside the PMS on a sessional or even a full-time basis:

> in a very short while the prison medical officer will be nothing more than a G.P. cum psychiatric registrar for the remainder of his life. Further, that this appalling state of affairs rests fairly and squarely at the feet of the Prison Commissioners and the little group of medical personnel at Horseferry House.[132]

The letter caused a flurry of correspondence in the medical press. Critics again pointed to the doctors' lack of psychiatric qualifications. The author of the original letter did not disagree:

> before the contribution psychiatry had to offer be assessed it should be practised by duly qualified persons in an adequate setting. At present the prison medical officer is being asked to undertake psychiatric diagnosis and assessment under very nearly impossible conditions: assessment being of necessity based on short interviews punctured by interruption, in many cases no social history and no corroboration of the prisoner's story, and a confusion of roles in which the 'psychiatrist/prison medical officer' is supposed to function.[133]

He proposed that the 'small and inadequate' PMS should be integrated with the NHS:

> [It] would do away to a large extent with the inflammatory bandying of words and concepts regarding 'fishes in small ponds' and the particular alphabet after one's name; it would all be irrelevant and the law of natural selection would maintain. We would all struggle in the same 'big pond', the better man would tend to win, and psychiatry, the Prison Service and the prisoner would benefit.[134]

The question of integration was taken up by *The Lancet* in October 1961, which pointed to a number of problems in 'this corner of medical practice – one might almost say a backwater – that receives little attention'.[135] These problems included the 'vicious circle of understaffing', the lack of formal training in psychiatry, psychology and sociology, the terms and conditions of service, and the isolation of the doctors:

> As with the military services (from which some prison doctors come) the organization is inevitably somewhat dictatorial. A man is 'posted' from place to place, and prison accommodation is not always in a district likely to prove acceptable to the doctor's wife or helpful to his children's education. Promotion by seniority is very slow and salaries are rather lower than NHS equivalents, despite a rise last January.[136]

The article concluded that amalgamation with the NHS would 'undoubtedly solve many problems' that a 'careful study of the situation is overdue' and that an interdepartmental committee should be established to review the position.[137] Once again the article provoked strong emotions in the letter columns. Richard Nunn, the General Secretary of the Institute of Professional Civil Servants, defended the PMS and asserted that recent developments meant prisoners were 'now afforded treatment which compares favourably with National Health Service standards, despite the overriding necessity for security'.[138] He concluded that there was no advantage to be gained in amalgamation with the NHS. Nunn's letter was not the only response to the article. Other writers raised a number of further issues including the involvement of the doctors in the use of padded cells and straitjackets and their role in the execution of condemned prisoners. According to Frank Byram

> many, perhaps most doctors fight shy of a Service in which their patients may include a man or woman under sentence of death. The doctor may even be required to use his skill so as to ensure that his patient shall survive until execution.[139]

Two prison doctors responded to the question of the straitjackets and their role in supporting them. They felt it might be possible, perhaps even desirable, to abolish them. This could be done, however, only if some modified form of restraint was retained for use as a temporary measure 'with violent prisoners until the drug of choice has begun to take effect'.[140] Doctors also felt they were being undermined by the commissioners, who denied them specialist status:

> Specialist status seems to be deliberately withheld to prevent our acquiring a higher 'market value', and this is one reason why so many ambitious young medical officers resign while they are young enough to win their spurs elsewhere. One result is that P.M.O.s are mainly rather old or young and inexperienced. Even a single retirement causes a frantic reshuffle, and a number of my friends must retire in the next few years.[141]

Prisoners challenged the viability of the psychiatric practices of the doctors. In the early 1960s group counselling techniques were introduced to 'help correct, in some degree, the distorted view which many inmates have of themselves and of society and which is often responsible for the behaviour which has brought them into conflict with the law'. This technique *The Lancet* felt was working out into a 'kind of superficial and authoritarian psychotherapy rather different from its more psychodynamic origins in the USA'.[142] Prisoners increasingly refused to participate in the sessions. One doctor wrote in the commissioners' report for 1961 that 'there has been a noticeable decline in the number of volunteers and most groups have had to be made up by persuasion'.[143] Similar views were expressed in the 1962 report. One of the writers pointed out that 75 per cent of all receptions

98

will be influenced by group counselling in varying degrees. On the negative side, and because the groups are completely voluntary, those who might benefit from, and need group counsel most are able to opt out right from the start. Thus the worst element with its anti-social, and vicious disruptive influences remains unaffected and continues to exert pressure on the rest of the inmates, thereby poisoning the attempt to further a constructive staff/inmate relationship.[144]

The application of these techniques, and the problems surrounding them, were worked out in the context of the increasing concern for security that began to intensify and ripple through the prison service in the early 1960s. In the summer of 1961 a wing was established at Durham for prisoners who needed special security conditions. Up to 31 March 1962 fifty-two men had been transferred to the wing. In the same year other long-term prisoners were transferred to two special units at Hull and Parkhurst. In this atmosphere, the commissioners urged that when groups met for counselling sessions, the staff member involved had complete discretion to use the information obtained 'either in the interests of security and good order of the institution or in the interests of a particular individual'.[145] The commissioners were quite clear where the direction of the sessions lay:

> The essence of the technique being to give inmates an opportunity to discuss frankly their difficulties and problems, it is to be expected that criticisms of the prison and borstal system generally, of the rules and of the people who administer them, may (not necessarily will) feature prominently among the topics in group counselling sessions. But since the sessions are not a channel for remedying grievances, and discussion of the system's and the staff's shortcomings will not, therefore, alter anything, groups may be expected to forsake this topic for the more fruitful one of what group members themselves should do to solve their problems.[146]

The prisons were also beset by a number of disturbances and strikes during the early part of 1961. In their annual report for the year, the commissioners discussed the cases of indiscipline that had occurred. Prisoners had used the tactic of 'standstill' when ordered to proceed to work after exercise:

> The first of these received considerable publicity in the national press; and a wave of imitative hysteria affected other prisons until it came to be realised that group disobedience has to be paid for individually. Prompt and firm measures were taken by Governors in dealing with such outbreaks and the epidemic died out. Although these demonstrations were described by some of the participants as protests against overcrowding, food, or earnings, they were, in fact, stimulated in each case by a small number of aggressive men as a deliberate challenge to authority, in which most of those taking part became unwittingly involved.[147]

Medical power was mobilized to deal with the most difficult prisoners. The security wing in Durham provided the means 'with the help of specially trained staff of attempting to find out why these men are violent and if there is any way in which we can modify their violent tendencies'.[148] It had a specially selected staff of hospital and discipline officers under a Hospital Principal Officer and the general oversight of a Medical Officer who was also responsible for case-work.

Again in December 1962 there was trouble at Dartmoor when eleven prison officers were injured. The commissioners blamed 'one or two aggressive men as part of an unremitting campaign against authority'.[149]

All of these issues – the general state of the prisons, the lack of research on and rehabilitation of the criminal, the apparent inadequacy of the PMOs' qualifications, the involvement of doctors in the control of prisoners – brought the question of what should be done about the Prison Medical Service to a head. In November 1962 Henry Brooke, the Home Secretary, announced the establishment of an inquiry into the structure and function of the PMS and its relationship to the NHS. The inquiry was to be conducted by officials from the Home Office and the Ministry of Health with the assistance of Professor Dennis Hill of the Middlesex Hospital Medical School and Dr Peter Scott of Maudsley Hospital. In welcoming the statement, Leo Abse, the PMS's most persistent critic hoped that full attention would be given 'to the manner in which the PMS was at the moment so totally insulated from all modern trends in the Health Service, so that they might hope to have a service in prisons which would help to prevent crime'.[150] It was a hope that was soon to be disappointed. By February 1963 he was already talking about the inquiry as a 'clandestine interdepartmental study'.[151] For Abse, and the other critics, there was to be no metamorphosis in the work of the PMS.

THE POLITICS OF GWYNN

Working parties, committees of inquiry, judicial inquiries and royal commissions, all have perennially played a part in the repertoire of responses commanded by the British state when an institution is in crisis. They have a long history in Britain and serve an important legitimizing function for political practice. The set agenda, controlled membership and the relationship between gathered evidence and the facts which form the basis for final recommendations are all part of a process in which fundamental alternatives to the prevailing orthodoxy are closed off and marginalized. They are part of the more general establishment of state practices in which particular definitions of reality are both forged and propagated. These definitions utilize

> an immensely powerful language, alternative representations appearing fragmentary and insecure in the face of this massively authoritative organization of what is to count as reality. This system of power is inseparably also a system of knowledge, both in terms of quantity . . . and quality. Recall the long, long history of surveys, commissions, inquiries,

inspections, the establishment of authorised facts, in England, from Domesday to the Blue Books.[152]

Allied to this is the individual membership of the committees, 'social individuals in historically constructed relations' whose own background experiences and ideological preferences are crucial determinants in the construction, direction and final form reports and inquiries take.[153] The history, work and final report of the Gwynn Inquiry was no exception to the thesis outlined above and provides a good example of state management at its best in dealing with an institution in crisis.

First, there were no women on the working party which had eight members and a secretary. Four of the eight were members of the medical profession and included H. K. Snell, the current Director of the PMS. A second member, Professor J. D. N. Hill, had been involved in the debates about, and research into, the causes of crime since the early 1950s. He had published research on electroencephalography and contributed to a number of publications which were forensically oriented in both their theories of and policy prescriptions about criminality. He was also a member of the Eugenics Society.[154] Dr P. Scott, the other external adviser, was closely associated with the PMS both as a visiting psychotherapist at Brixton and as a psychiatric adviser in Grendon Underwood, a post to which he was appointed in 1963. He had also published work in the area of crime and deviance including 'Homosexuality, with Special Reference to Classifications', 'Treatment of Psychopaths' and 'Psychopathic Personalities'.[155]

Among those who gave both written and oral evidence was T. C. N. Gibbens from the Institute of Psychiatry, who was heavily involved through the 1950s in attempting to construct forensically based prediction tests to identify those who had propensities towards future criminality. In giving evidence, Gibbens's work was not finished. The report, containing eleven pages of text, was received by the Home Secretary in February and published in April 1964, seventeen months after the working party was established. On 23 April Brooke told the House of Commons that in principle he accepted the recommendations 'subject to consultation with the interests concerned'. To do this, he had established another committee on which

> officials of the Home Office and the Ministry of Health have the assistance of Dr T. C. N. Gibbens of the Institute of Psychiatry and of Dr P. Scott of the Maudsley Hospital in dealing with the implementation of these recommendations.[156]

The report contained fifteen recommendations. It rejected full integration with the NHS despite evidence from the Royal College of Physicians, the Royal Medico-Psychological Association, the National Association for Mental Health and the Institute of Psychiatry, which favoured complete integration. The BMA and the doctors' own union, the Institution of Professional Civil Servants, did not. To cope with this the working party recommended the continuation of the dual system with more NHS appointments in the prisons but the preservation of the full-time doctors in the PMS who would remain responsible for organizing medical services inside. In addition, it recommended a system of joint appointments where the Home Secretary and hospital boards would appoint psychiatrists to work part-time in the PMS, the remainder of their work being in hospitals or clinics outside the forensic field. The *British Medical Journal* concluded that the 'increased experience that joint appointments would allow the holders of them to acquire should prevent forensic psychiatrists from becoming too cut off in their speciality within a speciality'.[157] *The Lancet* was more critical in its appraisal for while it argued that the report was 'remarkable for its clear examination of the issues', it raised a number of other concerns which were to prove prophetic in the ensuing years:

> whether the proposed remedies will sufficiently stimulate recruiting may be doubted: indeed, the working party expects considerable delay before enough doctors are trained. It recognises also the possibility of friction in a dual-control system unless all concerned make an effort to work together. Furthermore the report hardly gives due weight to the need in prisons for full-time doctors who are deeply involved in the life of the prison, its climate, and its morale. Unfortunately little is said about the work being done by the present service, and the extraordinary difficulties of meeting the demands of a distressed, exasperated, and commonly abnormal population.[158]

The Gwynn Inquiry was the last review of the work of the PMS until the May Inquiry was established in the winter of 1978. In the fourteen years between Gwynn and May other issues were to impose themselves into the lives of the managers of the prison system and their medical employees. The opportunity that Gwynn missed to address the questions confronting the PMS was to prove costly. The doctors and their subordinates, far from being allowed to develop their occupational roles harmoniously as Gwynn had hoped, were to become embroiled in even greater controversy in the following two decades as prisoners' rights organizations focused their attention on the role of the PMS in the struggle to maintain order in an increasingly brittle and fragile prison world. The search-light of scrutiny that these organizations operated once again raised serious questions about the medical treatment of the confined and the role of medicine in maintaining order inside. The blanket of secrecy which covered the prisons was to be torn throughout the 1960s and 1970s. Through the gaps and into focus came a medical world which was caught up in the crisis that gripped the prison system in those two decades. The response of the PMS was forged on the anvil of that crisis. Increasingly however, it was prisoners and their supporters who kindled the fires on which the anvil stood.

CHAPTER 5

Medicine and regulation: from the 1960s to the 1980s

The modern prison, especially the training prison, uses more and more specialists, for training, supervision of work, education, group work, social case work, etc. Many of them have to find a place for themselves within the prison world. Like the chameleons we all are, they take on the colouration of their surroundings. The adjustment is always to the prison system, never in the other direction, because the individual comes into the system alone and unsupported. It has become, as a result, inbred and conservative. It never has to face a real challenge from outside; when challengers arise they are absorbed, and eventually become 'adjusted'.[1]

In Chapter 4 I indicated how, in the early 1960s, the government opened security wings in order to 'cope with what it took to be a new breed of "violent and dangerous" criminals'.[2] This development was to symbolize and illustrate the direction of penal policy throughout the next two decades. Security was increasingly the driving force behind penal policy. It was, in turn, underpinned by an intensification in the struggle to maintain order, especially in the long-term prisons. Before considering the dimensions of this struggle, and the role of medicine and psychology within it, it is important to recognize that both developments took place against the background of a major increase in the long-term prison population. A range of commentators have pointed to this increase and the acceleration in the population of long-termers from the 1960s.[3] Stan Cohen and Laurie Taylor have argued that all the prison statistics lead to the same conclusion. They 'document the rise in the long-term prison population and the continuing predilection of English judges, to hand out longer and longer sentences'.[4] This trend accelerated through the 1970s and 1980s so that by 1985 'more than a fifth of the adult male prison population' were long-term prisoners.[5] Within this population there were specific groups whose sentences added to the increase. Those sentenced in connection with political violence in

Northern Ireland was one such group. By 1980 over forty of those sentenced in England had received sentences of either life or twenty years or more. Another forty had been sentenced to ten years or more with 'only a handful [being] sentenced to less than ten years'.[6]

The number of life sentence prisoners also dramatically increased. In 1957 there were 140 lifers; by November 1986 this figure had increased fourteen-fold to over 2,000.[7] For women prisoners, there was a similar trend, the number of lifers increasing from seven in 1957 to fifty-seven in 1986.[8] Life sentences were increasingly used for offences other than murder. In February 1980 there were twenty such offences ranging from murder through to grievous bodily harm and using firearms to resist arrest.[9] By January 1983 77 per cent of male lifers had been convicted of murder, 11 per cent of manslaughter and 12 per cent were sentenced for other offences.[10] The processes were compounded by the number of prisoners serving sentences that carried minimum recommendations attached by the trial judge. Between 1964 and 1987, 244 sentences with minimum recommendations were passed by the courts. In only seven cases were individuals released before the minimum time expired.[11]

The build-up in the number of long-term prisoners was accompanied by a major increase in the security and control aspects of the prison system. The developments around security following the Mountbatten and Radzinowicz reports in the mid-1960s have been extensively documented elsewhere.[12] The emphasis on security and classification which flowed from the reports had a major impact on the prison system. It percolated through the penal estate underpinning, directing and dominating penal policy in both long-term and short-term prisons. Between 1962 and 1977 there was a 5,833 per cent increase in maximum security places compared with a 41 per cent increase in long-term prisoners in the same period.[13]

Despite this massive increase in security, problems of internal control not only remained but also substantially increased from the late 1960s. Through the 1970s and into the 1980s there were major demonstrations in the majority of the long-term maximum security prisons. Between 1969 and 1983 there were ten disturbances alone.[14] Significantly these problems were blamed on a small number of difficult, subversive prisoners, who manipulated an otherwise quiescent prison population into riot and demonstration.[15] These prisoners were regarded as a new breed, more recalcitrant and subversive than anything previously known.[16]

The managers of the system concentrated their efforts on a range of policies designed to individualize and isolate the prisoner or prisoners responsible for 'riot'. The prison doctors themselves had identified the existence of such a group around 1965. In a memorandum to the Royal Commission on the Penal System (established in August 1964 but abandoned without reporting within eighteen months), they argued that

In view of the increasing number of difficult and disturbed inmates in Prisons and Borstals we believe that the role of the doctor is of increasing importance in penal treatment and furthermore we consider that medical opinion should be represented in policy making on the Prison Board (in the person of the D.P.M.S.) as, until comparatively recently, it used to be represented by the Medical Commissioner on the former Prison Commission.[17]

In 1970 the Chairperson of the Prison Officers' Association talked of the 'sophisticated, dangerous, psychopathic villains who make full use of the misguided and the inadequate to achieve their own evil ends'.[18] The previous year the Home Office maintained that 'there will always be a small minority of offenders needing strict control and supervision'. Such prisoners, it was felt, if given 'any opportunity to do so will dominate the larger group of which they form a small part'.[19] The ex-prison governor, Alastair Miller, pinpointed the 'disastrous effect that some wicked men can have on the morale and well-being of their fellow-prisoners hundreds of whom are fully co-operative'.[20]

In 1972 there were over 100 demonstrations in British prisons.[21] Robert Carr, the Home Secretary, responded in May 1973 by announcing a number of measures designed to improve 'our facilities and techniques for containing violent and dangerous men in prison'.[22] These changes included expanding the number of dispersal prisons to nine (there were then six) and building segregation units in each of them. The demonstrations had come on top of a major disturbance in Parkhurst in 1969 and were to be followed by an attempted break-out and trouble at Gartree in November 1972. Against this background Carr announced the establishment of

two additional facilities for dealing with the small core of intractable troublemakers. Two control units would be set up in existing separate accommodation within the present dispersal prisons to accommodate such 'thoroughly intractable troublemakers'.[23]

The Home Secretary had established an eleven-person committee of inquiry, which was chaired by W. R. Cox of the Prison Department. The committee produced a 20,000-word report, which 'was never published and even the governors themselves were refused permission to see it'.[24] The report claimed to have pinpointed a rise in 'anarchist attitudes' in the prisons. Additionally there were '72 particular trouble-makers in the system, many of them young men serving long sentences'.[25] After an internal bureaucratic battle, the Home Office established the control units. Details for implementing the units were contained in Circular Instruction 35/1974 circulated in June 1974 'and approved by the Secretary of State though it was not sent to the House of Commons and consequently Members of Parliament remained ignorant of any details of the regime'.[26] The unit at Wakefield was opened on 1 August 1974 and three prisoners were received on 23 August. There was a fourteen-page supplement known as Annex D to CI 35/1974 *Notes for Convicted Prisoners in Control Units* (Cell Information Card). Paragraphs 1 and 6 were blunt:

You have been brought here because it is considered that you have been disposed deliberately to try to undermine and disrupt the pattern of life in the prison from which you came and have shown by your behaviour that you were not prepared to co-operate with the normal prison regime. . . . If at any time you fail to co-operate, to work satisfactorily or to behave yourself you will move back to the beginning of Stage 1 and have to start all over again.[27]

The regime was based on sensory deprivation. There were no windows in the cells and 'no noise could be heard within them':

White light was continuous and inside they were painted brilliant white. Prison officers who manned these cells were given special training in avoiding any personal involvement or conversation with the prisoner. Officers were equipped with special footwear so that they made no noise while approaching the cells. Over a number of meetings, a list was drawn up by the Home Office and the prison administration of those prisoners whom they felt represented the most difficult management problem. The prisoners, once in the cells, were presented with a rigorous behaviour programme. They were placed on a graduated scale of privileges which they could 'earn' during successive ninety-day periods. If at any time they 'misbehaved' or were put on report, they reverted to day one of the scale and had to begin again. The point of the experiment was to break the will of recalcitrant prisoners.[28]

The sensory deprivation involved in the regime and its strategies of isolation were successfully challenged by prisoners' rights organizations. While the units were officially phased out in October 1975 they were

not to be dismantled as such, but reserved for those prisoners who had to be removed from the rest of the prison population 'in the interests of good order and discipline'. Not surprisingly, perhaps, this announcement left some groups in the penal lobby wondering whether they had simply won a battle but lost a war. Discipline through segregation was still officially favoured and who could be sure what this might mean in the future?[29]

Mick Ryan's question was to be answered by prisoners who described the segregation techniques that were utilized. After protesting about visiting conditions in Albany, Raymond MacLaughlin was moved to Wakefield's 'F' Wing in 1979 where he was held in

the control unit for three months. When he was removed from it he was completely dis-orientated and had lost all track of time. For a time afterwards he suffered from dizziness and inability to speak properly.[30]

In his autobiography MacLaughlin described a further spell in 'F' Wing when he was transferred there after a major disturbances at Albany in 1983:

It was designed for maximum isolation. For example, the windows are about three foot deep, two foot wide and one foot high, made up of three inch square tiles of frosted glass. There was no glass in two of these tiny squares and that doubled as my source of fresh air and my view. This view consisted of the twenty foot white wall that surrounded the unit. This wall was painted with abstract lines of the most dismal colours, i.e., grey, dark green, and black. The official explanation for these abstract designs was that the exercise yard that ran between the white wall and the unit was so narrow, that the designs helped give the illusion of more space!![31]

The use of segregation did not defuse the problems in the long-term prisons. In 1975 Irish prisoners caused £25,000 damage to the roof of Wormwood Scrubs. In September 1976 there was trouble at Albany when six Irish prisoners erected barricades in support of one of their number who had been placed in the punishment block for refusing to clean his cell. There were claims, partly endorsed in a joint report compiled by Amnesty International, the National Council for Civil Liberties and the Howard League that prisoners had been assaulted.[32] In the same month there was a major disturbance at Hull Prison which lasted for three days. In the aftermath of the disturbance prisoners, particularly those who were Irish or black, were subjected to violent abuse by prison officers. Eight prison officers were subsequently found guilty of conspiring together with others to assault and beat prisoners.[33] They were all given suspended prison sentences of which one was overturned on appeal. At the original trial at York Crown Court in January 1979, the judge and jury heard from a 'procession of prisoners':

> One told how a jug of urine was poured over him, others described how they were pulled along by the hair or were beaten on the way to being transferred. Many prisoners, in their evidence, observed how the IRA and black prisoners were especially humiliated. One of the former, for example, was made to sing 'God Save the Queen'. This man was held down and told to sing. He replied, 'Go play with yourself, you puff' [sic]. An officer then said, 'Hold his legs open', and then 'he put the boot in my testicles'. Later he was told, 'You Irish bastard; you'll remember me for the rest of your days.' One of the black prisoners stated that he had been kept awake on the night of the surrender by officers switching on his light, kicking his door and shouting: 'National Front rules, big black bastard.' After being beaten, this prisoner went to breakfast when an officer said: 'What does this black bastard think he is going to get?' When he did get breakfast, another officer hit his hands and the food went all over him. After being made to run the gauntlet to 'see if you can run like the other black athletes' he was put in his cell. There another officer poured the contents of a chamber-pot over him. The other black prisoner had the same kind of treatment. He was the man that the PEI had failed to knock down, and he confirmed Unwin's version of this particular assault. He also alleged that an officer had said: 'You flash cunt. If you're not quick with this slopping out, you'll be a sorry nigger'.[34]

The majority of prisoners were reluctant to complain to PMOs. As J. E. Thomas and Richard Pooley have pointed out:

> With regard to the doctors, the prisoners' views on medical treatment were repeated many times in the court. At the present time medical care of

prisoners is a matter of public concern on several accounts. The over-use of drugs is constantly being commented upon, and the right, or rather absence of it, to consult a second medical opinion is a target for the human rights movement. The assumption of most institutional doctors, including those in the prison service, is that people who report sick are malingering. If these facts are borne in mind, and if the mood at the conclusion of the riot can be imagined, the reluctance of prisoners to complain to medical officers can be understood.[35]

Following Hull, there were further disturbances at Gartree in October 1978, at Parkhurst in March 1979, Hull in April 1979 and Wormwood Scrubs the following August.

This last disturbance was notable because of the intervention of the Minimum Use of Force Tactical Intervention Squad (MUFTI). The squad was trained in riot-control and developed out of a working party established in 1978 'to give guidance to prison governors on the minimum use of force, tactical intervention . . . following serious disturbances including that at Hull Prison in 1976'.[36] Although it had been in action prior to August 1979 it was the squad's intervention in that month at Wormwood Scrubs which brought it to public attention. On 21 October after a number of prevaricating statements by the Home Office concerning the injuries prisoners had sustained, Christopher Price MP elicited from Ministers' statistics which indicated that a total of fifty-four prisoners 'incurred injuries consisting of cuts, bruises and abrasions. Eleven prison officers incurred similar injuries'.[37] The Prison Medical Service came in for particular attention in relation to how the prisoners were treated after the disturbance. The National Prisoners' Movement (PROP) provided a commentary on the official inquiry into the disturbance.[38] PROP argued that the inquiry highlighted some serious deficiencies in the Service's response to the injuries:

> At the regular Board of Visitors meeting on 5 October, *six weeks after the event*, the PMO reported that 'four or five prisoners had required sutures for head injuries out of a total of 55 prisoners reporting sick'. Pressed for more details the PMO 'left the meeting to check his figures' before giving 'a revised set of injury figures' which included 16 prisoners sutured. As the Report makes clear, none of the figures were accurate.[39]

Kay Douglas Scott described her visit to one prisoner. She told Granada's *World in Action* she was

> really shattered by his condition. He had stitches in his head, arm . . . and he limped very, very badly . . . he was made to walk down . . . four flights of stairs . . . to the ground floor where two hospital officers sutured his head . . . After they put the stitches in, his head hurt considerably. They neither offered him or asked him if he wanted any pain killers of any kind.[40]

Dr Eric Beck, a consultant physician at Whittington Hospital in London did not treat any of those hurt but after studying the Home Office report into the incident, noted that nineteen prisoners required stitching. He told the programme he was

> particularly surprised to see that the stitching was done by prison hospital officers without the injured prisoners being seen by a doctor first. And this is completely at variance with any practice in the National Health Service. The whole area about stitching by nurses . . . is very carefully laid down that it can only be done after a patient has been examined by a doctor who then may authorise a nurse, who will have had to have had at least three years' experience, be a state registered nurse, unlike the prison hospital officers who may have had as little as three months' medical training of a sort of first aid nature, and I think there is considerable potential hazard in this being carried out in this way.[41]

Alistair Logan summed up what he saw as the central issue involved pointing out that the PMS

> is not there to serve the prisoner it is there to serve the prison service. Many of the people working in the field have a great deal of sympathy and competence. A lot of them I believe do not have as much competence as others. However, anybody who has worked in connection with prisons for any length of time realises that a good number of them believe that their first duty is to the prison medical service, and the prison service, and their second duty is to the prisoner.[42]

It was not only the development and deployment of the militarized MUFTI squad which provoked medical controversy. The use of drugs as mechanisms of control was a fundamental concern for prisoners in the 1960s and 1970s. The formation of Radical Alternatives to Prison in 1970 and the National Prisoners' Movement in 1972 provided a forum for prisoners to articulate their concerns. As the crisis of containment intensified so the allegations became stronger that drugs were being used for disciplinary purposes.

THE POLITICS OF DRUGS

The use of drugs in institutions was not a phenomenon that emerged in the 1950s. Prisoners in the nineteenth and early twentieth century described what they termed 'sleeping draughts' to alter behaviour. What was different in the 1950s was the manufacture on a large scale of powerful new combinations of chemicals involving multinational companies. Chlorpromazine (marketed in Britain under the trade name of Largactil) is a good example of this process. When introduced in 1954, it had been tried on 104 psychiatric patients in the USA. A year later, it was being administered to 2 million people alone in that country. For the manufacturer, Smith, Kline and French, the commercial impact was equally great. Within a year of its introduction, 'Largactil had increased the company's total sales volume by one third. Between 1957 and 1970 net sales increased from 57 million dollars to 347 million dollars'.[43]

As Chapter 4 indicated, the prison doctors were remarkably frank in the late 1950s and early 1960s about the impact that drugs had on their ability to control difficult prisoners. When the Home Office took responsibility from the Prison Commissioners for the administration of the prisons in 1963, the tone of the official reports changed. There were no longer unsigned statements from doctors, psychologists and chaplains discussing their role inside. Instead, the public was given the 'facts' about the prison service and little else. This placed further restrictions on the quality of information coming from the inside. Despite this control, different accounts still emerged about the impact of drugs.

In his account of the Great Train Robbery, Piers Paul Read described life for the men in Parkhurst security wing in 1966 where 'those whom this living entombment made frenzied were quickly dosed with Librium and Valium'.[44] Wally Probyn, who was in the prison at the time described the case of a prisoner who

> attempted to cut his own throat shortly after arriving at the block. Ted had no one in the outside world to care about him or to protest on his behalf, so he was an ideal subject for experimentations. Despite Ted's chronic depression, which was caused by the oppressive and claustrophobic conditions of the block, he was coldly observed and recorded. Ted remained in his cell most of the day and night. He was taking powerful drugs that sent him to sleep all the afternoon and another dose that sent him to sleep all night. He became totally dependent on the drug and on the one occasion that it wasn't readily available, he became extremely distressed and began pleading and threatening until it was at last produced. Ted became more and more like a zombie over the months. By the time he was moved (to where, no one knew or yet knows), he was just a human wreck. His eyes were lifeless and vacant, it seemed amazing that he still lived at all. Ted was just one of the casualties of the programme for new psychological control of prisoners.[45]

In his autobiography Alastair Miller, the ex-governor of the prison also discussed the regime in the 1960s. In the case of an 'aggressive psychopath' who assaulted another prisoner:

> He had to be restrained. He was extremely violent and would have damaged anyone in sight. He was firmly dealt with and was hit during the restraining. This brought him to what sense he had. The member of staff who hit him reported this to higher authority. While in the cells he was constantly under sedation and under the Medical Officer's supervision.[46]

As in the 1920s and 1940s concern about the situation led to the formation of a pressure group to highlight the issues involved and to challenge the involvement of medicine in the process of discipline and control. In November 1977 the National Prisoners' Movement initiated the formation of the Medical Committee Against the Abuse of Prisoners by Drugging. The committee was made up of representatives of the National Prisoners' Movement, the National Council for Civil Liberties, the National Association for Mental Health, the Standing

Council on Drug Abuse, Radical Alternatives to Prison and Release. A number of consultant psychiatrists were also involved as well as David Markham, the Chair of the Bukovsky Committee and Victor Fainberg, the Chair of the Campaign Against Psychiatric Abuse. Its purpose was to monitor the allegations that were emerging and to 'campaign for the dissolution of the Prison Medical Service and its replacement by a health service for prisoners free of Home Office control and administered, instead, by the NHS'.[47]

The controversy was compounded further in the autumn of 1978, when it was revealed that a prison doctor had written an article in *Prison Medical Journal* which concerned the treatment of psychopaths with the drug Depixol:

> For some years we have had the problem of containment of psychopaths who, as a result of situational stress, have presented the discipline staff with control problems for which there has been no satisfactory solution. . . . From a medical angle these men show no evidence of formal illness as such, but, clearly, are characters having a lot of nervous tension, a certain amount of depression, considerable frustration with a low flash point who, until the situational stress can be removed or modified, are potentially either very dangerous or in the case of the more inadequate, an unmitigated nuisance.[48]

He added that these men 'are considered by the governor and discipline staff as medical problems [and were] regarded purely as discipline failures'.[49]

From the summer of 1979 through to the summer of 1980 there were a series of Parliamentary questions about the issue of drugs. It was revealed that Benperidol had been used on sex offenders by a doctor working in a prison in 1971.[50] While the Committee on the Safety of Drugs had authorized the manufacturer to dispense it on the prescription of any registered medical practitioner, its product licence was not issued until July 1973.[51] Renee Short followed up this revelation with a series of questions. She asked the Home Secretary to disclose 'the list of drugs, without product licence tested on prisoners in Great Britain'. William Whitelaw replied:

> Cyproterone acetate (Androcur) which was granted a product licence in January 1974, was used by one consultant psychiatrist working in prisons between 1970 and 1974. Benperidol (Anguil), which was granted a product licence in July 1973, was used by doctors working in prisons between 1971 and 1973. . . . Both drugs had been used overseas and in the National Health Service before they were used in prisons. I am not aware of any other drugs having been prescribed by doctors working in prisons in England and Wales before they had been granted product licences.[52]

These questions also brought into focus the issue of drug treatment and sex offenders. As Chapter 4 indicated, sex offenders had been a particular concern for medical personnel in the 1950s. This continued into the 1970s when chemical treatment was used to control their sexual urges. A number of them underwent profound changes. Between November 1975 and November 1978, 138 prisoners received one or more types of chemical treatment. Within this group, fifteen had operations to remove breasts and two others underwent the operation after their release.[53]

Once more, a number of outside commentators focused on this issue and raised what they regarded as fundamental questions which were relevant to the prisoners involved. In May 1979 contributors to *Probe*, a journal for probation officers discussed the ethical issues involved.[54] In 1981 Radical Alternatives to Prison (RAP) also discussed the issue and raised questions about the role of the PMS:

. . . we are clear that the present status of the prison medical service places prison doctors in an impossible ethical position in which they are unable to distinguish between treatment and control; we feel that the parole system and the associated pressure put on prisoners by their doctors to accept treatment makes it impossible to talk of consent to treatment in a meaningful way; and we are totally opposed to the use of prisoners, by unaccountable prison doctors, as guinea pigs, on which to experiment with new drugs and therapies. All this leads us to conclude that a greater degree of independent advice and consultation must be available to men who are recommended for behaviour therapy and drug treatment because they have committed sexual offences.[55]

The more general question of the use of drugs for disciplinary and control purposes continued to rumble on. Under pressure, the Home Office released statistics apparently detailing the amount of drugs in prisons. This was first done in 1979 and repeated in 1980 and 1981. Although welcoming the release of the statistics, RAP, in a series of carefully researched briefing papers and articles, illustrated how the presentation of the statistics still left a number of basic questions unanswered. The group made three broad criticisms of the presentation. First, the classification between 'Psychotropic drugs' 'Hypnotic drugs' and 'Other drugs affecting the Central Nervous System' was meaningless 'without further elaboration from the Prison Medical Service on exactly what drugs they place in each category'.[56] Second, the broad band of categorization 'disguises the fact that some drugs are far more dangerous than others while falling in the same division'.[57] Third, the figures lumped together the number of drugs dispensed in

two, three and in one case 42 prisons. The explanation for this practice is that in 'those establishments in which medical services are largely provided by a single doctor . . . it is not considered appropriate to publish information about an individual doctor's prescribing practice'. . . . Such an explanation typified the atmosphere of secrecy and the lack of public accountability that surrounds every aspect of the work of the Prison Department. The net result of the Home Office's desire to protect its employees from public scrutiny is that for 90 different penal establishments it is impossible to make accurate and meaningful comparisons between dosage rates.[58]

Two significant points did, however, emerge from the release of the figures. First, there was the question of the differential dosage rates in women's prisons.[59] This is considered in greater detail in the next chapter. Second, there were wide variations in dosage rates for male prisons. Brixton, a remand prison, had the second highest dosage rate per prisoner while Grendon Underwood, the psychiatric prison recorded the lowest dosage rate of any prison, remand centre or Borstal. According to RAP, Grendon's low dosage rate indicated that there were methods that could be used to deal with those who were suffering mentally without using

> heavy doses of behaviour modifying drugs. If Grendon is able to contain its population without the widespread use of drugs why, then, do other prisons with proportionately far fewer mentally disturbed prisoners need to prescribe as many as 300 doses of drugs per man per year? It is important to stress that RAP is not saying that there is a 'normal' acceptable dosage rate for our prisons which is being exceeded in some instances. Such a dosage rate is impossible to give. What we are saying is that there are certain dosage rates which cannot be explained by the Home Office's covering statements; indeed some of the dosage rates clearly contradict those covering statements. The Home Office must be pressed to give a fully adequate explanation of their statistical information. At present, the statistics they have provided confuse rather than clarify and beg more questions than they answer.[60]

CONTROLLING THE CRITICS

The debate about the use of drugs in the prison system in the late 1970s and early 1980s was not straightforward. Those outside the walls who were interested in researching and discussing the impact of drugs were themselves subject to severe controls not only in terms of the Official Secrets Act but also by the application of the libel laws. There were a series of libel proceedings initiated at this time against newspapers,[61] academics,[62] magazines[63] and publishers.[64] The use of the libel laws, however, did not suppress the criticism which came not only from those outside the prison service but from within the state itself. In October 1983 Benjamin Lee who was the medical adviser to the Prison Inspectorate before he resigned, outlined his views on the subject:

> prison doctors have become so sensitive to media criticism that they are just as likely to withhold doses of psychotropic drugs. It is true, though, that doctors may administer, or countenance the administration of, psychotropic drugs, to achieve what the disciplinary staff want – a quiet prison.[65]

In July 1984 MPs Gerry Bermingham and Alex Carlile again pressed for more information on the issue. Douglas Hurd told Carlile that psychotropic medicines could be 'administered by hospital officers who do not have nursing qualifications but who will have received appropriate training.'[66] Bermingham also elicited the information that twenty-one prisoners had received electro-convulsive therapy in 1981, four in 1982, and seven in 1983 while during the same period no prisoner had received either sex hormone implants or psycho-surgery.[67] Prisoners themselves engaged in litigation. In at least one case a prisoner successfully sued the Home Office after being injected with Largactil without his consent while on remand in 1978. He was awarded £600 'for his hurt feelings'.[68] The Prison Reform Trust brought a number of these themes and issues together in its 1985 publication *Prison Medicine: Ideas on Health Care in Penal Establishments.* In his contribution to the book, Dr Tony Whitehead pointed out:

> It would appear that there is evidence that drugs are, at least sometimes, used for disciplinary rather than therapeutic reasons. No doubt such allegations will continue to be denied, but the evidence, though limited speaks otherwise. It also appears that the use of drugs is less prevalent than previously. It would also appear that this reduction in the use of drugs has been a direct result of agitation by certain groups of individuals and, but for that agitation, would not have occurred.[69]

Whitehead's statement apeared to receive support from Phil Hornsby, the Assistant General Secretary of the Prison Officers' Association. In January 1986 he was interviewed on the ITV programme *Insiders* in which the following exchange occurred:

> INTERVIEWER: There is however a fine line between the use of drugs for therapy and their use for control.
>
> HORNSBY: Certainly there are cases in prison, quite a lot, where we would suspect drugs have been given to prisoners for no other reason than for control measures, because, quite simply, prison officers do not have the training and the ability to nurse these people properly.
>
> INTERVIEWER: So, in a sense it could be officially therapy of some kind, for medical reasons but the reality is, as it is I would suggest in many mental hospitals, . . . to do with control.
>
> HORNSBY: Yes, I wouldn't argue against that.
>
> INTERVIEWER: When you were an officer yourself, were you aware, I mean was that one of your impressions from the eleven years that you spent as an officer?
>
> HORNSBY: Yes, I mean it has to be said that it is vital for the prison officer to be in charge of the situation in prison otherwise we'd have total disruption and anarchy but how that is best achieved . . . with a normal prisoner we do it by the normal methods and there is a normal expectation that people will behave and conform to regimes. With the mentally abnormal offender he doesn't know any better and by hook or by crook he has to be controlled. I'm not sure that's right, the way we do it.[70]

DEATHS IN CUSTODY

In the early 1980s the issues around the use of drugs was compounded by the questions which were raised concerning deaths in custody. As previous chapters have shown this issue has itself had a long and controversial place in the historical debates around penal policy. Prisoners' rights organizations, academics, Members of Parliament and the relatives and friends of the deceased focused their attention on a number of deaths which occurred at the time. The concerns articulated by these individuals and groups led to the formation of the pressure group *Inquest* which was established in 1980. The group's brief was to campaign on behalf of the relatives and friends of those who had died 'suddenly, violently or inexplicably in police and prison custody'.[71] The initial focus for the campaign was a series of contentious deaths in police and prison custody in the late 1970s and early 1980s. Within the prisons, the case of Barry Prosser who died in the hospital wing of Winson Green prison in August 1980 was particularly controversial. In April 1981, after an inquest lasting seven days, the jury after hearing from nearly 50 witnesses, took 15 minutes to reach a verdict that the prisoner had been unlawfully killed.[72] Among his injuries was a burst stomach and oesophagus. In March 1982 after a series of legal twists and turns three prison hospital officers were tried at Leicester Crown Court. They were charged with Prosser's murder. After nine hours of deliberation the jury found the accused not guilty. Two of the three officers gave evidence at the original inquest, the third declined. One of the officers described how 'eleven or twelve officers' went to Prosser's cell where 'as many officers that could entered the cell'[73] The purpose was to give the prisoner an injection. He testified that:

> None of the officers drew their sticks. It is true that hospital officers do not carry sticks. I do not feel that any undue force was used by anyone at the time. I do not know who was holding his abdomen. . . . I did not see anything that could have caused any of his injuries. What I saw was simple restraint with no violence offered by one side or the other and no necessity for violence on the part of the prison officers.[74]

At the conclusion of the inquest the coroner took the opportunity to comment on the way that the prison hospital was organized:

> One of my concerns is the manner in which the drugs were prescribed and recorded, and the manner in which the administration was recorded. You will recall there were four different forms in use at the time. This was very confusing with staff coming on and off duty. Shift people and those working part time should know what is happening. . . . There was no proper document for ready reference by anybody visiting an inmate of the hospital having to order treatment. I think this was a failure at that time. It was below the standards one would expect for this day. I do not think the manner in which the medication was prescribed or recorded was a factor in Barry Prosser's death, but I think they should be looked at and I think that modern methods should be adopted as Dr Woods recommended. I am pleased to hear that this is the intention.

I think I should make some reference to the regulations regarding physical force. It does seem rather ludicrous that Home Office regulations are being ignored, and there seems to be a need for some regulations to be enforced in the hospital about when physical force is used. I must state that this is as much as anything for the protection of the men working there. The fact that no physical force form was used did affect the enquiries that the police made. It delayed the enquiries in the fact that the authorities at that time were quite unaware that physical force was used to restrain a man who died. The deputy governor was not aware of this, because no record was made. I think this ought to be looked into in the hospital.[75]

The Coroner felt that there should be much greater interchange of nursing staff between the hospital and prison service:

I think it is most important that there should be hospital qualified nurses available in the prison hospital. My remarks about the nurses will also apply to doctors. There would be great advantage if they had appointments outside in National Health hospitals as well as their appointments in the prison. This would raise professional standards.[76]

Finally, he pointed out that there were several questions that remained unanswered. There was no record of force used in the hospital occurrence book, no initials were 'recorded in the remand ward occurrence book that night [the 18th] as if something unusual had happened'.[77] Additionally, no records were kept of a fresh injury to one of the accused 'when he had only given an injection to an unresisting prisoner'. He went on:

I certainly look on another unanswered question with some horror. Nobody at the prison knew how seriously Mr Prosser was injured until the post mortem was carried out. It is extraordinary.[78]

The controversy over prison deaths continued into the late 1980s. There was particular concern over the question of prison suicides and suicide prevention measures. Between January 1987 and December 1988 159 prisoners died in English and Welsh prisons. Table 2 indicates the principal causes of death.

Of the sixty-seven prisoners who committed suicide, two-thirds (44) were prisoners on remand. However, as *Inquest* pointed out, remand prisoners only

Table 2   Deaths in prison in England and Wales 1987–1988[79]

Cause of death	No.	%
Suicide	67	42
Natural causes	57	35.8
Inquest to be held	16	10
Misadventure	7	4.4
Open verdict	6	3.8
Natural causes/lack of care	4	2.5
Suicide/lack of care	1	0.6
Lack of care	1	0.6

make up a quarter of the prison population.[80] Furthermore, they experienced some of the most horrendous conditions in the system:

> The severe overcrowding in most prison establishments means that many prisoners are kept banged up in their cells 23 or 24 hours a day, unable to take proper exercise or make use of prison facilities. This type of situation is obviously going to aggravate the mental condition of people already anxious, depressed and separated from their families, many of them in custody for the first time in their lives. It is interesting to note . . . that in 1986 and 1987 only 56% of the men and 36% of the women remanded in custody eventually received custodial sentences.[81]

In June 1988, the Board of Visitors at Armley prison, which was the most overcrowded in Britain, pointed out that staff shortages had led to a breakdown in suicide prevention measures. The number of prisoners had risen from 1,307 in 1987 to 1,380 in 1988. This was 111 per cent over the prison's theoretical maximum complement:

> . . . the most serious shortfalls stemmed from shortages of medical staff, including intermittent closure of the gaol's hospital and failure to comply with the suicide instructions which require the interviewing of every new inmate to gauge the suicide risk.[82]

In July the question of suicide risk came into sharper focus, when the Chief Inspector of Prisons revealed that staff at Risley remand centre had ignored the mandatory instructions governing potential suicide risks. Six suicides had occurred in the previous twelve months in conditions the Chief Inspector described as 'barbarous and squalid'.[83] Two of the prison's wings were

> filthy. Cells were small and dimly lit. Corridors were narrow. The low ceilings added to the oppressive atmosphere. Inmates spent the majority of the day in their cells. . . . A sense of squalor inside the wings could be gained by walking outside. We were told that the walls had recently been cleaned in order to remove deeply ingrained excrement and other foul matter which had for years been thrown out of cell windows by inmates. In an attempt to stop this practice metal mesh grilles had been placed over the windows. The response of those inside was frequently to smear these substances onto the grilles and to deposit other rubbish between the windows and the grilles. . . . The absence of integral sanitation through-out the prison is a major factor in the overall lack of human dignity.[84]

When four prison officers were asked about a standard form relating to suicide risk the inspector reported they 'did not know what we were talking about.'[85]

Finally, the Chief Inspector raised serious questions about the design of the prison which through its lack of integral sanitation 'laid the foundation for hopelessness and apathy'.[86] The Home Secretary responded to the report by indicating that £50m was to be spent on redeveloping the prison which would secure a better future for the prisoners. This was to be part of the new prison building programme for the 1990s. However, there were already serious questions being raised about the programme. In May 1988, the Board of Visitors at Full Sutton, which had opened in 1987 drew up a list of eighteen design faults in the prison. The Board accused designers of wasting public money in following 'an already discredited design' in the computerized alarm systems. The hospital wing was also criticized for lacking integral sanitation, dental cover and equipment.[87]

In 1989, a further group of cases and statistics emerged which indicated the seriousness and depth of the problem. At the end of May two prisoners committed suicide which brought the number of deaths so far for the year to twenty-nine.[88] In September the Howard League for Penal Reform published the report of an independent inquiry into the remand wing at Leeds where five young men hanged themselves between May 1988 and February 1989. The League condemned the Home Office for 'crisis management' in dealing with suicidal behaviour in the prison. It pointed out that despite the different calls for clear suicide prevention policies there had been a further forty-two suicide attempts and nineteen cases of self-mutilation on the wing 'in seven months this year [1989]'.[89] As The Independent argued:

> The report describes Leeds prison as a grey, forbidding building where highly vulnerable teenagers are locked up for as much as 18 hours a day often in degrading conditions with little supervision and little activity. Conditions there have been repeatedly attacked by prison inspectors as inhuman.[90]

In October it was announced that the Home Office had established an inquiry into the professional conduct of a prison doctor at Brixton which was known as the 'suicide capital' of the prison system. Eight prisoners had committed suicide in the prison since the start of the year, the inquiry was concerned with four of these cases.[91] Three members of staff at the prison committed suicide in the same period. One prisoner described 'F' Wing which contained prisoners with psychiatric and drug problems in the following terms: 'if you can think of constant screaming, banging and stench then that's what it's like. You wouldn't believe that anyone could scream continuously for eight hours but some of them do'.[92] Finally, in November it was revealed that the family of a prisoner who had died in the prison in January 1982 was suing the Home Office and the prison governor for damages. The family claimed that Paul Worrell's death could have been avoided if he had received better care in the prison. After hearing evidence which both criticized and defended the Prison Medical Service a High Court Judge rejected the family's claims. He ruled that the psychiatric wing at Brixton 'did not have to give the same standard of care as an outside mental hospital.'[93]

DISCIPLINING THE MAJORITY

The question of maintaining order in the long-term prisons, and the issues around medicine that flowed from this, was accompanied by the ongoing concern over short-term and remand prisoners and the conditions in which medical treatment of these prisoners took place. As I argued in previous chapters, medical treatment for the confined in the nineteenth century was constrained and determined by the impact of less eligibility on the philosophy and practice of penology. Discipline and regulation were corner-stones of penality which in turn meant that the physical conditions were, for many, purgatorial. This discourse, and the policies and practices that were generated continued into the twentieth century. Prison regimes for the short-term confined remained disciplinary in their orientation and philosophy. The conditions in which the incarcerated lived and worked began to decline still further from the 1940s as overcrowding rose. By the 1970s overcrowding and the often appalling conditions in which prisoners existed was a major cause for concern in the debates around the prisons. At the same time, this was a central element in the crisis that gripped the system during the decade.[94] Reports by academics, prisoners' rights groups, the media, politicians and prisoners themselves all highlighted the often gruesome and depressing conditions in which short-term prisoners lived. Prison medicine was caught up in these conditions. While the rhetoric of rehabilitation had allowed the managers of the penal estate to argue that prison health care was similar to that provided by the NHS the reality for those behind the walls was a health care system caught in the disciplinary vice of appalling conditions and the legacy of less eligibility. The evidence from the Royal College of Psychiatrists to the May Inquiry in 1979 caught the flavour of this inter-relationship:

> Since prisoners are already disadvantaged, the facilities available for their treatment should be at least equal to those in the community. However, the high morbidity of those imprisoned, which can be compounded by disabilities induced by the process of imprisonment itself, is met by a general tendency to reject and scapegoat prisoners so that the services provided for them are often minimal. . . . The Prison Medical Service is isolated within the medical profession, and doctors in prisons sometimes bear the brunt of the hardening of attitudes which results from criticism of prison officers and administrative staff. The recruitment of suitable Medical Officers remains inadequate and both full-time and part-time staff are about one-fifth below complement. Although some Medical Officers have a diploma in psychiatry, there is a tendency tor promotion to be weighted in favour of administrative posts so that the best qualified Medical Officers are not engaged in clinical work. Unfortunately many of the Medical Officers with psychiatric qualifications are expected to retire in the next few years and is very unlikely that they will be replaced by colleagues with similar experience. The working environment for Medical Officers is poor both in terms of physical amenities and back-up services (e.g. secretarial), and their clinical practice is restricted largely to males of one socio-economic group. Medical Officers are unable to follow up their prisoner-patients into the community, or be involved in work with families or offenders who receive sentences other than with imprisonment. Ethical problems are raised by the demands of non-medical staff but the isolated Medical Officer tends to meet these by denying that there is conflict.[95]

The Howard League for Penal Reform also raised significant questions about the Service at this time. The League argued that complete integration into the NHS was 'an ideal to be aimed for':

> Problems arise if an institution makes unreasonable demands that conflict with the doctor's duty to provide medical care, such as asking the doctor to certify his patient as fit to undergo cellular confinement. There is a strong ethical case for arguing that punishment is different from everyday matters like sickness certificates, and that prisoners, like other people, should have a doctor whose undivided commitment is to his patient. In prison practice such conflicts might be more readily exposed if the doctors involved were no longer prison service employees.[96]

The issue of prison conditions and the impact on the health and safety of prisoners continued to be a dominant theme in the 1980s. The Chief Inspector of Prisons wrote in his first annual report that the conditions were 'degrading and brutalising' and that key aspects of fire precautions 'were often missing' in the prisons he visited.[97] This omission was due to the fact that prisons fell under the category of Crown Immunity which meant that prison buildings were immune from fire and environmental health regulations. In other inspections the Chief Inspector found

> hygienic conditions in many jails are appalling. At Birmingham, for example, the food store was found to be dilapidated and dirty water ran down the walls and 'there were regular, infestations by vermin.'[98]

In August 1985 the Home Secretary confirmed that prison dentists were to be asked to 'limit the treatment of inmates and work within the financial constraints of the prison service'. Prison dentists themselves complained that they had been unable to complete treatment because the overcrowding in the prisons meant

> large numbers of prisoners were regularly moved round the country at short notice. They have also protested about being asked to break their terms of contract with the National Health Service to provide treatment on grounds of need and not on grounds of cost. One Home Office remand centre near Wigan with 350 inmates has set a budget of £2,595 for dental treatment for the present financial year. The prison dentist estimates that it will be exhausted by October, after which time prisoners would have to be refused treatment.[99]

The following year, the House of Commons Social Services Committee published its report on the Prison Medical Service. In May 1985 the Committee had decided to undertake an inquiry into the PMS in the course of which members visited 19 prisons. Additionally, it received 'much written evidence . . . from people working in the Prison Medical Service and their organizations, from a wide variety of other bodies both medical organizations and bodies concerned with the welfare of prisoners, and from a large number of former prisoners'.[100] The Committee pointed out its inquiry was not the first but that 'various select committee reports have identified deficiencies in Prison Medical Services and made recommendations to improve them'.[101] It also indicated that the report should not be 'construed as further criticism of prison doctors' but was written 'in the spirit of planning health care for the future'. Members were clear on where they stood on the issue of health care for the confined:

> In view of some of the rumours we had heard, we were surprised at the generally good standard of care for physical ailments and the fact that access to treatment is often at least as readily available as for those outside prisons. We have taken as a starting point in our inquiry the principle that prisoners are entitled to the same standard of medical care as would be available to the community as a whole under the National Health Service. The PMS is at present understandably open to criticism that such standards are not maintained in prisons. Whether such criticisms are founded on fact or on rumour is not the point. The Government needs to be seen to be beyond reproach in its provision of medical care to prisoners.[102]

This curious paragraph was followed by a series of comments on the conditions inside and the impact that these conditions had on the treatment of the confined. The committee argued that 'prison inmates are being kept in conditions which would not be tolerated for animals'.[103] These remarks were directed at a number of practices inside including the unhygienic and degrading daily process of slopping out which because of the lack of fixed sanitation meant that in Norwich prison.

> the prisoners queue up with their pots for the few toilets on the landing. The stench of urine and excrement pervades the prison. So awful is this procedure that many prisoners become constipated – others prefer to use their pants, hurling them and their contents out of the window when morning comes[104]

The committee's views were supported by a Health and Safety Report for Bedford Prison, which was submitted to members as part of a memorandum from the Royal College of General Practitioners. The report began by pointing out that life in a building which was over 100 years old and contained more than double its capacity could not 'be in any way healthy or safe. The overriding health problem is overcrowding'.[105] The report then detailed a grim series of often appalling conditions, including the bathhouse where

> in one corner there was mould between the tiles and the tiles themselves were dirty. The fact that prisoners are only allowed one bath per week I suppose dates back to the time when people were sewn into their under-clothes for the winter. It is dirty, unhealthy and unacceptable. Prisoners should have at least one bath every day[106]

The conditions in the hospital were also highlighted:

> There has still been no action taken about moving the dental surgery to alternative accommodation. Various plans have been discussed but not come to fruition. Thus the hospital continues to have extremely bad staff

facilities. Despite having to deal with dirty infections, violently ill patients, staff have no changing or locker room and no staff shower. The association room for the inmates is totally inadequate. There is no drain outside the strip cell, into which dirty water can be washed when cleaning out this cell when it has been fouled. In consequence the foul water contaminates the main hospital corridor. The cell itself has chipped flaking paint making efficient cleaning of the walls impossible. [107]

The committee further argued that the lack of prison officers affected both 'health in prisons and the availability of medical treatment'. Members heard from the Institution of Public Servants, who stated

If there are no prison officers available to bring an inmate from the cell to the doctor, the inmate does not see the doctor. If there are no prison officers available to escort the inmate to a hospital appointment, the inmate does not get to the hospital appointment[108]

Similarly the number of prisoners coming through the system meant that medical examination for new inmates was 'often perfunctory to the point of uselessness'. [109] The Association of Members of Boards of Visitors told the Committee that at Wormwood Scrubs it was not unknown for upwards of fifty prisoners to be examined in the space of an hour. The Committee found that this was 'deplorable clinical practice and a waste of time'. [110] In its evidence the Prison Reform Trust pointed to an important implication for the PMS with regard to the conditions:

. . . our awareness of how institutions work suggests that it is likely that, for example, medical officers do not speak out loudly enough against living conditions in prison, which no one disputes are bad, sometimes appalling. It is inconceivable that an individual, however professionally dedicated, who works solely within and owes his loyalty and career prospects to, an enclosed organisation such as the Prison Service, could retain the independence of mind necessary to develop and express cogent and effective criticism of the same organisation. [111]

Evidence from a range of groups including the Prison Reform Trust, the National Association for the Care and Resettlement of Offenders, the Howard League for Penal Reform, MIND, and the National Association of Probation Officers raised a number of serious questions about the role of the PMS and the issue of integrating the service with the NHS. The Royal College of General Practitioners supported this and outlined what it termed as eleven 'objectives for change'. These included an end to overcrowding, the disassociation of prison doctors from supervising punishments, the urgent upgrading of the notes and records in the PMS and the development of a directive role for the prison doctor concerning the environment of the prison 'including the content of the diet, smoking in the prison, and the level of occupancy which is tolerable':

Prison doctors must recognize and treat serious disease and at all times maintain the priority of the needs of the patient over that of the establishment. This would be a reversal of the present instructions as spelled out by Mr C. J. Train at the 1985 Prison Medical Officers' Conference. . . . The whole work of the prison medical service should be audited. This should not be hidden behind the Official Secrets Act. The audit should preferably be done by groups of peers but it should be seen to be done and the results published. A comparison with medical care in the community would be easier if prison doctors were employed within the National Health Service. . . . The whole morale of the prison medical service needs to change from defensive paranoia to aggressive investigation, standard setting and openness to outside scrutiny.[112]

The Royal College of Psychiatrists was more circumspect in its recommendations but did argue that the PMS should be managed by a single body which would be either a joint board of the DHSS and the Home Office or by the DHSS itself. Such a move would mean that 'there would be less conflict of roles for prison doctors'.

The Home Office should recognize that both administering a system of punishment and at the same time procuring the health of those being punished are incompatible objectives. . . . Historically, the prison medical officer's role has developed into that of a referee who could be relied on to support the home team. The prison doctor's role outside the provision of health care needs reviewing.[113]

The Social Services Committee, for its part, made fifty-eight recommendations which members felt when taken together 'can transform the Prison Medical Service into a prisoners' health service, less doctor-dominated, more professional, primarily concerned with the delivery of multi-disciplinary health care and in good working contact with the NHS, universities and the probation services'.[114] The government's response to the report was published in March 1987.[115] It set the committee's recommendations within the more general context of the new prison building programme which had been announced in October 1983. This programme, it was argued, would ease prison overcrowding and increase the access that prisoners had to sanitation facilities. The response conceded that 'conditions in local prisons and remand centres are far from ideal particularly so for the purpose of conducting medical screening examinations'.[116] The government maintained that the building and refurbishment programme would in time 'provide some easement' but added ominously 'the Department will continue to explore what further measures might be taken, though it must be realistic about the prevailing constraint on resources'.[117] Such future projections were doing little to alleviate the difficulties prisoners were experiencing. In the spring of 1987 Chris Shaw highlighted a range of areas affecting the health care of the confined. These included the lack of opportunity for prisoners to take responsibility for their own health; prisoners who reported sick and stopped work losing a day's pay; medical records for prisoners serving less than two years not being requested by the PMS; losing the medical records of long-term prisoners as they moved around the system;

and the inability of prisoners to bring medicine prescribed by outside doctors into the prison. Finally, there was

> no confidentiality between doctor and prisoner, medical notes are part of the prison record and used in management and allocation decisions. A doctor can, at one and the same time, treat a prisoner for a medical condition, comment on his/her suitability for parole and sanction punishment. Prisoners therefore can have no confidence in the doctor's independence, for the prisoner's interests cannot be exclusive, or even paramount, in the doctor's decisions. Prisoners have no choice of doctor and cannot, in any circumstances, ask for a second opinion.[118]

By February 1988 the increasing number of individuals being remanded in custody meant that there were no places available in the remand centres. Consequently prisoners were being held in police cells. One prisoner who was regarded as mentally ill was held in a police cell in Grimsby with two others. The man's lawyers successfully applied for leave to seek an order compelling the Home Secretary to arrange adequate medical and psychiatric supervision as well as suitable accommodation for him. The judge was troubled by the fact that 'remand prisoners were not getting medical reports and the treatment they needed for their own and the public's safety'.[119] Prisoners thought to be suffering from mental illness were also being moved between police stations with the result that doctors could not find them in order to assess the state of their mental health.[120] In May 1988 the annual report from the Board of Visitors at Wandsworth was published. It described the level of the sanitation in the prison as 'disgusting, degrading and a public disgrace'.[121] It also warned that the prison faced the possibility of a serious outbreak of infection and disease. Prisoners were being forced to wrap excrement in pieces of paper and throw the package from cell windows. When cell buckets were emptied in the morning,

> prisoners and officers frequently have to paddle through other men's urine towards the end of the slopping out session as the drains cannot cope with the volume of use . . . men are issued with only one shaving bowl. . . . They not only wash their faces and shave in the bowls but they also wash their hands in them after using the slop buckets in their cells. If their hands have faecal matter on them, contamination of the bowl would then take place. As there is inadequate disinfectant this would present risks when eating utensils are washed in the bowls later.[122]

Prison medical policy and practice was therefore caught up in the continuing debates about the adequacy of medical care for the confined. As this and the previous chapter has shown, this question has had a long and controversial history within penality. As I have also indicated, the issue of the conditions of care, discipline and regulation ran parallel with debates around the role of psychiatry and psychology within prisons and the relationship between the ideology and practice of these discourses and the normalization of the confined. The issue was again to surface in the 1980s over the relationship between state psychiatry and black prisoners.

MEDICALIZING BLACK PRISONERS

An increasingly important dimension in the debates around British prisons in the 1980s has been the question of the incarceration of black people and their subsequent experience behind the walls. That experience has been less well documented than the experience of black people in other parts of the criminal justice system, most notably their relationship with the police.[123] Indeed, until 1986, it was difficult to obtain bare statistical information on the number of black people in prisons. In that year the Home Office released figures which indicated that about 8 per cent of male and 12 per cent of female prisoners were black while the same groups comprised 1 and 2 per cent of the population respectively.[124] These figures however, need further elaboration. As the GLC Ethnic Minorities Unit has pointed out, there is a concentration of black prisoners in the south-east of England and the population is largely young, with particular prisons such as Ashford and Wormwood Scrubs holding high numbers of black people. Furthermore, the lack of monitoring made it more difficult to obtain accurate figures for women:

> A psychiatrist put the figure at 44% but there have been reports of 60% of women being from ethnic minorities. This would also include women who are being detained under the immigration laws prior to deportation – of whom there are an average 8–9% at any one time.[125]

More recent figures, gathered by the National Association for the Care and Resettlement of Offenders (NACRO) indicated that 14 per cent of prisoners in England and Wales came from what the Association described as the 'ethnic minorities'. This was more than twice the percentage in the general population. Differentiated by gender, NACRO's figures showed that on 30 June 1987, 13.6 per cent of the male prison population were from the 'ethnic minorities' while the corresponding figure for women was 22.7 per cent.[126] The study indicated that sentenced black prisoners had fewer previous convictions than white people convicted for the same kind of offence. They were also less likely to be granted bail. The director of NACRO commented:

> Taken overall, the evidence strongly indicates that black people are unfairly treated by our criminal justice system. The figures do not show that they are more prone to crime than white people but they do suggest that black people who offend are more likely to go to prison.[127]

Within this general context, the relationship between black people and medicine has been a contentious one. In particular, it has centred on the question of mental health and Afro-Caribbean prisoners. From the mid-1960s a number of cases emerged which illustrated the interrelationship between the penal system and the psychiatric network and how the powers given to criminal justice personnel under the 1959 and 1983 Mental Health Acts were being used:

> the rationale governing usage of this cluster of powers is almost always framed in terms of 'protecting public interests' and is dependent on assessment of the person's 'dangerousness' – a term so general and

125

inclusive as to offer law-and-order agencies a wide scope for acting pre-emptively against what they consider to be potential disruption.[128]

According to the Black Health Workers and Patients Group when non-medical or biological concepts such as 'personality', 'normal thought' and 'appropriate conduct' are involved in the assessment of individuals psychiatry 'is "influenced by prevailing social categories and expectations, by the whole gamut of discourse and institutions concerned with policing and checking abnormality"'.[129]

During the 1980s there were a number of cases involving black prisoners which raised issues around the psychiatric assessment of these prisoners, the medical treatment they received, the question of force-feeding, the use of drugs as controlling mechanisms and their certification as either mentally ill or insane which meant that they could then be transferred to state mental hospitals.

A number of studies provide support for the prisoners' contention that psychiatry and psychology as disciplines are working within a set of parameters which generate stereotypes about ethnic cultures. As the Black Health Workers and Patients Group has pointed out, the nature of psychiatry itself has to be questioned in this process:

> does it have a methodology or merely an arbitrary conglomeration of rules and techniques dating back to its origins in an earlier period of crisis when the workhouses disintegrated and their populations were redistributed in prisons, asylums, voluntary schools etc; does it have a theory or does psychology provide it with a series of pseudo-scientific hypotheses which are both anti-working class and racist; is it as it claims to be, a scientific area of study or a twilight zone where pseudo-science begins to shade into myth?[130]

In November 1987 a three-year study by MIND indicated that the additional powers granted to the police under Section 136 of the 1983 Mental Health Act were being used 'more against members of the black community than white in proportion to the population of ethnic groups'. Additionally the number of police referrals to mental institutions was far greater than was officially recognized by government statistics and that the police abused areas of the Mental Health Act.[131] This conclusion was supported by another study by Roland Littlewood, a consultant psychiatrist at Middlesex Hospital which showed that black people were over-represented in regional secure units and high-security units such as Broadmoor. Littlewood's study itself paralleled a West Midlands research project which indicated that Afro-Caribbean blacks were twenty-five times more likely than white people to be placed under psychiatric care by the courts.[132] Littlewood had also conducted a survey some years earlier. He found that black people were given heavier dosages of drugs than their white counterparts. He concluded that not only was there a tendency to view acute stress reactions in black people as symptoms of schizophrenia but also there were real problems of mental illness in the black community:

> It's not just a question of poverty. It is a question of racism. A large proportion of people in any society are vulnerable to mental illness but

many of them live with stresses without becoming ill. My strong feeling is that black people are being driven psychotic by our society, that racism is indeed causing these high rates of mental illness.[133]

McGovern and Cope also found that males of West Indian origin were 'significantly over-represented' in the psychiatric hospital they studied. This was particularly true for compulsory detainees in the category of offender patient. They cited a number of reasons why this might be so. They did not offer firm conclusions but argued that more research and further study was needed.[134]

Whatever the conclusion of academic studies, accounts by black prisoners of their experience continually reinforce and underline the pressure imposed upon them within the prisons. Describing her experience of twenty months in custody, one ex-prisoner indicated that

about two-thirds of the Black women prisoners were drugged. In prison there's a system and if you don't play it they beat you up and attack you. And if you're black you get more pressure because you're not only fighting for prisoners' rights, you're fighting for your Black rights. The treatment of prisoners is so bad. I think on the whole the way women prisoners are treated is a reflection of society. Most of the drugging is to do with that. People are going around like zombies. You get institutionalized so that when women come out they crack up and commit more crimes.[135]

CONCLUSIONS

These controversies have, as I have indicated, a long history and have been an identifiable element in medical practice within institutions since the late eighteenth century. The most recent demands for change provide a focus for raising more fundamental questions concerning the reasons and rationale behind the reform of prisons in the late 1980s. As I indicated above, the government's response to the report by the Social Service's Committee was to point to the prison building and refurbishment programme that had been underway since October 1983. Officially this programme was designed to deal with overcrowding, improve conditions and, by extension, alleviate the unhealthy environment within which many prisoners existed. It was also designed to confine the increasing numbers of individuals whom the courts were incarcerating. By 1988 the prison population was hovering around the 50,000 mark. The UK had the largest number of prisoners per 100,000 of the population than almost any other Western European country. The government's building programme was costing £1 billion which was 'more expensive in relation to gross domestic product than any other developed country'.[136] By the end of the century, the prison system will have the capacity to hold 80,000 prisoners.

A critical reading of these expansionist reforms requires moving beyond the narrow view that they are concerned with alleviating appalling conditions or even dealing with the crime rate. Sociologically there is little evidence that this has ever been or indeed will be the case.[137] Rather, when more prisons are built more individuals are likely to be incarcerated. The penal estate grows while conditions for many remain primitive. Within the UK the work of Steven Box and Chris Hale has been important in illustrating how the expansion of the prison system has been tied to the maintenance of order through disciplining surplus populations rather than with any simple desire to improve conditions or fight crime.[138] Sentencing policies

> are not that concerned to control serious crime. Rather they are more concerned to instil discipline, directly and indirectly, on those people who are no longer controlled by the soft-discipline machine of work and who might become growingly resentful that they are being made to pay the price of economic recession.[139]

This analysis has been supported by the work of Nicos Poulantzas, Stuart Hall, Paddy Hillyard and the Centre for Contemporary Cultural Studies, all of whom have traced the emergence of the strong or authoritarian state.[140] I have written elsewhere about the consolidation of this state form and the establishment of a much more integrated and less informal process of justice in the UK.[141] It is in this context that the prisons can be understood, being concerned with both individual regulation and with the policing of wider social divisions. Discipline, individualization and normalization are corner-stones of these institutions within which the emphasis on security, order and control invariably vanquish any notions of rehabilitation and reform.

The prisons in the late twentieth century are themselves prisoners of a past and of a history in which discipline and the protection of wider social relations of private property provided the mainspring for social policy and action. This is not to impose a deterministic reductionism on to social formations nor to adopt a fatalistic, non-contradictory analysis of how institutions work. Rather it is to point to the often overwhelming sense of discipline and regulation, which is deeply embedded in the programmes and policies of penal institutions and engraved in the consciousness of those who staff them. As Michael Ignatieff reminds us, a historical perspective is crucial in helping to

> pierce through the rhetoric that ceaselessly presents the further consoli-dation of carceral power as a 'reform'. As much as anything else, it is this suffocating vision of the past that legitimizes the abuses of the present and seeks to adjust us to the cruelties of the future.[142]

Medical and psychiatric discourses within penal institutions are a good example of Ignatieff's point. Through articulating ideas of benevolent care and the ceaseless but ultimately doomed search for individually located causes of crime, medical professionals have consolidated their position within prisons and the criminal justice process. However, as both this and previous chapters have shown, a critical reading of the history of medicine reveals the strong dialectical relationship between prison medicine and wider social processes. It has been this relationship built around the iron therapy of discipline, regulation and normal-ization which has been the propelling force in its development. The next chapter which analyses the question of women, confinement and medicine illustrates still further these disciplinary processes.

128

CHAPTER 6

At the centre of the professional gaze: women, medicine and confinement

[Dr Knox] wished people suffering from psychopathic illness could have a separate form of identification so that they could get the special treatment their condition deserved. He would like to see them 'coloured green or with two little horns on their heads' so that they could be distinguished from other offenders and treated with the particular care they required. 'The majority of our female psychopaths at Holloway look sweet and homely. They are pretty little girls. We try to treat them with special attention to bring down their tension and aggression but it is very difficult'.[1]

Criminal women have been a central concern for prison managers and medical and psychiatric professionals since the emergence of the modern prison system at the end of the eighteenth century. They have been studied, probed and tested not only because of their supposed uniqueness but also because of the threat they posed to the social order of stable, family relationships. As with male prisoners, regulation, discipline and normalization were key weapons in the prison's struggle with imprisoned women. However, it was a regulation, discipline and process of normalization quite different and distinct from the experience of male prisoners. And at the centre of this iron therapy stood the figure of the medical man.

There is a further dimension to this process which is also important to note. While medical and psychiatric professionals were central to the lives of women prisoners, they should be seen as part of a wider professional network whose concern with returning criminal women to their 'normal' role legitimized a level of intervention and surveillance which was much more intensive than that experienced by criminal men. From their initial contact with the Criminal Justice System through to imprisonment and on to release, these women were confronted by a series of interlocking rules and regulations, programmes and practices administered by a range of groups and individuals and targeted to controlling, constraining and remoulding their behaviour. More particularly it was the personal and moral life of the women which was at the centre of the professional's gaze. Liberal notions of rehabilitation and reform therefore masked a deeper, more fundamental strategy, namely to reshape the very spirit of the criminal woman back to the role for which she was seen to be biologically and sociologically suited – that of wife and mother. The concept of femininity built 'around notions of domesticity, sexuality and pathology' was a central element in the relationship between professionals and incarcerated women.[2] This relationship was in turn increasingly shaped by the interventions of the state whose 'key site of intervention is always the woman as mother':

> It is . . . the mother herself who requires education and supervision – not directly but through the medium of social work and child psychiatry. . . . The discourse of domesticity is legitimised by privileged (predominantly male) professionals who are empowered to circumscribe the behaviour of women through alliance or tutelage.[3]

Finally, as with the male prisoners, confined women did not easily accept the imposition of medical or state power into their lives. This power was again challenged from within and without the walls. There were also contradictions in and conflicts over penal strategies for women offenders. Medical and legal discourses had their own theoretical, practical and political limitations. As Hilary Allen has noted, while these discourses have a 'poignant' and 'violent' impact on female offenders, professionals are also constrained. They cannot

> just make *any* decision; they cannot even make what they perceive to be the *best* decision. They too are constrained in their social actions by the discourses they speak but cannot own.[4]

The relationship between confined women and medicine is more complex than has been recognized either in conventional evolutionary accounts or in the work of Foucault discussed in Chapter 1. The historical evidence in this chapter illustrates the complexity of the processes involved.

PRISON MEDICINE AND THE 'MOST DANGEROUS OF THE DANGEROUS CLASSES'

Chapter 3 questioned the conventional account of the history of criminology which put the Italian positivist Cesare Lombroso at the centre stage of the discipline's development. As it noted, Lombroso's theories built around *Criminal Man* (published in 1876) were greeted with scepticism by the British medical establishment. While acknowledging that biological explanations of criminality could have some relevance, the men who populated the profession recognized that his reductionist views constrained their power to intervene and influence both individual treatment and wider social policy. Conventional accounts have missed this important theoretical and political point. There is a second dimension which has also been missed, which relates to the question of gender. Traditional accounts of the history of women's criminality begin with Lombroso and Ferrero's book *The Female Offender* (published in 1895). However, as Susan Edwards points out, a closer and more critical reading of this history reveals that it was the medical profession who set the parameters for and responses to women's deviance:

> The real and pragmatic influences on the criminal law and the administration of justice during the nineteenth century were in fact medical and gynaecological theories on women and crime. They too were based on the tenets of biological positivism but were exerting an influence in the courts well before the advent of Lombroso's work on the female offender and, indeed, long after. From the beginning of the nineteenth century, medical practitioners, mental health physicians and gynaecologists conceded rather more specifically that criminality in women could be explained by the physiological episodes to which they were subject.[5]

This development underpinned the emergence of a network of institutions and practices designed specifically to deal with deviant women who were classified into different social groups: the prostitute, the criminal, the lunatic and the undeserving poor. This classification was in turn underpinned by a system of disciplined morality, women in whatever moral group they inhabited were subjected to the surveillance and gaze of medical professionals and concerned reformers eager to rescue them from debauchery and deviance.

Elizabeth Fry's interventions into the prisons in December 1816 are a good early example of the above points. As Michael Ignatieff indicates, women in Newgate were separated from male prisoners. Regular work patterns were introduced, particularly sewing. Fry also changed their appearance to make them appear more decorous and domesticated:

> in place of the idleness, fighting, and swearing she had substituted quiet industry and prayerfulness. As her brother-in-law, Thomas Fowell Buxton, put it she had turned a 'Hell on Earth' into a 'well-regulated Manufactory'.[6]

Fry formed the Association for the Improvement of the Female Prisoners in Newgate. She informed the Aldermen of the City of London that 'women should have no male attendants other than medical men or ministers of religion'.[7] In 1827 she published *Observations of the Visiting, Superintendance and Government of Female Prisoners*. The booklet advocated a change in the status of women in terms of urging that there should be opportunities for them outside the home. At the same time, this suggestion was set in the context of the duties of women in the hierarchy of society:

> I wish to make a few remarks . . . respecting my own sex, and the place which I believe it to be their duty and privilege to fill in the scale of society. . . . Far be it for me to attempt to forsake their right province. My

131

only desire is that they should fill that province well; and although their calling in many respects, materially differs from that of the other sex and is not so exalted a one yet . . . if adequately fulfilled, it has nearly, if not quite, an equal influence on society. . . . No person will deny the importance attached to the character and conduct of a woman in all her domestic and social relations, when she is filling the station of a daughter, a sister, a wife, a mother or a mistress of a family. But it is a dangerous error to suppose that the duties of females end here . . . no persons appear to me to possess so strong a claim on their compassion . . . as the helpless, the ignorant, the afflicted or the depraved of their own sex.[8]

The development of prison and asylum regimes based on domestic routine and paternalistic surveillance was not accepted easily by confined women. In 1817 women in Millbank engaged in a number of protests concerning food and the 'overzealous punishment of two prisoners'.[9] These protests were followed by a general disturbance which was broken up the following day through the intervention of the male-dominated Bow Street Runners:

The 'ringleaders' of this uprising were punished, but it did not stop the general protest and resistances of the women. In 1823 another general disturbance broke out, accompanied by attacks on wardswomen and the matron. According to the governor's report, this uprising included a plan to murder the matron, one female officer and the chaplain.[10]

As Chapter 2 indicated, individual women were also severely treated. In October 1811 Hester Harding was arrested for want of sureties and sent to the infirmary in Gloucester Prison. The prison doctor, thinking she was feigning insanity, ordered a cold bath with 'a little hot water added as it was December'.[11] When this failed she was put in a straitjacket. Martha Jeynes was also suspected of feigning insanity:

an electric shock was tried instead, which the surgeon noted 'I am pleased to say produced an immediate desired effect . . . The 'Electric Machine' was used again when she became obstinate but without effect so the surgeon directed the Turnkey to drench her with Beer Caudle and this proved effective. She was serving two months for stealing butter.[12]

Women's behaviour, particularly when they rebelled, was discussed in explicitly moral terms by male commentators of the time. In September 1850 when workhouses committed refractory paupers to Coldbath Fields, George Chesterton remarked that 'the inconceivable wickedness of those girls was absolutely appalling. Their language, their violence and their indecency shocked every beholder'.[13] In 1855 the Directors of Convict Prisons talked in their annual report about 'the problems of "reckless" women and their "violence and passion"'.[14] When transportation was replaced by penal servitude there were a number of collective protests between 1853 and 1859. Clothes were destroyed, bedding torn and windows smashed. Religious sermons were rejected, the silent system was subverted by the use of the knocking alphabet and the women continually struggled to find new methods of undermining the spartan regime which the authorities attempted to enforce.[15] Singing loudly, shouting and smashing the cells were also common forms of protests. Finally, there was self-mutilation and suicide as the last response to the pressure of the regime:

> Penal authorities sometimes demonstrated considerable insensitivity to this behaviour, describing such women as 'troublesome prisoners' who were merely attempting to gain entry into the infirmary where they might converse with other women and receive an improved diet. One woman who covered her body with her own excreta for six months was described by the Brixton medical officer as engaging in 'deceitful behaviour'. He was referring to what he judged as her attempts to feign madness, and it seems not to have occurred to him that her persistent behaviour could have anything to do with the nature of her confinement.[16]

The mid-Victorian predilection for institutionalizing deviant women was thus marked by stiff resistance to the regime and to its managers. This occurred across institutions. The Contagious Diseases acts of 1864, 1866 and 1869 allowed for the confinement and isolation of women and the medical policing of their behaviour. The disciplined programme of the Royal Albert and Royal Portsmouth hospitals followed a similar regime to the women's prisons:

> The women could only be transformed if order was put into their lives and a strict regime enforced. Accordingly the inmates were subjected to work and time discipline; their daily lives were punctuated by work, prayers, mealtimes, lessons in ablution and reading classes.[17]

They had been in the words of one contemporary 'desexed' and therefore the domestic and hygienic direction of the regime, led by the nurses and the matron, was designed 'to inculcate the women in moral and social values',[18] including

> deference and subordination. The social world of the hospital reproduced the patriarchal and class order of Victorian society. The male doctor was to reign supreme as the chief disciplinary and medical officer. The matron usually a middle-aged spinster or widow would act as his subordinate and female role model to the inmates.[19]

Here too, resistance was a central part of everyday life. At the Royal Portsmouth Hospital there were frequent disturbances between 1873 and 1883. For those who resisted, dark cells and solitary confinement were used. In the 'soup riot' of January 1873, which lasted for two days, seven women were arrested and eight placed in the confinement cells. After five days, a police inspector was called in to question those involved:

> After further questioning, the meaning of the 'soup riot' became clear. The resident medical officer had been 'too readily disposed to adopt coercive measures in the repression of any acts of insubordination.' Because he felt some of the women had been 'saucy' with him, the doctor had refused to examine them the next week. Angry and disappointed, the women lashed out at the conditions most immediately intolerable: watery soup, restricted

access to their mail, and generally harsh treatment. Fundamental, though, was a simple desire to get out.[20]

By the 1850s women formed the majority of the population in asylums.[21] There was also conflict in these institutions:

since women were accustomed to being ordered to submit to the authority of their fathers, brothers and husbands, doctors anticipated few problems in managing female lunatics. Yet rebellion was in fact frequent. Victorian madwomen were not easily silenced and one often has the impression that their talkativeness, violation of conventions of feminine speech, and insistence on self-expression was the kind of behaviour that had led to their being labeled 'mad' to begin with.[22]

This behaviour could have serious consequences. In Bethlem solitary confinement was used, while in Colney Hatch 'they were sedated, given cold baths, and secluded in padded cells, up to five times as frequently as male patients'.[23]

For the managers of prisons, asylums and workhouses the cause of ill-discipline was seen to lie in the peculiar temperament and biology of women criminals. This allowed them to call for medical and psychiatric intervention. Arthur Griffiths, a prison governor, pointed to his own experience with women prisoners:

I forbear to enter into any psychological enquiry into the causes or reasons, but will merely state the facts drawn from my own experience, that the female 'side' of a prison gives more trouble to the authorities than the male. It has been officially recognized nowadays that the most effective government is that exercised by a doctor; so many questions of hyper-emotional temperament, of hysteria, of peculiar physical conditions arise, that the chief official in every large prison today is invariably a medical man.[24]

He maintained that 'the intractability of the female candidates for reformation was painfully shown from the earliest days' of Millbank prison. The first prisoners

were found to be suffering from fits, imaginary as it proved. The affliction promptly disappeared when the Governor stated that the best treatment was to shave and blister the heads of all who were attacked. But a number who refused positively to have their hair cut were removed to the hulks. The female prisoners were fanciful about their food, refused to eat brown bread, and raised an uproar in chapel, chanting 'Give us our daily bread'. . . . Violent outbreaks were of continual occurrence in the female pentagon.[25]

Griffiths also discussed the problem of 'breaking out', which was the tendency of the prisoners to demolish furniture, smash windows, destroy clothing, barricade doors and use 'strident and offensive language'.[26] There were also fights between the prisoners and assaults on prison staff.

The conflict between the prison and one prisoner continued for a year. Julia St Clair Newman confronted the authorities at every turn, including throwing a can of gruel over the governor. While there were doubts concerning her sanity, she was none the less removed to the dark cell, where she sang songs, blackened her eyes, beat herself on the cell floor and attempted suicide:

> To curb her violence the surgeon devised a special strait-waistcoat, but she was no sooner placed in it than she released herself and tore it to ribbons. No means of restraint would hold her. A strong strait-wasitcoat was slashed to ribbons, and it was found she had secreted a pair of scissors under her arm. Not strangely, she was a terror to the whole place.[27]

She was transferred from Millbank to an asylum and then back to the prison when the authorities decided she was not insane. Here the pattern was repeated with further medical intervention:

> she was tied to a bedstead with strong webbing, but got out of it. The surgical instrument makers invented a new kind of waist-belt combined with handcuffs, but all to no purpose. At last she was fastened to the wall by a chain passed through a ring and padlocked. This security was of short duration; before morning she had slipped through the chain. It was again placed upon her in a more effectual manner, under instead of outside . . . a pair of leather sleeves were constructed of extra strength, which came up to her shoulders and were strapped across, also strapped round her waist and again below, fastening her hands to her sides, yet in the night she extricated herself from this apparatus, and it was found she had cut it to pieces with a bit of glass.[28]

She was eventually exiled to Van Diemen's Land.

Griffith's response to women prisoners was based on a particular view of their nature:

> Wise men will freely admit that the management of the softer sex by the stronger presents peculiar, it may be insuperable difficulties, but these are enormously accentuated when the moral sense has been weakened and the women have lapsed into evil ways.[29]

He pointed to the 'spirit of imitativeness' which 'is strong in women' and using a medical metaphor discussed how 'quickly the contagion of misconduct spreads'. This 'imitativeness' developed into more collective forms of protest in a northern prison where the population was 'a rough, headstrong lot, very difficult to manage'. When twelve of their number took to the roof, Griffiths left them for the night and then sent in male prison officers, who after 'a sharp scuffle' brought the women down.[30] In an earlier book he devoted a chapter to women and included a discussion of insubordination:

> a really bad woman can never be tamed, though she may in time wear herself out by her violence. We shall see more than one instance of the seemingly indomitable obstinacy and perversity of the female character,

when all barriers are down and only vileness and depravity remains. . . .
No doubt when a woman is really bad, when all the safeguards, natural and
artificial, with which they have been protected are removed, further
deterioration is sure to be rapid when it once begins.[31]

In 1864 another state servant, 'Prison Matron', published an account of prison
life. The description of women in Brixton and Millbank is similar to that of
Griffiths: 'desperately wicked', 'deceitful', 'crafty', 'malicious', 'lewd' and 'void
of common feeling':

> all the vices under the sun are exemplified in these hundreds of women,
> with but a sparse sprinkling of those virtues which should naturally adorn
> and dignify womanhood.[32]

The 400 women in Millbank were subjected to a strict regime and routine from
5.45 am when the morning bell rang, to 8.45 pm when lights went out. The day
was punctuated with work, chapel, exercise, prayers, reading and eating. The
women were productive. In 1860 they made 50,822 shirts for one city firm and
mended 96,541 bags for another.[33] Conversation was prohibited. Within this
regimented vice the prisoners were allowed to receive one letter a month and
after six months to see their families once every three months. If they
complained about those who supervised them then it was assumed that 'the
woman as a rule is always in the wrong and has invented the charge as an excuse
to see the director'.[34] Given the regime it is hadly surprising that they presented
problems and difficulties for prison managers.

A number of strategies were mobilized to deal with the women who smashed
windows, tore blankets, barricaded cells and set fire to them. They included
straitjackets, male officers who were 'cruel and vindictive' and used 'their giant's
strength tyrannously', dark cells and the mobilization of psychiatry.[35] 'Prison
Matron' pointed to the 'restlessness and excitability in the character' of the
female prisoner which 'flies in the very face of prudence and acts more often like
a mad woman than a rational reflecting human being'.[36] Those who engaged in
'breaking out' were a particular problem. The matron saw this behaviour as
'altogether distinct from the raving and violence of the inmates of a lunatic
asylum and appears very often to be a motiveless fury'.[37] None the less,
Broadmoor which opened in 1862 as a criminal lunatic asylum, was used to
control them:

> the principle is attempted there of treating all 'refractories' – women prone
> to break-out – as lunatics. It held the most dangerous of the 'dangerous
> classes'.[38]

The women were subjected to a battery of surveillance from 'observant officers,
surgeons and physicians taking note of every sign of mental weakness or of
every pretence thereof'. Professionals felt it was difficult to know 'where sanity
ends and where madness is likely to begin',[39] as a number of women feigned
madness, for the purpose of association. Women in desperation at the regime
also attempted to obtain a place in the infirmary through self-mutilation and

personal damage, which would mean 'a few privileges and a higher scale of diet'.[40] However, the Matron was not impressed:

> taking the infirmary patients altogether, there is not much difference in the character between them and their more robust sisters doing prison work. The same ingratitude, and selfishness, and callousness are evinced towards each other; and to the prison officers, the same duplicity, craft, and vindictive feeling. There are women whom nothing will soften, whom no kindness will affect.[41]

Prison Matron's account provides a valuable insight into how women prisoners were regarded by state servants and particularly how the root of their criminality was conceptualized. It also shows the deep and often violent level of tension and confrontation in Millbank and the increasing intervention by medical men to deal with it. R. F. Quinton, the MO in the prison, described his relationship with the 250 women who were kept in a special pentagon:

> The governor at the time, who could manage quite successfully 600 military prisoners and 500 male convicts, was as wax in the hands of the females. If they were at all refractory, his sole idea was to hand them over to the medical officer as patients requiring medical care and treatment, and so to get them out of his jurisdiction for the time being. He seemed to have an idea that all women were mad. His plan led to friction, and did not work well. Violence frequently took on an epidemic form, and too often the female pentagon was a pandemonium.[42]

He based his views on the peculiar aspects of female nature contending that women drunkards were 'much more hopeless to deal with than men, and that it is very difficult to wean them from evil habits'. He saw young women as 'peculiarly susceptible to contaminating influences'. This contamination came from confirmed female criminals who were 'specially dangerous as corrupters of novices':

> It is a disagreeable characteristic of some of these vicious female criminals that they seem to derive a mysterious satisfaction, amounting almost to a delight, in corrupting their younger companions. The characteristic is certainly not so common with men.[43]

Quinton's solution involved

> unrestricted intercourse with Lady Visitors, who can give them sensible ideas and straight talks, and at the same time show them sympathetic consideration, [it] will be of much more practical value in effecting their moral improvement than cycles of short sentences of imprisonment.[44]

He advocated a different institution for women with 'weak intellect[s]' who engaged in petty thieving, drunkenness and prostitution. They needed

> not only preventive, but protective detention in some kind of institution other than a prison for a much longer period than any term of penal sentence their offences would justify.[45]

The increasing importance attached to the doctor's role in prisons for women was reflected in the appointments of medical men to head the establishments. In March 1885 the *BMJ* commented on the recommendation made by the Directors of the Convict Prisons that the prison for women at Woking should be placed under the charge of 'an experienced medical man'.[46] The writer could see no objection to this, the common response 'that discipline cannot be intrusted to a medical man is frivolous'.[47] This was to continue into the twentieth century. In 1909 the governor and deputy governor of Aylesbury were medical men. In 1916 another deputy governor was appointed. She was Selina Fox, who was the first woman to hold this position; she was also a doctor. When Dr Winder, the governor was transferred, she was promoted to governor, a post she held for 3½ years. After the First World War, Dr John Hall Morton became governor of Holloway. He was succeeded by Dr John Muir Matheson, who was both governor and medical officer. He was assisted by two other medical officers: both were women.[48] In 1920 it was decided to employ fully trained nurses. They were introduced by Beryl Carden, who was a qualified nurse. She replaced prison officers in the hospital at Holloway and other women's prisons with trained nurses. The post of Nursing Matron-in-Chief was created and through this the Prison Nursing Service was established. The nursing service was linked to the commissioners by a voluntary Advisory Nursing Board (ANB). Those involved were 'mostly matrons of the large London hospitals'. The ANB's role was advisory, discussing with the commissioners 'the conditions of service of the nursing staff and on nursing matters generally'.[49] It was not until 1945, with the appointment of Doctor Charity Taylor, that a woman became governor of Holloway.[50]

CONSOLIDATING PROFESSIONAL POWER

Between 1859 and 1866 Dr Issac Baker Brown carried out a number of operations in his surgery in London. These operations revolved around the surgical practice of clitoridectomy. Madness in women, Brown believed, was caused by masturbation so that 'the surgical removal of the clitoris by helping women to govern themselves could halt a disease that would otherwise proceed inexorably from hysteria to spinal irritation and thence to idiocy, mania and death'.[51] He also carried out operations for the removal of the labia and operated on girls of 10, those whom he considered idiotic, epileptic, paralytic and

> even on women with eye problems. He operated five times on women whose madness consisted of their wish to take advantage of the new Divorce Act of 1857, and found in each case that his patient returned humbly to her husband. In no case, Brown claimed, was he so certain of a cure as in nymphomania, for he had never seen a recurrence of the disease after surgery.[52]

Brown's savage intervention into the lives of his patients, and the ruination that followed, was based on the presumed relationship between women's sexuality and deviance. The control of that sexuality became a central concern for the male medical profession. It turned on preventing women, especially degenerate women, from procreating and at the same time introducing programmes and policies inside the walls of institutions to regulate the body, discipline the mind and produce the industrious, sexually controlled female subject. While Lombroso published photographic studies of the faces of female degenerates, in England it was doctors such as Henry Maudsley and A. F. Tredgold who pushed the argument forward to include not only outward physical stigmata but also internal defects which could be passed on to the next generation. In 1895 Maudsley urged husbands to scrutinize their prospective partners for

> physical signs . . . which betray degeneracy of stock . . . any malformation of the head, face, mouth, teeth and ears. Outward defects and deformities are the visible signs of inward and invisible faults which will have their influence in breeding.[53]

Dr L. Forbes Winslow contended that abnormal criminal women were far more 'vindictive and cruel' than males and had 'badly shaped heads . . . large projecting ears and flat foreheads'.[54] The surgeon at Queen's College, Birmingham, argued that the delicate skin, thin eyebrows and sharp tongue of women 'made men unable to resist hitting them'.[55] A. F. Tredgold outlined a typology of the morally defective, which included the 'facile type' mainly composed of women whom he judged to be 'lacking in will power' and 'unable to steer a right course', while the trouble with girls was usually sexual deviance. He maintained that around half of the girls admitted to Magdalen Homes 'and a considerable proportion of prostitutes . . . belonged to this class of morally defective':[56]

> discovering physical signs provided doctors with 'scientific' confirmation of the hypothesis that lunatics were actually degenerates. Contempt for the insane as evolutionary failures characterized the discourse of psychiatric Darwinism. The rhetoric of heredity, inheritance and degeneracy which appears obsessively in the medical literature of the time is also closely linked to class prejudice and to ideas of race superiority.[57]

This ideology allowed for particular interventions to be made into the lives of women, both confined and otherwise, for it was they as a social group who were held responsible for the transmission of such defects from one generation to the next. At the BMA Conference in August 1900, the Psychology Section discussed the causes of insanity which included 'the marriage of the neuropathic, and hereditary transmission, alcoholism and syphillis'.[58] Dr Mac-Naughton-Jones detailed the correlation between insanity, vice and crime 'and pointed out the importance of co-operation between the alienist and the gynaecologist'.[59] He maintained that

> Insanity might arise from masturbation as well as from the changes attending the onset of sexual life (puberty and adolescence) or its close (the menopause). Psycho-pathology and gynaecology had a common meeting-ground in the sexual ailments of women.[60]

Some speakers deprecated the routine vaginal examination of female lunatics, arguing that it increased their hypochondria. Overall, however, it was the biology of women which was the focus of attention. This was underlined by Dr Wynn Westcott, a coroner who had conducted inquests on 200 women and concluded that 'the majority were at the "change of life" and that the younger of these appeared to be menstruating'.[61] Similar views were expressed the previous January at the annual meeting of the British Gynaecological Society, whose president was MacNaughton-Jones.[62]

The idea that women caused criminality and degeneracy was taken up by the medical journals. In May 1902 *The Lancet* discussed the problems of feeble-mindedness and degeneracy. The journal argued there was ample evidence that 'the offspring of feeble-minded persons, both men and women, usually inherit their defectiveness in some degree and that is the way that the evil is perpetuated'.[63] Two weeks previously in an article entitled 'Undesirable Marriages', its writers agreed with Sir James Crichton-Browne's proposal that 'large classes of the most degraded of the people should be restrained by law from [the] possibility of propagating their kind'.[64] In its 1904/5 session the *Transactions of the Medico-Legal Society* reported on a meeting that had taken place to discuss 'the proposed sterilization of certain degenerates'. Sir James McDougall told the assembled men that physical means 'should be adopted to prevent "degenerates" from propagating their like'. While Bernard Shaw raised questions about the ignorance of the medical profession in this matter, the mood of the majority favoured some form of direct action including removing degenerates to a 'colonial situation' and sterilization.[65] Arnold White pointed out that he had recommended the sterilization of the unfit nearly two decades earlier. He had visited different countries and concluded that Britain's sovereignty in the world would end by 1925 'unless something practical was done to reduce the number of inefficients'.[66] Dr Robert Rentoul was more specific:

> Degenerates who desired to marry should be sterilized after a written direction by the Commissioner of Lunacy. The necessary operation was continually and legitimately performed now to protect the personal health of the man or the woman concerned. It should be *voluntary*, in the case of the sane – here vasectomy would suffice; with the insane it should be *compulsory* – spermectomy. The sterilizing effects of X rays were considered. A heavy punishment should be inflicted if notice of previous sterilization was withheld from the other party to the marriage. Dr Rentoul exhibited an elaborate series of diagrams and tables in support of his thesis.[67]

Rentoul's book, *The Proposed Sterilization of Certain Mental and Physical Degenerates*, was published in 1903. He argued there should be compulsory sterilization for the 107,944 inmates in asylums, those suffering from congenital heart and lung disease, venereal diseases as well as 'the 36,000 to 50,000 tramps and the 60,000 prostitutes who had so manifestly shown their mental defectiveness through their choice of life-style and profession'.[68] In 1910 Winston Churchill, then Home Secretary, wrote to the Prime Minister pointing to the 'multiplication of the unfit' which clearly constituted such 'a very terrible danger to the race'. Until the British public accepted a policy of sterilisation of the unfit it was Churchill's opinion that the feeble-minded would in the public interest have to be segregated both from the general public and from the opposite sex.[69]

William Bateson, Professor of Biology at Cambridge, was more forceful in his imagery:

> The union of such social vermin [the feeble-minded] we should no more permit than we should allow parasites to breed on our bodies. . . . Further than that in restraint of marriage we ought not to go, at least not yet.[70]

Women were at the centre of this debate. In 1906 Aylesbury Prison was established for weak-minded women,[71] while those in Broadmoor convicted of infanticide were detained until the menopause occurred.[72] The *Report of the Royal Commission on the Care and Control of the Feeble-Minded* (published in 1908) supported the view that 'feeble-minded women were more fecund than normal women'. There was 'near hysteria' in public debates about them.[73] In 1912 A. Lyttleton told Parliament 'these women have no control over themselves . . . they transmit loathsome diseases throughout the country'.[74]

The Eugenics Education Society was an important focal point for the dissemination of these ideas. Founded in 1907, by 1913–14 it had over 1,000 members. At the International Eugenics Congress in London in 1912, A. J. Balfour and Winston Churchill were included in the list of vice presidents.[75] The leadership of the society was dominated by the educated middle class, particularly from the fields of medicine, university teaching and science. The society was concerned about the decline in Britain's imperial role which was propelled by

> the flourishing in the hearts of the great cities of a group of people tainted by hereditary defect. They were unemployed because they lacked the health, ability and strength of will to work. Hereditary weakness turned them to crime and alcohol. Their constitutions inclined them to wasting diseases such as tuberculosis. This group of degenerates was out-breeding skilled workers and the professional middle class. . . . Social control was to be imposed by the detention in institutions of the habitual criminal, the alcoholic, the 'hereditary' pauper, and so on. Prevention of parenthood in these institutions would mean the eventual disappearance of the residuum as a group.[76]

As Donald MacKenzie makes clear it is important to see the links between these proposals and the development of rationalized systems of mental testing in the period after the First World War. Eugenists such as Francis Galton and Karl Pearson aimed for 'the provision of a rationalised system for ensuring that occupational positions at the various levels of the hierarchical division of labour were adequately filled'.[77] Cyril Burt was an important figure in the debates at this time. He published *The Young Delinquent* in 1919 which 'was widely read and went through several printings'. He paid particular attention to the deviance of girls, arguing that women were ruled by their biology. Delinquency in girls could be explained 'by the onset of puberty and periodicity'.[78] For women who were not dangerous Burt advocated 'temporary segregation in training colonies operated like a "normal family . . . with grown house parents"'.[79]

In his study of the development of psychology between 1869 and 1939, Nikolas Rose sets these developments in their political and institutional context. He argues that the eugenic strategy provided the conditions which allowed the question of feeble-mindedness 'to take the form that it did and to offer to psychological discourse a particular object around which it would begin to regularize and institutionalise itself as a practice'.[80] This strategy was one element in the struggle around the nature, objectives and practices of social policy. This is an important point for, as Rose notes, there were other discourses operating and challenging the eugenics movement. In particular, the issue of the environment and the discourse of social hygiene that flowed from it was important. Doctors in journals such as the *BMJ* proposed interventions in the lives of the poor, 'breaking down . . . the opaque masses . . . into visible units' and instigating 'action upon the efficiency of the population at the level of the household'.[81] While the eugenic and neo-hygienist strategies appeared to be in opposition,

> this opposition was by no means an absolute one: not only could these strategies be combined into a single schema of administration, but such a schema illustrates exactly the key point at which an individual psychology was to try to establish itself. For what became central were techniques of individuation and assessment which would enable a rational distribution of individuals, amongst a variety of social institutions and practices special-ised to deal with them according to their personal characteristics, problems and difficulties in order to produce the most efficient and productive population.[82]

Rose's point is encapsulated by an editorial in *The Lancet* in April 1905. The journal was circumspect in calling for all-out eugenic intervention, fearing that in the present state of knowledge it would be 'hazardous' to interfere with individual lives. This circumspection, however, allowed the writer to call for more general interventions which did not preclude eugenics but which

> might raise the moral and the physical condition of the masses, if so raised, would in time supply the country with children prepared for still further advances in the same direction. . . . The influence must . . . be exerted rather upon the community than upon individuals.[83]

This emphasis on the community meant, in practice, a series of interventions such as the establishment of special schools for feeble-minded children.[84] At the same time, the attribution of physical signs and bodily shapes to criminality and deviance declined and instead the link between mental powers and behaviour was increasingly emphasized. Modes of assessment, pioneered by Alfred Binet in France, set the parameters for the debates on intelligence. The Binet–Simon test held a potent promise in its ability to transform previously unmanageable attributes into assessable calculable quantities. The first extension was from the pathological to the normal. What was originally a device for diagnosing the defective became a device for hierarchising the normal.[85]

The quantification of behaviour in women's prisons was reflected in the work of W. C. Sullivan, the MO in Holloway. He visited Binet to study his methods and produced his conclusions in *The Lancet* in March 1912. Sullivan felt that the test 'supplements the clinical investigation and enables its results, so far as the facts of intelligence is concerned, to be presented with a clearness and an objectivity which must considerably enhance their value'.[86] By 1921 he was the Medical Superintendent in Broadmoor and was lecturing at London University on a postgraduate course in mental deficiency. He reiterated the view that the 'critical study of individual cases' should be the basis for researching criminality.[87] Dr Norwood East, the SMO in Brixton, discussed the case of a 'moral imbecile' named Jane in the same journal. Not surprisingly, he found a history of 'early sexual delinquencies'. From an early age she 'possessed a personality which fascinated those men she elected to attract'.[88] He concluded:

> The instincts of sex, acquisition and exhibition are uncontrolled, and result in sex immorality, fraud, and theft in the wearing of her hair in a long false plait, and in her exalted impersonations. The maternal instinct is defective, the social instinct which should express itself in a desire for companionship, in consideration for and duty towards other members of the community is undeveloped.[89]

This individualization through the measurement of character or temperament meant that prison medicine and psychology developed a 'behavioural rather than a therapeutic rationale for detention'.[90] At the same time, it supported an intensification in the level of probing, testing and surveillance strategies to which criminal women were exposed. This surveillance and the drive to normalization that underpinned it was based on an interrelated network of professional and class power. Women prisoners were the object of a range of strategies, more intensive and well-developed than those to which male prisoners were subjected. The strategies met on the same policy terrain, saving the soul of the deviant woman for the heaven of normal motherhood.

SURVEILLANCE AND THE DEVIANT WOMAN

In 1901 the Lady Visitors Association was formed. Its president was Adeline, the Duchess of Bedford. She was succeeded by the Hon. Lady Cecilia Cunliffe.[91] The association was described as 'a body of earnest and devoted ladies with experience of rescue work and a keen sympathy even for the most degraded of their sex'.[92] The Duchess of Bedford regularly visited Aylesbury Prison and it was 'on her advice that the first trained nurse was appointed to the Prison Service'.[93] *The Lancet* felt that the association had done 'magnificent work in persuading convicts who have expiated their offences to desire a better life'.[94]

The journal set this praise in the context of the 'psychical fact that a woman criminal is far more difficult to reclaim than a man'.[95] The prison governor, Mary Size, described the dynamics of the meetings:

> At the first meeting she introduces herself in a cheerful kindly manner and puts the woman at ease. They discuss everyday things that concern the housewife; cost of living, fluctuating prices and so forth. A friendship is established at the first meeting usually, and afterwards visits become events to which the woman looks forward. During the ensuing period the woman generally thinks up what she will discuss with her visitor next time. She collects the letters and photographs of her family to show the visitor. These create topics of conversation for the woman, and incidentally give the visitor an insight into the character of the home and the relationship between the woman and her family.[96]

The work and surveillance of the voluntary associations extended beyond the prison walls. The Holloway Discharged Prisoners' Aid Society was formed in 1922 by Lady Carter and Lady Humphries. The Lord Mayor of London chaired its annual meetings.[97] In Liverpool, Walton Prison also had a society: its patron was the Earl of Derby and its president was the Lord Mayor of Liverpool. Women and girls were placed 'in suitable homes and refuges and [found] situations . . . where possible'.[98] In 1916 it placed 41 per cent of women who came to them in employment including domestic service, factories, charring, shop-work and weaving.[99]

The interventions by outsiders reinforced the domestic discipline of the prisons. In August 1904 *The Lancet* commented favourably on lectures given by Miss Charlotte Smith-Rossie to women in Portsmouth Gaol. The lectures were concerned with hygiene and the care of children. The journal supported Smith-Rossie's argument that these women should be placed in a separate class from the ordinary criminal 'as for the most part they are respectable married women and an attempt should be made to teach them home duties'.[100] It believed that the classes acted as an incentive to good conduct:

> The ignorance of the poorer classes about the management of their houses and their children, about hygiene, and about housekeeping is, after 35 years of compulsory education, simply astounding and anything which will tend to remove this ignorance is to be welcomed. Miss Smith-Rossie expresses a hope that such lectures will be initiated in every local prison and we echo her wish.[101]

In 1922 the Prison Commissioners supported by the Board of Education organized classes run by voluntary teachers. An educational adviser was appointed to each prison, who with the governor constructed a syllabus and employed teachers. There was a weekly, one-hour lecture:

> These lectures came from the medical profession, from universities, high schools and from domestic science centres; there were social workers also, who spoke on health, housing, nursing and citizenship. . . . Two volun-

tary teachers conducted a class of twelve women in embroidery, quilting and children's dressmaking. The senior officer in the work-room acted as a voluntary teacher and taught advanced needlework and dressmaking. I conducted a leather class. All classes were purely voluntary, but practically all the convict women wanted to attend them.[102]

In March of the same year, the commissioners announced that they 'cordially' supported a suggestion by Miss Olga Nethersole of the People's League of Health for a series of lectures in London's prisons. Doctors were involved at a number of prisons and Borstals lecturing on elementary principles of health and the body. Col. Knox, a Prison Commissioner, wrote to Miss Nethersole and emphasized that

> the lectures must be on the *simplest lines*. There are but a few of our population who even understand what psychology means and whose only idea of 'Health' is to have a beano and sleep it off.[103]

It was also felt that lectures on health led to introspection among the prisoners and to a rise in the numbers complaining sick. The League itself had wider objectives and principles. It emphasized the importance of heredity and the transmission of hereditary defects, the selection of suitable and healthy partners in marriage, the importance of worthy and responsible parenthood, the care of mental defectives, the use and abuse of alcohol and its relation to crime and disease and physiological and environmental influences on the human organism. In its first annual report it described how

> the rungs of [Galton's] ladder are fashioned out of the laws of heredity, the laws which transmit physical and mental characteristics from one generation to another.[104]

QUESTIONING MEDICAL POWER

From the prisoners' perspective hygienist philosophy and practice and the medical education that flowed from it provided no answer to the problems they experienced either inside or outside in terms of their objective position in the gender stratification of English society. It was also clear that despite official discourse, many prisoners were not prepared to accept the prison regime and raised serious questions about its impact on their lives. This often involved questioning the standards of medical care and medical treatment. Susan Willis Fletcher's autobiographical account, *Twelve Months in an English Prison*, was published in 1884. Fletcher detailed the terrible conditions in Westminster Prison. She had three blankets, which were washed once a year. Her sheets and sawdust pillow were washed once a month. She had no mattress. In winter, the cells were cold, damp and dark:

> the healthiest nearly perish of cold. Of course they are sent there – some thousands of women every year, an average of five or six hundred at a time – to be punished, but not, I think to have their health destroyed by being

145

kept twenty-three hours out of every twenty-four in solitary confinement in dark, cold, damp cells, like so many tombs.[105]

She described the death of a 60-year-old prisoner. A jury was 'summoned from the neighbouring public houses' for the inquest:

> The testimony of the physician was given, and, in accordance with it, a verdict of 'death from old age' – old age at sixty! We who had watched her knew that she had died from the exhaustion of grief, cold, and an insufficient and inappropriate diet.[106]

In 1905 Florence Maybrick published her account of the fifteen years she spent in prison. The book detailed a range of issues affecting women prisoners including solitary confinement, hard labour and strip-searching. She discussed the constant supervision where the prisoner was 'always in sight or hearing of an officer . . . the rule of supervision is never relaxed'.[107] While the prisoners were guarded and controlled by women it was men who 'make the rules which regulate every movement of their forlorn lives'.[108] Maybrick also described the role of the prison doctor in the apparatus of punishment which included solitary confinement, bread and water, the loss of marks and the use of straitjackets and hobbles:

> Hobbling consists in binding the wrists and ankles of a prisoner, then strapping them together behind her back. This position causes great suffering, is barbarous, and can be enforced only by the doctor's orders.
>
> To the above was sometimes added, in violent cases, shearing and blistering of the head, or confinement in the dark cell. The dark cell was underground, and consisted of four walls, a ceiling, and a floor, with double doors, in which not a ray of light penetrated. No. 5 punishment was abolished at Aylesbury, but in that prison even to give a piece of bread to a fellow prisoner is still a punishable offence.[109]

Finally, she discussed medical treatment. In Woking, women who were removed to the infirmary experienced a particular sense of desolation and alienation. This was compounded by the lack of nursing care:

> The prisoner must attend to her own wants, and if too weak to do so, she must depend upon some other patient less ill than herself to assist her. To be sick in prison is a terrible experience. I felt acutely the contrast between former illnesses at home and the desolation and the indifference of the treatment under conditions afforded by a prison infirmary. To lie all day and night, perhaps day after day, and week after week, alone and in silence, without the touch of a friendly hand, the sound of a friendly voice, or a single expression of sympathy or interest! The misery and desolation of it all cannot be described. It must be experienced. I arrived at Woking ill, and I left Woking ill.[110]

She concluded that 'women doctors and inspectors should be appointed in all female prisons'.[111]

146

In the early twentieth century some of the most bitter conflicts centred on the medical treatment of suffragette women, particularly those on hunger strike. Lady Constance Lytton provided a chilling account of the procedure involved at Walton in Liverpool. When her mouth was forced open, the prison doctor

> put down my throat a tube which seemed to me much too wide and was something like four feet in length. The irritation of the tube was excessive. I choked the moment it touched my throat until it had got down. Then the food was poured in quickly; it made me sick a few seconds after it was down and the action of the sickness made my body and legs double up, but the wardresses instantly pressed back my head and the doctor leant on my knees. The horror of it was more than I can describe. I was sick over the doctor and wardresses, and it seemed a long time before they took the tube out. As the doctor left he gave me a slap on the cheek, not violently, but, as it were, to express his contemptuous disapproval, and he seemed to take for granted that my distress was assumed.[112]

This controversy spilled over into the general question of the medical treatment of the confined. In May 1919 the Duchess of Bedford chaired a committee of inquiry into 'various matters concerning Holloway' and in particular the arrangements for nursing and medical care.[113] It found that there was no ambulance at the prison and a lack of trained nursing staff which was 'a serious defect in the prison administration'.[114] This had fatal consequences. The committee focused on the deaths of two prisoners. Ellen Sullivan, a pregnant 17-year-old remandee, was continually vomiting and was 'attended by the wardresses on duty at the hospital, of whom not one was a trained nurse'. She was eventually left with an officer who had only a few months' experience:

> At about 3.15 a.m. on the morning of January 18th, this officer noticed the girl Sullivan on the night-chair. She got her back to bed, and gave her some milk. The patient made no complaint of pain, and nothing was to be seen in the night-chair. The officer then went upstairs in the ordinary course of her patrol duties and on returning a few minutes later found the patient again out of bed and on the night-chair. This time she suspected something wrong and roused the day hospital officer who slept on the upper floor, having to leave the patient to do so. On returning to her she found she had given birth to a child. The child had fallen on the wood floor of the cell, the cord being ruptured by the fall. The officer got the patient, who was still on the night-chair, back to bed and picked up the child. She then left her to the day officer while she summoned the midwife and doctor. The child lived only for a few minutes and was dead when the midwife arrived.[115]

The prisoner died the following evening. She was remanded for using insulting language in a public place and had been refused bail 'because the magistrate could see no reason for granting it'. The second case concerned 19-year-old Rose Land, serving two months for theft. When she became ill on the morning of her release the authorities decided to admit her to an outside hospital. One refused while another could not obtain an ambulance. After a three-hour delay the prisoner was taken by cab as her condition was deteriorating:

On arrival at the Infirmary at 8.15 p.m. the girl was in a state of collapse and no operative treatment was considered possible. She died at 2 a.m. the next morning. The post mortem examination showed death to have been caused by intestinal obstruction from inflammatory glands constricting the ileum about 6 inches from the ileo-coecal valve.[116]

The commissioners wrote to the governor of Holloway about the report and noted:

The section of the report dealing with verminous and dirty conditions should be carefully noted. It is evident that there has been a want of care and thought amounting to neglect in these matters . . . the Commissioners must express their great regret that it has been necessary for them to admit that certain irregularities have crept into the administration of Holloway in essential matters eg due segregation of convicted and remands, cleanliness, clothing etc.[117]

Prisoners and their supporters protested against the conditions. The commissioners report for 1923 pointed to 'smashings-up' at Aylesbury Borstal.[118] In the same year, Jane Cormack brought an action against the Home Office for being illegally detained in an asylum. One of the points in the writ was that she was forcibly conveyed to Hellingly Asylum, where

she was detained for about one year and . . . drugg[ed] several times a day with force intent to deprive her of sound reason, judgement etc.[119]

When the report of the Prison System Enquiry Committee was published in 1922, the authors Stephen Hobhouse and Fenner Brockway devoted a chapter to women in prison. The committee found the most common crime committed by women was drunkenness with aggravation followed by prostitution, offences against public regulations, simple drunkenness, simple larceny and assaults. It also discovered that magistrates were using the prisons to sentence prostitutes for compulsory examinations and treatment for venereal disease. These women would ordinarily have been released on bail, fined or discharged. Sentences, the committee felt, were too short for effective treatment:

All the evidence goes to show that even those women who serve their full sentence go out but little improved in health, and soon return worse than before. . . . The recognition of the futility of short sentences has led to a deplorable custom. Some magistrates, instead of passing sentence on a woman suffering from V.D., remand her from week to week for treatment – a grave evasion of the safeguards of personal liberty.[120]

The figures for remands supported this point. In 1919, 4,511 women were remanded. Of these 1,622 (36 per cent) were sent to prison while 2889 (64 per cent) were either acquitted or were given a non-custodial sentence. Accounts by women indicated how the remand process was being used. Two who had been arrested during Easter 1917 for 'using insulting words or behaviour' were remanded in Holloway 'with definite instructions from the magistrates that they were to be examined for venereal disease, bail being refused until the result of the examination was known'. The women had two examinations, the ordinary one and then a full internal and external examination:

> On Thursday (April 12th), after we had been in prison two days, we were sent to the doctor and were both stripped of everything except our chemises. My friend was examined first and I found her crying. The nurse said 'K—— is all right'. Then I was told to lie down on my side and take off my chemise. The doctor and the nurse examined me and the nurse called attention to where I had been torn when my baby was born.[121]

For convict women serving long sentences, these processes were significantly intensified. They frequently complained of hunger, there was little variation in the food and they spent eighteen hours out of every twenty-four in the confinement of their cell. The allowance of a third remission (as opposed to a quarter for men), their daily gratuity and the privilege of spending the last nine months of a sentence (if well-behaved) in an approved refuge or home were scant consolation for the pressure of the daily regime.

Other prisoners complained about the lack of privacy and the fact that little attention was paid to the special medical needs of women during menstruation. At a conference organized by the Penal Reform League in June 1917, one ex-prisoner captured the relationship between the women and the all-male network of power with which they were confronted:

> Owing to prison negligence I became ill and only left my cell for four hours' exercise on four different days – during the whole of my sentence. My cell was, therefore, my dining-room, my bedroom, my bathroom and my water-closet, and I was always just in my nightdress. I must, of course, leave a good deal to your imagination, but can you realise what it meant when the male governor, male deputy-governor, male doctors, male chaplains, male visiting magistrates, male inspector, all apparently have the right to plunge into your cell-bedroom without the slightest warning, or even knocking, or even asking your permission! The wardress certainly unlocks the cell for these men, her superiors; but as you seldom hear their approach, and practice has made her a lightning-speed key-fitter, a prisoner may be caught in the most embarrassing situations. I do not want to labour the point, but I say that there is not one woman in this audience – whether single or married – who would like to think that any strange man could burst into her bedroom in that way.[122]

The report by the Prison System Enquiry Committee was a crucial document for raising the issues around the prisons. The breadth of its research and the fact that it allowed the prisoners to articulate their views and feelings about life inside stood in marked contrast to official accounts of the day. However, despite the radical direction of the report, it too could also fall into stereotyping the lives and behaviour of confined women. Thus in discussing cruelty to children, the authors pinpointed its causes as lying in 'utter neglect, ignorance and bad conditions' and complained that in the present system 'no real effort is made to give such women any training in home duties'.[123] The report noted:

> as a rule the medical officers of prisons do not appear to be encouraged to use their position with a view to research into the immensely important bearing of physical conditions upon crime. In view of the fact that the emotions are so profoundly affected by the sex instinct, it might reasonably be supposed that the incidence of crime, particularly of those forms of it which are more directly associated with emotional instability, would vary with the condition of the sexual life. It should be a comparatively simple matter to elucidate some of the efforts of this element in the causation of crime in women owing to the definite monthly cycle of the sexual life.[124]

There were critical voices raised from other, more unexpected sources. One of the strongest was Mary Gordon, who was the first female Inspector of Prisons. She held the post for ten years and after her retirement published *Penal Discipline* in 1922. Gordon was critical of a number of aspects of women's imprisonment. She was opposed to the compulsory examination of women with venereal disease. She introduced improved lighting and ventilation and substituted clear glass for the opaque variety in the windows.[125] She also raised serious questions about the relationship between prisoners and prison doctors, including the lack of confidentiality between doctor and prisoner. The doctor could take a prisoner's secrets and 'give them to the Governor of the Prison, the police, the court. The prisoner does not consult the doctor, the State pays the doctor and consults him about the prisoner'. His official position meant

> he is a constable as well as a doctor. He is endowed with very special powers over the patient's life. He is one, and a very important one, of his gaolers. He decides upon his fitness for work, fitness for dietary punishment, fitness for restraint. If corporal punishment is awarded he certifies the prisoner fit, supervises the punishment, and can stay it. He forcibly feeds the prisoner to prevent his determining his imprisonment, stops when he thinks he has done as much as he dare, carries out the 'cat and mouse' regulation. He is there when the prisoner is hanged.
>
> None of these disciplinary or penal events would ever be carried out at all, except under his aegis, and, but for his help, this part of penal discipline would absolutely disappear. If it is argued that he is there on the prisoner's behalf to see that he is as little injured as possible, nevertheless, he is the person who makes what happens possible. His is, therefore, very much the heaviest hand over the prisoner in the affair of penal discipline.[126]

The 'heaviest hand' could lead doctors into areas where their ethical code concerning the protection of life was compromised. In 1923 Edith Thompson was sentenced to hang for murder. Her lover had murdered her husband in a plot of which she had no knowledge. She was seen 'as an adulterous femme fatale urging her young lover to dispose of an unwanted husband, a view that the trial judge was only too happy to endorse'.[127] Immediately before the execution, John Hall Morton, the prison governor and Medical Officer, dealt with the prisoner's distraught protests by injecting her with drugs '1/100 grain of Scopalmine-Morphine (Purlight-sleep) and 1/6 grain of morphia'. She was carried to the scaffold and propped up on the trap door so that the noose could be fixed to her neck.[128]

Despite her critique of the PMS, Mary Gordon was clearly committed to the use of imprisonment for offenders. It was the principles on which confinement was based that she wished to challenge. While she was 'on the side of firm discipline',[129] she did not believe that a repressive, uniform regime could do much for the thousands of petty offenders who were incarcerated each year. It was a 'very expensive absurdity'.[130] She wanted a more individualized approach to criminality at the centre of which would stand medical psychology. For the 'drunken dissolute woman . . . we want our doctor to study and unravel her problem':

> What of the woman who has murdered her child because there is a man who does not want the child? Are we to shut her up for 16 hours a day, for an indefinite number of years, with nothing to think of except how badly she managed that she was found out, and how much less of a fool she will be next time – built on *this* time? Or shall we give her the doctor or educator who can show her where she is, and bring her to herself?[131]

The Lancet supported her views on 'the importance of substituting the spirit and methods of medical science for the rigidity of military and bureaucratic "systems"'.[132] So too did Calvert and Calvert, whose study, *The Lawbreaker*, was published in 1933. The Calverts discussed the women's prison of the future and cited the recently published report by the Departmental Committee on the Treatment of Persistent Offenders. The committee called for the establishment of 'a building of the non-prison type' for selected numbers of detained women.[133] The Calverts also called for the construction of two 'modern institutions', each holding 150 women. The institutions would be built on the 'cottage' principle, have small, self-contained units and accommodate between twenty and thirty women. This would enable

> the authorities to classify the offenders adequately, and the domestic work of each house would provide a good all-round training in house-work. There should be no wall and a minimum of locked doors. The buildings and equipment should be as pleasant as is practicable, for it has been found by experience that women offenders respond to small amenities in their environment. In such an institution a certain amount of psychological treatment, which would be wholly ineffective in the atmosphere of a present-day prison, could be carried out with success for those offenders who were in need of it.[134]

While these writers demanded a greater input from medical psychology in specially constructed prisons, it is important to note that in the 1920s and 1930s confined women still experienced a regime that was orientated towards them as individuals by emphasizing a rehabilitation specifically designed to socialize them into patterns of work, and a life-style, of the traditionally accepted female kind. In the late 1920s and early 1930s young, physically fit women in Holloway were employed in housework or gardening. They also had instructions in cookery and table service for two hours each week. There were classes in elementary education and in embroidery, current affairs and 'housewifery'. Finally, they received instructions in needlework and dressmaking.[135] Similar programmes existed for the adult women, who were classified into various groups and instructed in kitchenmaids' work and plain cookery. The commissioners commented that 'many of these women are capable of filling posts such as kitchenmaids, scullery maids, or as vegetable cooks in hotels, restaurants or hospitals'.[136] All women serving three months or over attended evening classes where they were taught embroidery, knitting, beadwork, toymaking, leather-work, weaving, rug-making, stool-making, basket-work and pottery. Those who did not attend had to accomplish twelve feet of sewing per night. Any women producing unsatisfactory work was cautioned by the trade instructor and then reported to the governor if her labour showed no sign of improvement.

Education classes were similarly restricted to infant welfare, mothercraft and first aid. At its annual conference in 1928, the National Association of Prison Visitors to Women complained about classes in current events and citizenship. Considering so many women in Holloway were mothers, the association felt it was 'unfortunate that certain classes are in subjects of an unpractical nature'. The conference also noted that in the commissioners' report for 1929 the daily proportion of prisoners under treatment in hospital was far higher in women's prisons. Whereas one in eleven males were under treatment at any one time, the figure for women was almost one in three. For Miss E. H. Kelly the figures were 'startling, but apparently there was nothing unusual from the prison point of view'.[137]

The issue of the psychological treatment of women offenders was given further legitimacy by the publication of a Medical Research Council report in 1933. Authored by the psychoanalyst Grace Pailthorpe, and focusing on delinquent women and girls, it had 'a profound impact on official thinking about women prisoners'. Pailthorpe studied 223 women and girls detained in prisons and preventive rescue homes and concluded

> deficient biological development was revealed in underdeveloped immoral sentiments and various psychopathologies. [They were] 'sick persons' who . . . should be regarded in the same light as people suffering from the various contagious fevers.[138]

She argued for segregation and psychological correction:

> Her ideal approach would involve extended 'Psychoanalysis [as] the only radical cure for all psychological maladjustments. For women described as passive mental defectives, prone to promiscuity resulting in pregnancy, permanent segregation could be useful but sterilization would be best since it would allow them some freedom.'[139]

Pailthorpe's work was important in that she can be linked with the early bio-psychologists such as Maudsley, Tredgold and Cyril Burt, who saw women's innate biology and sexuality as the source and cause of crime.

Other commentators made similar points. Calvert and Calvert cited Pailthorpe's study and in particular her view that 56 per cent of all the women she examined, excluding mental defectives, needed psychological treatment.[140] In 1937 Dr C. P. Blacker, the general secretary of the Eugenics Society, edited *A Social Problem Group?* The social problem group fell into two categories, the 'medico-psychological' and the 'sociological', with an intermediate group occupying an uncertain position between the two. The insane, mental defectives and epileptics fell into the first group, pauperism and slum dwelling into the second while 'recidivism, unemployability, inebriety and prostitution are conditions more or less intermediate between the medico-psychological and the sociological.'[141] W. H. De B. Hubert, the psychotherapist at Wormwood Scrubs, contributed a paper on 'Recidivism and the social problem group'. Hubert enlisted the views of the governor of Birmingham on alcoholic women, who saw them as 'a pathetic and hopeless collection of human wreckage. They come and go with unfailing regularity and are assisted again and again without making any effort to help themselves. It is doubtful if they are capable of effort'.[142]

By the 1940s and 1950s individual psychology and the family environment were the rocks on which professional and state intervention into the lives of criminal women was built. For individual women, they were also the rocks on which their chances of a fulfilling and free life-style were dashed and broken.

WOMEN IN POST-WAR PRISONS: 'A THOROUGH GROUNDING IN MOTHERCRAFT'

The regimes in post-war prisons were specifically designed to reform deviant women by resurrecting and reasserting their maternal and domestic instincts. The commissioners outlined how they conceptualized these regimes in their first post-war report. The direction of the women's 'training' was towards making them better citizens in the modern world. While some industrial training would be provided for younger women

> the greater part of the work will be domestic, though directed towards training better housewives rather than better housemaids. With the 'cottage home' as the background, every aspect of the domestic work, whether in shops or the service of the prison, should be made to serve one idea – that of instilling into the women the ideals of a good home and how they may be best achieved.[143]

Furthermore, the appearance of the women was to be reconstituted. They saw no objection to 'the use of cosmetics if the administrative difficulties can be overcome'.[144] The following year, the commissioners indicated that when

153

released young women, 'girls' in the words of the report, went into factory work, the catering trade, hospitals, clerical work and the women's services.[145]

Women categorized as neglectful mothers were a particular cause for concern. In 1945 the Women's Group on Public Welfare, together with the National Council of Social Service, appointed a committee to study and report on 'the neglected child and his family'.[146] The commissioners arranged for the study to be conducted in Holloway between 1947 and 1949. In June 1949 the governor of Holloway outlined some of the main findings of the study and concluded that 'poor intelligence is an important factor in neglect'.[147] This 'lack of intelligence' directly contributed to the fact that the women could not improve their already poor home conditions. Finally, irresponsibility led them to be either ignorant of, or ignore lessons in, child-care management:

> Their irresponsibility is a state in which responsibility is not realised, and the poor early environment of many of them may be a cause of this. . . .
> The domestic standards of some of these women were very low, and they regarded an appalling state of affairs as adequate.[148]

By February 1952 the commissioners, acting on conclusions drawn from the study, had introduced a special training scheme based in Birmingham Prison. Twelve women, serving sentences of three months or over, were transferred from different parts of the country to take courses in elementary housewifery and mothercraft.[149]

The course syllabus aimed to remove the problem by striking at its moral root. This centred on the women's inability to cope with the domestic environment. Each weekday from 9.30 am to 3.45 pm they worked in the Education Department learning housewifery, cookery and laundry work. The house in which the 'trainees' lived was cleaned throughout the day. On Monday and Wednesday evenings they were given a 1½-hour lecture, supported by visual aids, on a range of topics, including the bathing of babies, the physical needs of the child, antenatal care and 'the man's place in the home – given by a male lecturer'.[150] Other talks and demonstrations focused on the mental and emotional development of the child, how to care for the sick and on Thursday evenings 'one lecture in each course by an officer from the Gas Office – use of cooking appliances'.[151]

Psychological assessment by prison doctors legitimized the regime. In 1952 one unnamed doctor wrote that the 'salient features' in the case of neglectful mothers 'were the mental subnormality and general unfitness of such people to be parents'.[152] In 1954 another commented:

> Generally speaking the mothers were of low intelligence and although they maintained that they had learned a great deal from the course, it is doubtful if those of low intellect had the capacity to carry their teachings into practice after release from custody. The aftercare of these prisoners is extremely important in order to observe the results of the course.[153]

The scheme was extended to outside the walls. In Birmingham the local authority, the WVS and Probation Service were involved in guiding the 'mother through the difficult weeks that face her in having to return to a home as sordid, dirty and ill-equipped as it was when she left it'.[154] Lionel Fox, the Chair of the Commissioners, commented that a similar scheme at Askham Grange was *'training* [and of] real value to women who will for the most part return to their homes or be called on to make homes'.[155] Other state servants articulated similar views. The first governor of Askham Grange, Mary Size, maintained that

> Ignorance, inefficiency, selfishness, jealousy, bad housing, bad family relationships, and lack of Christian teaching, together with a certain degree of mental abnormality, are responsible for much crime amongst women.[156]

The commissioners were more succinct but no less directive in their views about the education of the prisoners. Educational programmes, they noted in 1960, 'are naturally more concerned with the home and the family'.[157]

The ideology behind the regimes was also legitimized by the conceptualization of the women as 'girls' whose mental capacity and behaviour had to be lifted to the standard of 'normal' adult women. In July 1957 Joanna Kelley, the governor of Askham Grange, caught this well in an article in the *Journal of the Medical Women's Federation*. For Kelley, the prison resembled 'a very strict boarding school':

> The women tend to respond to this Boarding School system by behaving rather like school girls, even if on the whole quite sensible well-behaved ones. Small events and sayings assume big proportions: there is childish excitement over treats, such as concerts, films, an extra cigarette each, outings. Like children, their voices are apt to rise. They are often over-whelmingly downcast by rebukes, their sense of proportion seems out of gear. They become absorbed in the day to day events of the establishment, which is like an isolated world, and any other life becomes to them as far away as 'when I'm grown up' is to a child.[158]

From the perspective of the 'children' the prison world was nothing like the reality articulated by Kelley and other state servants. As in the nineteenth and early twentieth century women reacted, sometimes violently, to prison regimes. In August 1949 a senior Home Office official visited Holloway 'as a result of recent disturbances among girl and women prisoners there and consequent complaints by the prison staff'. This visit followed a meeting held by the Holloway officers, who complained about general indiscipline. They asked that 'Borstal girls and girls who had their licences revoked should be transferred from the prison'.[159]

The regime in the prison had been severely criticized six years earlier in a report by the Prison Medical Reform Council. The conditions were appalling:

> In my cell, I found a tiny piece of soap, not more than 1 inch by 1 inch by ¼ inch in size (which had to last me for all purposes for over a week) and a very slimy rag, both left by the previous occupant. . . . Unfortunately, the rag and soap were not the only things left behind by my predecessor. On

the shelf were dried faeces, under the mattress were some grimy, hair-curling rags and on the floor, furniture and all the utensils was a layer of grease and dirt.[160]

The women also complained about prison labour. Many were employed as cleaners in the toilets which were 'always in a filthy condition and usually three out of four were stopped up'.[161] They cleaned the pails containing used sanitary towels:

Every morning these were taken down for the contents to be burned. There was no lid on any of the pails I had to empty; nor were they ever disinfected. . . . Much of the food was unsavoury. The greens were always dirty but I had to eat them, I was so hungry.[162]

Doctors and nurses regarded them as 'malingerers'. Illnesses were either ignored or there was a delay in receiving treatment. Pregnant women received the ordinary prison diet for six months and were then allowed two extra slices of bread and half a pint of milk daily. They spent twenty-three hours either sitting or lying down and were alone in the cells at night. This continued until the baby was due. It could have serious consequences:

The cell emergency bell often went unheeded especially during the night. One could keep ringing the bell for over an hour without having attention paid to it. On one occasion before I went to hospital the cries of one of the girls were pitiful. We could hear her calling for help and getting more exhausted. The whole landing was awake in the finish and several other prisoners were ringing their bells and calling to draw attention to her. I heard from several prisoners in the morning that when help came it was found that her baby had been born in the cell.[163]

Joan Henry's account of her experience in Holloway in the early 1950s covers similar ground. She was particularly critical of the medical treatment. Many of the women never had a normal period 'or perhaps only twice a year'. This was due both to the shock of imprisonment and 'possibly to a starchy diet and little exercise. The medical officers do not seem to worry about it at all'. She described the interaction between herself and the hospital staff:

That first morning I cleaned the cell with my handkerchief, and that was about all I could do. Hours passed, and eventually a doctor, accompanied by one of the hospital sisters, visited me on her morning rounds. I had never seen her before.

'Are you all right?'

I was to become accustomed to this phrase after a few weeks in the hospital. It was used in varying tones by the head sister, doctor, and matron on their separate rounds every single morning. The correct replies were:

'Yes, thank you, Sister.'

'Yes, thank you, Doctor.'

'Yes, thank you, Madam,'

even though you might be dying on your feet.[164]

Henry also pointed to the 'nerve storms' which women had. After 'smashing up' they were removed to the padded cells:

> This either quiets them down or sends them completely off their heads. It is not necessary to call in anyone from outside to certify a prisoner, as there are at least three doctors on the premises. It is an everyday occurrence in the hospital to inquire after someone only to find she has gone to Broadmoor.[165]

The research conducted by prison medical staff, academics and other medical workers helped to set the rigid parameters within which the women's actions were explained. It also legitimized individualized and often painful interventions into their lives.

RESEARCHING WOMEN: PSYCHIATRIZING BEHAVIOUR

The criminality of women in the 1950s was a special object of study. Female prisoners in both Borstal and adult institutions provided a focus for psychologists and medical personnel interested in what appeared to be the small number of women who could not adjust to their allotted domestic role in society. Hence, their criminality. Such women had to be readjusted to fit that role. The themes of individual and constitutional pathology, influenced by the wider familial environment, was the dominant explanatory framework within which the deviant behaviour of young women, in particular, was understood. Dr Phylis Epps, who worked in a Borstal and subsequently at the Institute of Social Medicine in Oxford, wrote a number of papers in the early 1950s which elided both themes. Between April 1948 and August 1950 she surveyed 330 young women committed to Borstal. While admitting the work was carried out during her 'very inadequate spare time', publishing in the *British Journal of Delinquency* provided an important academic forum for her ideas.[166] While 275 of the women were kept under daily observation, 25 were seen only once for 'a brief interview and intelligence testing'. Epps outlined a host of factors she considered to be important, including family history, illegitimacy, psychosis, menstrual function, school record, emotional instability and mental state. In the last two categories she reinforced many of the prevailing ideas about women's criminality: first, that they were less intelligent than the average non-delinquent and second, emotional instability in young women created disciplinary problems:

> Since the days of Lombroso immaturity has been noted by numerous observers . . . to be a common characteristic of criminals. It was particularly noticeable in this as in the prostitute group.[167]

She concluded that intervention should work at a number of levels. Citing John Bowlby, she called for social work intervention with problem families 'with a view to preventive treatment of other, probably younger, members of the family'. The women needed

careful individual investigation such as would be available at a well-equipped Allocation Centre in order that the correct factors in training and treatment may be provided. The danger of contamination among females is as great as, if not greater, than among males of this age group. It can be reduced by careful allocation to the appropriate establishment, which preferably should be small i.e. for 50 or under.[168]

In 1952 Epps collaborated with R. W. Parnell, the physician in charge of the student health service in Oxford, in publishing another paper in which they compared the physique and temperament of delinquents with undergraduates. This time the forum was the *British Journal of Medical Psychology*:

In studying two groups of young women, one delinquent and the other student, corresponding differences in physique and temperament were found. The delinquents were shorter and heavier in build, more muscular and fat; their temperaments showed a predominance of somatotonia and viscerotonia over cerebrotonia, broadly confirming Sheldon's work. . . . Old notions, in particular the one advanced by Lombroso, of a constitution disposed to crime, may be investigated with advantage by modern tools for the assessment of physique and personality.[169]

In 1954 she followed up the original study of the 300 Borstal women by analysing data on 100 of them for the *British Journal of Delinquency*. While larceny remained the commonest offence for which they were sentenced, 'continued social maladjustment' was the major problem. She called for more work on prediction tables, as the Gluecks had done in the USA. In addition, careful classification was needed to prevent the sexually promiscuous from 'unduly influencing the sexually inexperienced'.[170]

Family life was a particular focus of attention for the researchers. This research was boosted by the work of John Bowlby in the late 1940s, although he was only one of a range of individuals from sociology and psychology who placed the family at the centre of crime causation. Indeed family life and the criminality of young women was a central element in joint research by the British Medical Association and the Magistrates' Association conducted as early as December 1946.[171] This and other work readily found its way into medical journals, who commented favourably on it. The editorials 'Medical aspects of crime' and 'Mental health and the mother' written in March 1950 and May 1951 and carried in the *BMJ* and *The Lancet* respectively are good examples of this process.[172] The criminologist Howard Jones also supported this research in *Crime and the Penal System* (published in 1956). He maintained that measures should be introduced to ensure that the very young child was

not deprived of the love and attention he needs from his mother, by being physically separated from her. This is a very real danger in those parts of the country where women supply a large part of the industrial labour force.[173]

158

The research of professional psychologists confirmed this thesis. *Types of Stealing* by John Rich published in 1956,[174] and the monograph from the Office of the Chief Psychologist at the Prison Commission (published in 1958) underlined the family background of the criminal.[175] In January 1961 *The Lancet* reviewed the research conducted by leading British and American criminologists and concluded that 'the mother's personality seemed to be the most significant in the genesis of criminality'.[176]

This research coexisted with more biologically based theories which concentrated on the genesis of criminality within women. Katharina Dalton's study published in December 1961 noted that there was 'a highly significant relationship between menstruation and crime'.[177] The psychiatric social worker in Holloway, Moya Woodside, published the results of her research in November 1962. Again the forum was a medical journal. She emphasized the psychiatric history of the women and identified elements of 'social disorganization' in their lives. This revolved around 'irregular unions' with men and 'illegitimate maternities' which were 'frequently concomitant with delinquency'.[178]

Woodside's project was one of a number conducted at this time. Each had a strong medical and psychiatric input. The list of projects undertaken in women's prisons in 1961 indicates the kind of work being funded: the psychiatric social worker at Holloway published a paper on alcoholics, carried out research on abortionists and conducted 'a survey to discover which of the women might be suitable for psychiatric treatment'; the staff led by a senior psychologist conducted an exercise in Borstal allocation; the MO and one of the chief officers investigated the case histories of women sentenced to preventive detention. At Birmingham the psychologist examined the domestic training course 'investigating the intelligence, case-histories etc. of the women undergoing it and assessing the results'.[179]

Prison regimes directly reflected the drive to normalization inherent in the research. Group counselling provides a good example of this process. It was based on the idea that female prisoners could work in a community with other prisoners. Crucially it was a community based around the principles of motherhood and domesticity with the woman as the 'key site of intervention'.[180]

In 1963 the commissioners indicated that the group counselling class in Holloway had 'extended far beyond its original conception', which was to ease tensions between prisoners and staff. It was now being used as a 'means of communication' not only between prisoners and staff but also between prisoners and their husbands. Counselling groups were run by married women officers and their husbands. Prison managers sought to make womanhood the common link between prisoners and staff, a link that was to transcend the respective statuses of gaoler and gaoled. During the sessions

> frustrations are cured, difficulties are discussed and problems are shown to be something which all women may have and which all can share in attempting to solve; they are not isolated phenomena to be looked at in horror and then thrust away as soon as possible. Group methods are also used for social therapy. The reasons for social failure are being explored in

the hope that the women concerned may come to see their personalities and circumstances objectively, and to help each other avoid the same pitfalls in the future.[181]

The governor of Holloway at this time was Joanna Kelley. In 1967 she published her autobiography, *When the Gates Shut*. Kelley provides an illuminating insight into the nature of the psychiatric regime in the prison in the first half of the 1960s. The psychiatrist was responsible for diagnostic groups such as the Husband and Wife Group and the Young People's Group. In 1964 they were integrated and became the Family Group. Therapeutic sessions were designed to strike at the causes of crime:

A frequent cause of delinquency is inefficiency. Surprisingly, many women, although they have large families to cater for, are unable to cook and have little idea of marketing wisely or planning a budget. They may live in accommodation with no facilities for cooking other than a gas ring. One such woman and her family lived on bread and jam, fish and chips from the shop around the corner, tea, which she could make, and food out of tins: an extravagant way to live. She was ecstatic when taught in prison how to cook and to market.[182]

When a husband fell ill, became unemployed, deserted the family or died then 'at such a time the old-fashioned virtues of thrift, inventiveness and self-denial would be of value'.[183] In the Borstal wing there were often 'stories of rape, incest or cruelty'. Again, it was the prisoners who had to be changed by a regime which would 'help them to adjust themselves to their incapacities so as to be able to live as normally as possible'.[184]

A network of psychiatric personnel reinforced the direction of the regime. There were four doctors for the 300 women in the prison. They were supported by a psychologist, a psychiatric social worker, two part-time psychotherapists, a psychiatric social worker, a part-time physiotherapist, chiropodist, dentist, gynaecologist, venereologist, and optician. The hospital was staffed by

about forty sisters and nurses: two of these are male hospital officers whose presence has made a great deal of difference to the discipline of the hospital; without apparent effort they are able to quieten and control the most difficult patients.[185]

In spite of the image of psychotherapeutic togetherness, the reality was often more fractured and brittle. As in the 1940s psychotherapy and psychiatric intervention was resisted both by the prisoners and prison officers. Kelley points to continual conflict in the Borstal wing, where prisoners were aggressive towards the staff and other inmates. Furniture was broken and windows smashed. There was a 'phase of inward aggression . . . there was a great deal of tattooing, self-mutilation and swallowing of needles'.[186] Many of the older officers did not wish to become social workers nor did they support open wings or group counselling. For them, punishment should be the basis of imprisonment. They were 'sceptical of the value of rehabilitative work'.[187]

Overall, however, these contradictions and conflicts were not regarded by Kelley as the major problem. It was the women who were the focus of attention. In her view 'women who break the law and are sentenced are likely to be more disturbed than men who do so'.[188] Changing the behaviour of the prisoners and dealing with the disturbed rejection of their outside social role meant subjecting them to a domestic training course similar to the one at Birmingham described above. Between 1962 and 1964, 211 women participated in the course, 118 of whom had been sentenced for child neglect. The other participants were those 'with large families who are thought to be in need of such training'.[189] Kelley indicated how she gauged the success of the course in adjusting the women:

> Two women, for example, started leaving the prison at half past six in the morning, much earlier than was necessary for them to get to work in time. One it was discovered, was making her husband's breakfast and trying to get him off to work, the other was scrubbing her front step and cleaning up. This was heartening in a way, for it showed that their minds were working along acceptable lines; the difficulty was that they became so bitter and restive at having to come back to prison at night.[190]

Normalization through psychiatric counselling was supported by a process of infantilization. The relationship between the officers and prisoners was like that of a child to its nurse, 'nanny is kind and forgiving, but firm; she always knows what is best for her charges'.[191] Recidivists were 'immature, having the egotism of small children'

> and some of the small child's jealousy when too much attention is paid to someone else. . . . Their desires and emotions are of paramount import-ance to them and because they have little self-control, they give way to the impulse of the moment without hesitation. . . . They have become in-adequate to meet the normal demands of life and to shape their lives within the social framework.[192]

This process was described by other state servants. Between November 1961 and October 1962 A. M. Morgan, who had worked at Holloway for twenty years, conducted a survey of women sentenced to Preventive Detention. In discussing recidivism Morgan drew an analogy with children:

> A child who is learning to walk falls down continually at first. Should we not regard these lapses, in some cases, as the fall of a child till it has learnt where to place its feet? If a woman stays out of prison for a longer period each time between sentences – could it not be that eventually she will be able to walk without assistance?[193]

The unsigned comments of a PMO, written in the commissioners' report for 1961, also provided support for the normalizing direction of the regime particularly the domestic science courses. While the majority of the women were 'below the average of intelligence nevertheless they all appeared to benefit from the course in regard to housewifery and cooking'.[194] Prisoners, once again, described a different reality. They discussed the regimes in terms of the enforcement of petty rules, constant surveillance and rigorous discipline. This discipline was often tied to cleaning the buildings. For Joan Henry this meant that in Holloway 'the floor of the ward had to be polished and bumpered till it shone like glass, and matron always examined the window ledges for any specks of dust'.[195] Jane Buxton and Margaret Turner's experience was similar. Conditions were appalling, the discipline and regimentation severe, arm-slashing frequent, medical services poor and medical staff abrupt. As Buxton pointed out, she 'stopped looking for humanity or the normal consideration that civilized people give to those who are sick or in pain. As a prisoner I was apparently a second-class being, and didn't deserve such sentiments'.[196]

Xenia Field's account also raised serious questions about the PMS, which she felt should 'become part of the National Health Service rather than continue as an independent service'. Hygiene in Holloway was 'grim' while the hospital left 'much to be desired by doctors, nurses and prisoners alike, but shortcomings are largely due to the unsuitability of the buildings'.[197] The governor conceded that complaints were made about medical treatment but denied prisoners were automatically regarded as malingerers. In her view medical staff had 'to exercise some caution in dealing with a body of women of whom a large proportion are warped and thwarted'.[198] It appeared that less caution was used when it came to dispensing drugs. The prison employed two full-time dispensers, who dispensed between 'five and six thousand doses of medicine' each week to the 300 women. Kelley attributed this 'incredible' situation not to the medicalization of the women's behaviour but to the fact that the women would hoard the drugs if they were issued as tablets. Consequently 'a woman needing to take a medicine four times daily must be dispensed twenty-eight separate doses every week'.[199]

The criticisms of the PMS did not alter the psychiatric direction of the regime for women prisoners. As Field pointed out, while psychiatrists complained that women referred for treatment were not always suitable, none the less one member of the profession could state that

> virtually all women prisoners need some help. Women prisoners are not necessarily neurotics requiring psychotherapy, but many of them have badly organized and distorted personalities and need forward-looking management and support in life.[200]

The early to mid-1960s also saw the emergence of demands for tighter security and control in women's prisons. The female psychopath emerged as a folk-devil. They were women who smashed cells and were therefore 'not suitable to be among prisoners who are always an unstable community'.[201] In 1964 the annual Prison Department report highlighted the problem of those who would not adhere to, or accept the prison regime. They were arcanely described as 'too afflicted or inadequate to take part in modern methods of training not only in open prisons, where those who fail can be returned to closed establishments, but also in the semi-secure prison at Styal'.[202] It pointed to the changing 'characteristics' of the prisoners:

> A large proportion of the women are mentally unstable, alcoholic or drug addicted, or so inadequate in their daily lives that they need the skilled

attention of welfare and social workers before they can be considered fit to take a responsible part in their own training and rehabilitation.[203]

For those who were 'too afflicted' or 'inadequate' to participate in 'modern methods of training', the Home Office built a secure block at Styal. The block, however, was ineffectual in dealing with the problem, so prison managers considered a scheme for converting two of the houses into single-room accommodation. One of the houses would contain women serving very long sentences while the other would 'help the increasing number who prefer not to take part in community life'.[204] A closed wing was also established in Holloway.

Once again, the justification for these developments was the behaviour of the women. Any rational or logical rejection of the prison regime was interpreted as a further sign of psychological imbalance to be probed, tested, quantified and controlled. For some PMOs the emergence of the 'female aggressive psychopath' was tied to wider, sociological factors. Writing in the in-house *Prison Medical Journal* in July 1965, John Knox, the MO at Holloway, discussed some of these factors:

> What makes it so difficult for us in the Prison Service is that one of the most marked public attitudes to life in this century has been a general desire to emancipate the individual citizen at the expense of society itself. With one accord it seems that we have strained every muscle to reduce discipline everywhere. Schools, young people, factory workers, wives at work, easy divorce, condonation of murder and modifications to all kinds of institutions are to this end.[205]

In July 1966 Knox followed this article with a contribution to a conference organized by the Medical Association for the Prevention of War. The theme was 'the doctor and situations of tension'. Knox told the participants 'there may be no need for women's prisons in 30 years' and that 'quite possibly there will be other ways of dealing with women offenders'.[206] The memorandum submitted by the Prison Medical Officers to the abandoned Royal Commission on the Penal System around the same time succinctly stated their collective position: 'in view of the high numbers of mentally disturbed women offenders we believe that there might be a case for a women's prison under medical direction'.[207] In 1967 the Home Office gave official blessing to this view by arguing that

> Severe personality disorders and emotional disturbance are more prevalent among the women and girls than among the men and boys committed to custody. Whatever the factors contributing to the committal in custody of men and boys, it is clear that either the factors differ or they operate differently as regards women and girls.[208]

These comments were made in the context of a prison population whose crimes were overwhelmingly of a petty property nature and whose sentences were short.

In 1963 88 per cent of those imprisoned in England and Wales, without the option of a fine, served sentences of six months or less.[209] In her review of the position in 1965, Ann Smith provided a critical and alternative perspective to the official discourse of the period:

> One conclusion can be drawn from the statistics – that imprisonment provides no solution to the problems of large numbers of anti-social women in the community today. It is, however, much more difficult to suggest satisfactory alternative methods of dealing with the alcoholic, the prostitute and the neglectful mother. No solution is likely to be found unless the State itself, and indeed the community as a whole, has the courage to experiment and bear the cost of such experiment both financially and through the consequences of those failures which almost inevitably will occur. The special problems of the delinquent women have at all times been neglected – or glossed over by sentiment and unreliable male intuition.[210]

This alternative view was not to prevail. By the late 1960s security and control on the one hand and the psychiatrization of women's behaviour on the other were the dominant pivots in the regimes designed for women prisoners. On their own they did little to relieve the pain of imprisonment for the confined. Together, they propelled already damaged women still further into a pit of despair and individualized recrimination.

WOMEN AND THE CONTEMPORARY SYSTEM

On 10 June 1969 a conference was held at Haverigg Prison. In attendance were governors, deputy governors, administrative officers and the regional Medical Officer. Mr K. J. Neale of Prison Division 4 addressed the meeting. He pointed out that in December 1968 the Home Secretary had announced a comprehensive new policy for the treatment of women and girls. The numbers in custody at that point fluctuated between 800 and 1,000 'and it was not anticipated that these figures would vary very much for the rest of the century'.[211] He went on to announce that as women tended to be lodged further away from friends and relatives than men and because of the difficulty in maintaining the full range of psychiatric and medical services in more remote areas, the Home Office intended to divide the country into north and south. A full range of custodial establishments would be provided in each. While medical facilities would be made available on a broad basis it was Holloway with its 'sophisticated treatment and specialised functions' which would have a national role to make good any deficiencies in the regions. The prison was to have a large staff with approximately one staff member to each prisoner, and two medical staff to one discipline officer:

> Never before had there been a prison specifically designed for women and the new Holloway projected had necessitated much research. It would be orientated towards the provision of advanced sophisticated medical services and of the 500 places planned for women only 150 would be allotted normal prison accommodation.[212]

This view was consolidated in July 1968, when the Prison Department established the Holloway Project Group, which included representatives from the Prison Department and the Department of Health and Social Security.[213] T. C. N. Gibbens, the psychiatrist from Maudsley Hospital, conducted a medicosocial survey of women received into the prison. This was passed to the Home Office Research Unit. As Dobash *et al.* point out, Gibbens's methodology was problematic and unclear: he offered generalized and unsubstantiated comments on the nature of women offenders and provided no definition of personality disorder, although he maintained that 53 per cent of his sample suffered from it. Such problems did not, however, deter the Labour Home Secretary, James Callaghan, from announcing in December 1968 that

> the main feature of the programme to re-shape the system of female penal establishments in England and Wales was to demolish the existing prison at Holloway and build an establishment that was basically a secure hospital. The central features would be medical and psychiatric facilities and normal custodial facilities would comprise a relatively small part of the establishment. Moreover, the new Holloway was to be designed so that, if and when it was no longer needed as a prison, it could be handed over to the National Health Service and used as a mental hospital.[214]

In 1971 D. Faulkner, the chair of the Holloway Development Group and Assistant Secretary in the Prison Department, discussed its philosophy in the *Howard Journal*. Women were classified not in relation to 'their sentence or offence, but rather in terms of the treatment they required'. The building was to be constructed so that it would not resemble a prison:

> The entry point was to be made informal and reassuring and, according to Faulkner, the buildings were to be centred on a green 'to give an open aspect and an appearance of freedom while preserving a high degree of supervision'.[215]

People in Prison, an official Home Office report published in 1969, supported this view. While the anonymous authors pointed out that 85 per cent of women in prison were incarcerated for offences against property, prostitution and drunkenness, they concluded 'many women in custody are clearly in need of medical and psychiatric treatment'. They went on to note

> because most women and girls in custody require some form of medical, psychiatric or remedial treatment, priority will be given in the redevelopment of Holloway to the construction of a new hospital. It will thus become a medically-orientated establishment with the comprehensive, versatile and secure hospital as its central feature.[216]

By the early 1970s this medicalized view of Holloway's philosophy and practice had become institutionalized. John Camp's analysis of the prison (published in 1974) provides a good insight into the direction of the regime. He reiterated the view that the prison would be 'more akin to a hospital' than a prison and outlined the three main aims of the prison. First, any woman who had family problems would be assisted. This included meeting children from school and providing meals. Second, there was to be 'long-term treatment' when required and 'education for the illiterate and backward and various forms of group counselling and therapy'. Finally

> there is the provision of a community life in prison modelled on life outside which will prepare the woman for coping with a normal existence from the moment she enters Holloway and which will include tuition in various skills which may augment her income on release, improvement in her ability to communicate, introduction to hobbies which she can pursue in her leisure time and information as to where she can turn to for help in the community if she finds herself in difficulties. It is hoped that by this means she will be taught not only to lead an honest life but also a reasonably happy one, which so many women who come to prison have never known.[217]

From this perspective, the problem of women's deviance lay very much within the individual whose behaviour thus had to be normalized in order to return them as rehabilitated individuals into the community. Camp indicated how this perspective was reinforced by changes in the categorization procedures, where the women would no longer be grouped according to their sentence or offence, but 'in terms of the treatment they require'. Five main units were to undertake the 'various kinds of treatment'. These included medical, surgical and obstetric units for physical care, a psychotherapeutic unit for drug addicts and alcoholics and a unit for those 'who are not in need of definite medical treatment but who may benefit from the attention of a psycho-therapist'.[218]

Medical surveillance was to continue on the outside with the provision of an out-patients department, which would provide a 'full range of clinical services both to supply medical and psychiatric reports to the courts and also to provide continuing out-patient treatment for those who require and desire it after release'.[219] The staff too were to participate in medical training where 'great attention' was being given to the psychiatric approach to offenders. In particular, group counselling was an important part of the training which itself was to be augmented by two or three week secondments to institutions which specialized in psychiatric medicine including Broadmoor, the Maudsley Hospital and Grendon Psychiatric Prison. Camp was quite clear about the implications of such psychiatric treatment for women: 'she has committed an offence and is not fully responsible for her actions and must be taught what is best for her'.[220]

Carol Smart captured the essence of the debates around women prisoners at the time. Describing the development of the psychiatric regime at Holloway and the power of the medical profession within it, she contended:

> The aim of the programme of treatment in Holloway will be to achieve conformity in its inmates through modifying their personalities and attitudes. In embracing such a goal the role of the legal system, the police and courts, as well as an inequitable social system, in the process of criminalization, is entirely ignored. . . . policy makers like many

criminologists perceive female criminality as irrational, irresponsible and largely unintentional behaviour, as an individual maladjustment to a well-ordered and consensual society. Yet as well as sharing basic assumptions, criminological theories of female criminality may serve to legitimize the trends in penal policy, giving scientific justifications for the treatment of female offenders as 'sick' individuals.[221]

The final touch to the programme, and one which continued the tradition established in the nineteenth century, was the appointment of South-African-born Lady Megan Bull as prison governor. She had been MO at Holloway since 1967 and was appointed to succeed Dorothy Wing, who retired in February 1973.[222]

The appointment of a doctor to the post of governor has, as I have noted, a long history in women's prisons and symbolized the direction of prison regimes for women through the nineteenth century. At the same time Megan Bull's appointment did not herald a new beginning in the psychiatric treatment of confined women. On the contrary, by the late 1970s the ability of psychiatry and medicine to alter the behaviour of women prisoners was the subject of critical and often sceptical scrutiny. This is not to say that psychiatric discourse was eliminated from the penal regimes for women. It remained a central and contradictory element in the everyday lives of the confined. It did, however, take its place alongside other developments, most notably official pronouncements concerning the changing nature of women's criminality. Official spokespersons talked of the prison population as 'depressingly normal' or as the Assistant Director of Prison Medical Services expressed it in 1978:

> When the new Holloway was begun there was a very much higher percentage of female offenders who appeared to be psychiatrically disturbed, there are fewer who are psychiatrically disturbed in relationship to the total number than there were before. There are normal but difficult people in the system.[223]

Other evidence to the House of Commons Expenditure Committee in 1978 re-emphasized the disturbed and inadequate nature of the female prison population. One sister from Holloway told the committee that 'perhaps five per cent are normal. The rest are disturbed'.[224] Such contradictory perceptions were to underpin the responses and programmes that women in prison were to face in the late 1970s and through the 1980s. Either as individuals or in groups, the women were continually under the penal microscope with every movement, gesture and response magnified and recorded by those who observed them.

CONSOLIDATING CONTRADICTIONS

The Fifteenth Report of the House of Commons Expenditure Committee was published in 1978. The introduction to the report called for a separate inquiry into women's imprisonment which the committee undertook in late 1978 and early 1979. However, because of the 1979 general election the report was never written. The National Association for the Care and Resettlement of Offenders (NACRO) reviewed the evidence to the committee in its fourteen-page document *Women in the Prison System* (published in 1980).[225] NACRO's report pointed to a number of areas of concern including a major increase in overcrowding, the problems of mothers and babies in prison, and the distance from family and friends which led to a lack of contact with the outside world. The report also highlighted the continuing disruption in the prisons. This disruption took different forms including assaults, self-mutilation, ear-piercing and self-strangulation. As in the nineteenth century such behaviour was explained in psychiatric terms, the women were treated as abnormal with drugs being used in some prisons to regulate and discipline their behaviour. NACRO pointed out that there was no consensus that the majority of women prisoners were in fact mentally ill. The Prison Officers' Association (POA) saw them as 'sophisticated, callous and cunning', while the Home Office argued that the female prison population 'is depressingly normal and that a large number of the women are normal women'.[226] In January 1981 the Home Office confirmed the new direction that Holloway was to take. In an internal memorandum sent by P 4 Division to, amongst others, Dr Orr, the then Director of the Prison Medical Service, the writer pointed out that delays in the building of the prison had allowed the Prison Department to take account of the changed situation. In particular 'it has become clear that the needs of the female inmate population have changed markedly since 1968'.[227] The department pinpointed three main changes. First, the rise in the female population to a figure of over 1,500. Second, the number of women being sentenced to longer terms of imprisonment: the memorandum indicated 'the number of prisoners serving over four years has trebled since 1970'.[228] Finally, the department argued that the nature of the prison population had changed and that 'in many ways' the women had 'characteristics similar to that of the male population'.[229] From this overview, it concluded

> these factors and the realisation that psychiatry has little to offer in the treatment of criminality, have combined to make it impossible to justify the high expenditure and heavy emphasis on medical and related facilities and have made it necessary to allow for the development of a training regime for a larger number of women.[230]

The department maintained that while Holloway would continue to play a central role in providing the required medical and psychiatric facilities for both young and adult female prisoners

> that will no longer be, however, its sole or primary focus. Its primary intention will be to provide a training regime for sentenced prisoners, and remand facilities and services as a local prison for unconvicted and unsentenced inmates. The prison will therefore share with other local and training establishments in the prison system the objective of providing for

the positive custody of its inmates, with education activities and occupational employment provided within a disciplined but caring regime.[231]

One further consequence of this shift was that the level of security was being enhanced while 'provision is also being made for a segregation unit'.[232] The fact the department had declared that Holloway was now to be a 'disciplined but caring regime' did not prevent the utilization and application of psychiatric and psychological concepts within the prison setting. At the same time the resurrection of security and control in the context of the 'normal' dangerous woman offender meant that prison managers could also legitimately increase and intensify the level of regulation and surveillance to which the women were subjected. As I have indicated, such individualized surveillance strategies have been an integral part of female prison history. By the 1980s electronic monitoring had augmented the gaze of the professional prison visitor and the medical doctor. The experience of women in 'H' Wing of Durham Prison is a good illustration of the twin processes of individualization and surveillance. According to one ex-prisoner:

> The only way I've ever been able to describe Durham is like a submarine – I've never been in one but I imagine that's what it's like. You couldn't see daylight. It felt like you were buried alive. That was your life in there. It was as if the world outside didn't exist. . . . When you went out on exercise, it was just in a concrete yard with a wire fence round it, no trees, no grass. There were dogs and male officers patrolling with walkie-talkies around the outside and the inside. Four cameras watching you, following you. All you could see were brick walls. The men from the men's part of the prison had their cells overlooking the yard. They'd shout remarks as we walked round. Sometimes they could be very abusive. In Durham you weren't allowed to think for yourself, you couldn't do anything. Everything you did was monitored, you couldn't get away from it.[233]

In March 1984 the wing held thirty-six prisoners, three of whom were in the top security Category A.[234] During the year the women had to slop out; cell association was limited to three at a time with the doors continuously opened; food, drink and conversation was prohibited in the two main TV rooms; cooking facilities were not allowed; education was basic and exercise was taken in a tarmac yard, which was surrounded by a twenty-foot wire fence topped with coils of razor-sharp barbed wire and a high perimeter wall. Overall

> The keyword is perpetual surveillance, there is little privacy, even the toilets are fitted with half doors, leaving a psychological impact on the mind with the very real effect of constipation, one of the many problems of life on 'H' Wing. . . . The women are monitored by closed-circuit TV cameras, female officers and male officers regularly patrol the area between fence and wall with ferocious-looking guard dogs.[235]

Former prisoners have indicated that the conditions had a detrimental effect on their physical and psychological health, including loss of energy, hair and memory, becoming withdrawn, eyesight problems from the fluorescent lights and skin changes in colour and texture.[236]

> I am having to come to terms with a recurring urinary tract infection and hormone problem. But this isn't surprising considering the strain put onto the bladder, kidneys and bowels by being made to wait in turn one at a time to use the toilets in the workroom and trying to avoid the potty during lock in. There is the unavoidable further degradation of the slop out when unlocked, usually whilst the food is being set out directly below the slop-out recess. No light penetrates within 'H' Wing walls: fluorescent lighting has to be in continual use. I entered the prison with 20–20 vision and had to wait nearly 5 months before an optician examined me. I am now having to adjust to wearing glasses for the rest of my life. Many women's periods stop and schizophrenia and paranoia are prevalent.[237]

The stress generated was compounded by the enforcement of petty rules and regulations. Furthermore, the use of strip and cell searches had become part of the daily routine. The searches were carried out after visits by probation officers, solicitors, friends and relatives while rub down searches were employed daily when the women entered and left the workroom, the exercise yard and the gymnasium. The prisoners protested at the conditions. Early in 1984 twenty-three of the thirty-five women on the wing engaged in a hunger strike.

For younger women, debilitated by the 'dreary monotonous routine and £100,000 of space age technology' underpinned by the imposition of petty rules and regulations 'it is small wonder they usually end up behind their doors on report, or get "doped" up to dull their minds.'[238]

Accounts by others confirm the constant and complex series of rules and regulations which govern their behaviour inside. At a general level women are disciplined more than twice as often as men. In 1986, as Una Padel and Prue Stevenson have pointed out, '3.6 offences were punished per head of the female prison population as against 1.6 per head of the male prison population'.[239] Many of these disciplinary infractions could be seen to arise from the intensive enforcement of the petty rules and regulations:

> Every morning, even Saturday and Sunday, we were woken at seven. We had to be washed, dressed, have our hair immaculate (which was difficult because I had to plait mine), strip all the bedclothes off our beds (which seemed a totally pointless exercise and got right up my nose the entire time I was at Styal), and fold them to a complicated and immaculate design – sheet, blanket, sheet all wrapped round with the counterpane and put at the end of the bed. All that and down to sign the time book by 7.20. You had to queue to sign the book as only one inmate was allowed in the office at a time. If you're late twice you're put on report, and girls often lost remission because of that. Twenty-two women, eight wash-basins, two toilets, it's just impossible; twenty minutes to do all that and bunk your bed as well, and if you're sleeping in a bunk in a crowded room you're

falling over each other trying to fold your sheets and blankets at the same time. I got it down to a fine art, but it was all additional pressure.[240]

As Pat Carlen has indicated, the enforcement of hierarchical discipline in this way combines

> with the domestic work programme, with the denial to prisoners of sociability and adult womanhood and with the organization of women into small family units, to ensure a mental and bodily surveillance which denudes the prisoners' daily life of all dignity and independence.[241]

In the majority of prisons hierarchical authority retains its nineteenth-century legacy in that the positions of power are occupied by men. When Polly Toynbee visited Bullwood Hall in March 1983 she found the young women were faced with a hierarchy in which the governor was a man as was the person in charge of the kitchen, the factory, the workshops, physical education and the probation and religious services. The doctor was also a man who visited the prison two half days a week to operate the therapeutic unit. When it was pointed out that men were set above the prisoners to the possible detriment of their self image he argued:

> 'you couldn't have all women! The place would be rife with pre-menstrual tension and no sanity anywhere!' Here he mentioned in passing that he had thought of instituting menstrual charts to see if there was a correlation between violence and menstruation but this had to be abandoned according to the deputy governor since girls kept asking for Tampax to use the outer wrappers as cigarette papers.[242]

What is clear from these accounts and recent research on women in prison is that the long march of medicine from the beginning of the eighteenth century to the present is still a central factor in the response of the criminal justice system in general and prisons in particular to criminal women. Medical and psychiatric power pervades and percolates the institutional practices and individual ideologies of state personnel. This cuts through all aspects of imprisonment. At the pre-trial stage, remanding women for medical reports mobilizes a series of comments and images from prison medical personnel. It is a set of images quite distinct from those which find their way into reports on male prisoners. As Hilary Allen has noted:

> . . . the medical reports on women prisoners are complex documents, containing statements on a whole range of biographical, social, moral, criminal, psychological aspects of their subjects' lives, as well as a detailed discussion of their mental condition. . . . In these reports one rarely finds the dismissive formula that concludes so many male reports: 'I can find no evidence of mental disorder *and have therefore no recommendations to make'*.[243]

The use of psychiatric labels such as 'personality disorder' continues to reinforce the subordination of the women. As Pat Carlen has argued, although it cannot be defined the application of the label makes imprisoned women . . . feel 'quite horribly at home' within psychiatric careers . . . whilst both the history and the present organization of psychiatric and penal internment in Britain are particularly suited to disciplining women into what is still regarded as being Scottish woman's most proper role, that of the child-rearing home-maker. [244]

Normalization through psychiatry is underpinned by other medical mechanisms for maintaining order and control. As Chapter 5 indicated, psychotropic drugs have become an important element in that control. In women's prisons, such drugs have been used disproportionately in terms of the rate of prescription per head of the prisoner population. [245] Carlen described how one doctor saw this process:

PAT CARLEN: Do you ever give drugs for control purposes – for controlling violent prisoners?
DOCTOR: Yes. We have to take the staff into consideration when selecting a drug. Some people we've had in eight or ten times in two years and you know they can be pretty wicked without the drug. [246]

More recent research in the area has confirmed this view. Mandaraka-Sheppard observed what she described as the use of 'heavy sedation' in the course of her research. The drugs were part of a network of control designed to prevent escapes and quell disturbances by

so-classified 'hard core troublemakers'. This research has shown that such classifications (at least as far as women prisoners are concerned) are arbitrary and have negative repurcussions. There was no evidence by which to identify such troublemakers; they are, it would appear, likely to be the result of the system's use of harsh social control and labelling procedures which are negatively perceived by prisoners. . . . The argument concerning 'disturbed' prisoners has been accepted with complacency; the result has been to introduce psychiatric methods and psychotropic drugs of therapy in prisons, which, under the guise of 'benevolent treatment' have resulted in abuses for the purpose of social control and not for the genuine help of the prisoners. [247]

Elaine Genders and Elaine Player have indicated that between January 1984 and March 1985 over 145,000 doses of anti-depressants, sedatives and tranquillizers 'were dispensed to women in prison proportionately five times as many doses of this type of medication as men received in prison'. [248]

In this way the structural questions around the prison regime, its philosophy and practice are translated into individual psychological problems situated on a coping–non-coping continuum. The place of medicine in the everyday lives of confined women is compounded by the more general question of the medical treatment which they receive. As I have indicated, historically this has been a controversial issue in women's prisons. The doctrine of less eligibility analysed in previous chapters has been compounded by the refusal to acknowledge the particular problems which women experience with regard to health care. [249] As in the previous 150 years, the issue of health care has underpinned the more recent debates in relation to the deaths of women in custody. As previous chapters have shown, such deaths are not a recent phenomenon but stretch back to the early days of the PMS. According to Melissa Benn and Chris Tchaikovsky, behind the latest statistics 'is a story told by prisoners, ex-prisoners, prison reform groups and official sources, of fire hazards, medical neglect and preventable suicides'.[250] The report published by the Women's Equality Group in the London Strategic Policy Unit in 1986 highlighted a number of issues in relation to the deaths of women in custody:

> Nothing highlights the urgent need for a complete change in the use of imprisonment in this country more than this account of deaths in custody. Emergency bells bent back or not answered, access to doctors denied, suicide threats ignored, suicide attempts disregarded, and most fundamentally, women suffering severe mental or physical illness remanded in custody or even sentenced to imprisonment. Women are sometimes sent to prison in the mistaken belief that they will receive good medical care or to undergo psychiatric assessment.[251]

The report made ten recommendations with regard to these issues including a recommendation that women should never be remanded in custody for psychiatric assessment, prisoners should never be assumed to be malingering if they threaten or attempt to take their own lives and 'prisoners should be afforded the full protection of the NHS, the Prison Medical Service should be abolished'.[252]

While death has been the path chosen by some, others have engaged in disturbances and self-mutilation in response to the regime. As I have indicated, this pattern of behaviour also has a long history in women's prisons. Again, it continued into the 1980s. Holloway's C1 Wing, which opened in 1977, has been a particular source of controversy and concern. In October 1984 the *Guardian* reporter Polly Toynbee discussed the wing's problems.[253] She was distressed at the number of 'so many deeply deranged and disturbed women' in the prison and questioned whether they should be there at all:

> With some it is immediately clear that they are urgently in need of full-time psychiatric care in a secure hospital. For a prison 'psychiatric' wing is nothing more than a dumping ground, a containment for them. The atmosphere is punitive not therapeutic, the prisoners' mad outbreaks and attacks are regarded as punishable rather than treatable and the psychiatric care they can expect in any prison is nothing more than a parody of proper treatment.[254]

Since that time, the punitive and contradictory nature of the regime has been highlighted by MPs, newspapers, pressure groups and the prisoners themselves. They have focused on the recurring self-mutilations and suicides as well as questioning the nature of the disciplinary hearings at which women suffering from mental disorders have been punished. They also revealed that 'Home Office advice on the treatment of mentally ill inmates is being ignored by medical staff'.[255] For William Bingley, the Director of MIND, Holloway's problems were the same as those 'endemic in the rest of the prison system. They follow from the separation of the prison medical service from the mainstream National Health Service'.[256] In March 1986 Nick Davies, the *Observer*'s Home Affairs Correspondent, visited the prison and once again illustrated the inter-relationship between containment and medical therapy. While he noted that 'the last vestiges of a medical regime still survive on the wing' its philosophy was towards containment and control:

> Safe containment thus becomes the torment of hours alone in a bare cell with every potential distraction removed – an experience which inevitably makes sick women sicker. In an attempt to make it safer still, builders are now constructing a padded cell on the wing – the ultimate paradox of humane treatment as solitary confinement.[257]

Davies pointed out that the wing was staffed by prison officers who had no medical training and by nurses who had no psychiatric training. Additionally some of the nurses were employed for short spells from an outside employment agency. Finally, he noted that the women on the wing were punished 'more often than other prisoners, particularly for damaging prison property and disobeying orders'.[258]

The issues around self-mutilation continued into the late 1980s. Between April 1987 and March 1988 there were 429 self-injuries reported among adult women and 107 in young women's prisons in the same period.[259] Similar statistics were recorded for the special hospitals. In the year between December 1986 and 1987 the recorded number of self-mutilation in one of the institutions was 250.[260] In May 1989 it was reported that a 27-year-old woman had committed suicide in Risley remand centre. It was the eighth case in the prison in 18 months.[261]

CONTESTING POWER

As I have noted throughout this book, the Prison Medical Service has not developed and consolidated without challenge. I have indicated that during the twentieth century the challenges mounted by prisoners have been supported by groups outside of the prison walls. The work of the Prison System Enquiry Committee in the first decades of the twentieth century, the pamphlets of the Prison Medical Reform Council published between the 1940s and 1960s and the interventions of the National Prisoners' Movement and Radical Alternatives to Prison in the 1970s and 1980s have all provided alternative accounts of life inside in general and challenged medical hegemony in particular. In March 1983 the formation of Women in Prison (WIP) carried on this tradition. The ten-point manifesto of the group called for amongst other things 'improved medical facilities in general and specialized facilities for women during pregnancy, childbirth and menstruation'.[262] The manifesto contained a further ten points relating to prisoners in general. Point 6 of these demands argued for

[the] abolition of the Prison Medical Service and its replacement by normal National Health Service provision coupled with the abolition of the present system whereby prison officers vet, and have the power to refuse, prisoners' requests to see the doctor.[263]

The report by the Women's Equality Group of the London Strategic Policy Unit (published in 1986) had a strong input from the group. The report made ten recommendations around women's health in prisons. These included a call for the abolition of the PMS; the right of a prisoner to choose her own doctor; the non-involvement of doctors in discipline and the sanctioning of punishment; the rejection of the use of medicine for punishment, control or disciplinary purposes; and finally the call for women prisoners to 'have the right to ask to be treated by women medical staff'.[264] Since its formation WIP has been campaigning, holding public meetings, picketing prisons, appearing in the media and writing to MPs and prison officials about conditions in prison. It has gathered and disseminated a range of information and alternative accounts of life in the prisons. Since 1983, one forum for that dissemination has been a regular contribution to *The Abolitionist*, the journal of Radical Alternatives to Prison. The group has produced accounts by prisoners of life inside in general, and prison medical facilities and treatment in particular. Various issues of the journal have contained powerful accounts of medical treatment and the lack of sensitivity to the medical problems facing imprisoned women.[265] The group also launched a project on women in special hospitals in the light of the fact that 'prisoners are regularly transferred from prison to special hospitals under a variety of orders'.[266] It noted that there were 400 women in special hospitals at any one time and illustrated the relationship women have had with these institutions. In 1983, of the 297 men and women discharged, 69 per cent of men and 80 per cent of women were 'conditionally discharged and therefore liable to recall. Two per cent of men and five per cent of women had been detained for over 30 years, that is since their original committal or last recall'.[267] WIP has also highlighted the issues around the question of mothers and babies in prison as well as the disproportionate use of strip-searching on women prisoners, an issue which signifies the surveillance and continuing scrutiny of the minutiae of their existence. As with the previous campaigning groups that I have highlighted, the work of Women in Prison has provided a focus for resistance and a forum for women prisoners to articulate their grievances around medical care and conditions inside. The group has, in short, challenged medical power and provided a counterweight to the development of a full-blown medical hegemony in women's prisons.

The relationship between prison medical power and confined women, is, as I have indicated, a complex one. From the historical and contemporary material presented in this chapter it is possible to discern a number of themes running through this relationship: the individualization of women prisoners; the drive to normalize their behaviour; the close interconnection between different, usually male-dominated professional groups whose activities have been built on the perpetual surveillance of the women's physical and psychological response to imprisonment; the advent of intensive technological control from the 1960s; the resistance of women to that control and to medical and psychiatric categorization; and the continuing entrapment of women within catch-all psychiatric categories such as behavioural and personality disorder. As Pat Carlen has pointed out:

> As it is not acceptable to say publicly that people are sent to prison because of their social circumstances, the actual social reasons for imprisonment . . . are, in public, displaced on to the psychiatric category of psychopathic personality disorder and this category is then used by prison personnel to justify all aspects of the prison regime. Women are actually sent to prison because of either their domestic circumstances, the failure of non penal welfare or health institutions to cope with their problems . . . or their failure to comply with socially-conditioned female gender-stereotype requirements. Once there, they are treated to a disciplinary regime which engenders confused states of consciousness by contradictorily defining them as both within and without family, femininity, adulthood and sanity.[268]

It is within this disciplinary matrix that medicine operates in women's prisons, ultimately reinforcing the fragmentation that imprisonment engenders in the already fractured psyches of the women at the centre of the professionals' gaze.

CHAPTER 7

. Conclusion

At the beginning of his *Discipline and Punish* Foucault puts the question to himself, why, now, write a history of the prison? 'Simply because I am interested in the past? No if one means by that writing a history of the past in terms of the present. Yes if one means writing the history of the present'.[1]

Chapter 1 noted that this book owes a theoretical debt to the work of Michel Foucault. His analysis of the disciplinary genesis of institutional medicine, resistance to domination and the non-reductionist nature of power has been central to this dissection of medical power in English prisons. At the same time, the substantive material in the book has raised some important questions about Foucault's conceptualization of power within institutions. This concluding chapter explores three issues – gender, violence and the state – which are important to consider if the full complexity of the processes surrounding medicine in prison are to be appreciated and understood.

GENDER AND CLASSIFICATION

The issue of gender and classification has been marginal to traditional and radical accounts of medicine in prison. Yet, as Chapter 6 illustrated, medical and psychiatric classification procedures had a differential impact on male and female prisoners. The essence of their criminality and the threat they posed to the social order was perceived differently by the professionals who analysed them, the courts which sentenced them, the gaolers who confined them and the medical personnel who categorized them. This interlocking network of power responded to what were understood to be important differences in the origins and impact of male and female criminality and legitimized the construction of different regimes to suppress it.

The process of individualization was a corner-stone of women's prisons. State servants, professionals and prisoners themselves saw it as something which was more clearly articulated in relation to female prisoners than to their male counterparts. The surveillance which was integral to this process was carried out by different groups from chaplains, to lady visitors to medical personnel themselves. The latter group involving doctors, psychologists and psychiatrists as well as psychiatric social workers beyond the walls tested, probed and hypothesized about criminal women constructing quantifiable profiles of the bio-psychological and narrowly defined sociological factors, deemed to be lying at the root of their criminality. These investigations were further intensified when dealing with those who responded negatively to the prison regime. Throughout the nineteenth and into the twentieth century women reacted differently from men to the pains of confinement in terms of physical self-injury and psychological introspection. This was a central aspect of women's imprisonment, although it should also be noted that there was a strong element of collective support and resistance to the regime. Such individualized responses generated further medical intervention into their lives reinforcing the view that it was they rather than the pressurized structures and policies of the prisons that were at fault.

The generation of psychological profiles, the construction of a knowledge base and the implementation of different categorization procedures were orientated to normalizing the women back to domestic respectability. Rehabilitation meant the domestic normality of motherhood and home. The key Foucauldian concepts involving order, control, routines and timetables built around this knowledge base were therefore translated into very different practices in women's prisons in the shape of the work programmes, motherhood courses and domestic education classes.

THE QUESTION OF VIOLENCE

A second limitation in Foucault's thesis revolves around the issue of ethnocentrism and violence. The system of power he analyses and the relationships that flow from it are applied narrowly to Western Europe and North America. He fails to consider how the power to punish was exported to, and utilized in, colonial situations and in turn was reflected back on to the punishment apparatus of the original exporter. Violence was endemic to this process.[2] This has specific relevance for Foucault's idea that with the rise of capitalism and professional expertise punishment moved from the body to the mind. At one level, this conceptualization undoubtedly 'fits' with the emergence of psychiatric practice in Europe and America. However, it misses an essential point, namely that physical violence and punishment of the body did not, and has not, disappeared but retains a central place in the repertoire of responses mobilized by the state inside prisons. Autobiographical accounts by male and female prisoners from the mid-nineteenth century to the present which have been utilized in the book testify to the centrality of violence in the maintenance of order. Recent accounts of the operation of the criminal justice system in general,[3] as well as prisons in Scotland,[4] Northern Ireland,[5] and Nigeria[6] in particular, further emphasize the importance of violence in state practices.

Foucault overemphasizes the nature of the shift in punishment that has taken place and underestimates the complex and continuous interrelationship between punishment of the body and control of the mind. While displays of torture, violence and execution may have disappeared from the public domain they still exist and operate in the various institutions that have developed since the late eighteenth century. Medical and psychiatric discourses did not simply replace physical punishment of the body; the two continued to coexist with the latter strategy being mobilized when the order of the institution was threatened. Women's prisons in the 1950s provide a good example of this dialectic. It was at this moment that these discourses were operating at their most intensive. And yet, as Chapter 4 indicated, physical violence was still utilized to discipline and punish problematic behaviour. As Heinz Steinert has pointed out:

> Alongside the discourse on punishment, the prison and their scientific 'humanization' worldwide, we still have torture, people being beaten and dying in prison. We have concentration camps: we have the death penalty in the majority of countries. There remains a lot that is not accounted for by a Foucault-type analysis of history.[7]

THE QUESTION OF THE STATE

As this book makes clear, those who staffed the PMS from the end of the eighteenth century were important in the hierarchy of domination within prisons. In Foucault's terms they were 'front-line controllers'.[8] The early prison doctors emphasized a particular view of criminality together with disciplined health care for the confined. The doctors were powerful figures in both the understanding of, and treatment for, the confined. When there were major inquiries such as that conducted by the Carnarvon Committee in 1863 the evidence of the doctors was heard and treated with respect. Through working in the laboratory of the prison, medical personnel affirmed their status as the professional group who could speak with the authority that this access gave them. At the same time, their views did not diverge from those of the law-makers in Parliament nor an increasingly identifiable and powerful state bureaucracy. Disciplined regulation was the perceived strategy invoked to deal with the problem of criminality and potential disorder. From 1877 state intervention intensified through the centralization of the prison system. The work of prison medical personnel was increasingly co-ordinated by the state. The observations and research projects by doctors such as Quinton, Campbell, Devon, Sutherland and Hamblin-Smith, while emphasizing different aspects and facets of criminal behaviour, were united on an ideological terrain which saw the problem of criminality rooted in the individual's body, psyche, temperament or local community. The theories expounded derived from the observation of the criminal in the individualized environment of the prisoner's cell or the doctor's office. They reaffirmed the individualization of criminality and the need for professional intervention either into the individual's mind or into particular communities to prevent its contaminating spread. These views did not diverge from the analysis of the medical profession in general nor from state servants such as the Prison Commissioners, who were responsible for the management of the penal system. Indeed the apparent professionalism and scientific basis of the doctors' studies gave state intervention and regulation an added disciplinary legitimacy.

After the Second World War there was a close relationship between the work of professionals and intellectuals working in and around the prisons. This relationship was co-ordinated and facilitated by state bureaucrats who provided research funds, access and conference platforms for these groups to meet. The research conducted by prison doctors, psychologists and organic intellectuals reflected wider concerns around criminality and disorder that were prevalent at the time. This was particularly relevant to the criminality of women both as creators of criminals in terms of the thesis of maternal deprivation and to the internal constitution of the female criminal herself. The doctors and particularly the psychologists and psychiatrists who observed, probed and tested criminal women and the theories expounded from their empirical examinations did not simply reflect state concerns about order but reinforced them. The unfit and criminal mother was therefore not only the object of theoretical interest from prison doctors and psychiatrists but also at the centre of the state's concern with the maintenance of order in the post-war world. Here the interrelationship becomes complete in a political sense with the introduction of programmes in institutions designed to correct female deviance and reconstruct the supine and loving parent. The state's field of activity and its relationship to the criminal therefore also varied with gender. While both Catherine MacKinnon and Bob Connell have pointed out that 'feminism has no theory of the state',[9] it is none the less possible to discern important moments in its development in relation to medical discourse and imprisoned women. For example, the research into and the introduction of domestic programmes for women in the post-1945 prison system would not have been possible without the direct co-ordination and encouragement of the Home Office state bureaucracy, who above anything else provided access for research to take place. Similarly the surveillance of the women by male professionals strikes a theoretical chord with feminist work on the sociology of occupations and the state, where in the hierarchical division of labour men such as prison doctors occupy the dominant positions of power, authority and decision-making.[10] These processes not only allow the state to regulate institutions but also, according to Connell, help it to constitute 'social categories in the gender order'.[11] The early-twentieth-century degenerate woman and the post-1945 unfit mother are two examples in which medical discourse and the state's constitution of gender categories converged on a common theoretical and political terrain. Thus while the power of the doctors to manage the prisons and to make interventions into debates about criminality was a central element in the development of prisons in the post-war period, this power did not operate in a vacuum. It was tied to, and reflected in, the wider debates about criminality, social control and social order, which were an integral part of political discourse at the time. While they may have had autonomy, medical personnel did not stand outside or above these processes, which were conducted through or co-ordinated by the bureaucracy of the post-war state. As Bouventura De Sousa Santos has noted, while Foucault is correct to stress the existence of power relations which operate outside of the state's orbit

> he goes too far in stressing their dispersion and fragmentation. He is left with no theory of the hierarchy of power forms and no theory of social transformation. He obscures the central role of the power forms of the citizenplace and the work-place in our societies, domination and exploitation respectively.[12]

As state servants, medical and psychiatric personnel retain a pivotal position within the contemporary criminal justice system. They produce what Robert Nye has called 'metaphors of pathology' which, as Chapter 1 indicated, not only set the parameters for debates about offenders in prison but also seep into the public domain and play a leading role in discussions about social problems and responses to them.[13] Within the contemporary prison system bio-medical explanations of human behaviour continue to dominate the programmes and policies of the interventionist state. Recent proposals for the construction of new-generation Panopticon prisons, the introduction of electronic tags and the continuing emphasis on the identification and control of small groups of difficult prisoners testify to the power of bio-medical discourse.[14]

Contemporary prison medical workers would therefore find much common ground with those who worked in the prisons immediately after John Howard's intervention in the mid-1770s. The 200-year gap is bridged not simply by individuals who recognize themselves as *prison* medical workers (notwithstanding the fact that the majority of contemporary treatment is carried out by outside practitioners) but by the complex and interrelated set of ideologies and practices within which they work. Thus the issues around discipline, regulation and control and the individualized understanding of deviance that flows from them would provide one common meeting-point. Similarly the appalling conditions in which many prisoners exist in the late 1980s would be recognized by those practising in the 1820s and 1830s, the eligibility of the confined for the receipt of proper medical attention again providing a common terrain that bridges the 200-year gap. They would also recognize the continuing conflict around their role and the critical questions asked of them by prisoners and their supporters which over the last 200 years at times have fractured the medical gaze through social actions as diverse as ridicule, complaints, pamphlets, assaults and murder. There has been a clear and often uncompromising contestation of medical power.

Reading and analysing the history of the PMS in this way is in a sense a double-edged sword. Sociologically it allows for the identification of the long history of discipline within which prison medicine has operated, together with the continuities and discontinuities in medical and psychiatric practice. Politically, and here I return to Foucault and the quotation which heads this final chapter, conceptualizing history in this way means engaging in what Michael

181

Donnelly has termed the construction of a 'usable past . . . a past or a myth of the past useful in contemporary struggles against the prisons because it debunks the ideological justifications of the other side'.[15] In a society where media representations provide, indeed dictate, a short-term historical understanding of social action (with the notable exception of monarchical and heritage phenomena) the concept of the history of the present allows for not only an examination of the historical gestation of social phenomena but also the kind of political tactics and strategies which might be adopted to deal with processes that have been laid down over decades and centuries rather than weeks and months.

The issue of the use of drugs to control the behaviour of difficult prisoners provides a good example of this contention. While the controversy surrounding the issue in the late 1970s was given some media coverage it was generally portrayed as one which had sprung up overnight and involved a group of neutral professionals being accused by a deviant group, whose activities both within and without the penitentiary had placed them outside the law. If abuses had occurred then some mechanism for reform was needed to alleviate the situation. And yet, as this book has shown, the issues around control and regulation through medical practice are not new but have been deeply embedded in the discourse of institutional medicine since the late eighteenth century. The historical evidence in this work can therefore be seen as a challenge to the view of the benevolence of the medical scientific mission where abuses will be reformed if the profession or the institution or the state are left to their own incorruptible devices. The evidence indicts such a view and raises significant theoretical and political questions about strategies and tactics for changing long-established medical programmes, practices and ideologies. Ultimately this evidence can be seen as a contribution to Foucault's 'usable past', the uncovering and exposure of contemporary strategies which are orientated to the individual will to order rather than the collective need for liberation.

Notes and references

1 ANALYSING THE PRISON MEDICAL SERVICE: THE SOCIOLOGICAL CONTEXT

1. Schrag, P. (1980) *Mind Control*, Marion Boyars, p. 252.
2. Smith, R. (1984) *Prison Health Care*, British Medical Association.
3. Hinde, R. S. E. (1951) *The British Prison System 1773–1950*, Gerald Duckworth; Howard, D. L. (1960) *The English Prisons*, Butler & Tanner; Elkin, W. (1957) *The English Penal System*, Pelican.
4. Stratton, B. (1973) *Who Guards the Guards?*, PROP (National Prisoners' Movement).
5. Fitzgerald, M. (1977) *Prisoners in Revolt*, Penguin.
6. Wicker, T. (1975) *A Time To Die*, The Bodley Head.
7. Fitzgerald, M., op. cit; Boyle, J. (1977) *A Sense of Freedom*, Pan.
8. Fitzgerald, M., op. cit; Pallas, J. and Barber, B. (1980) 'From riot to revolution', in T. Platt and P. Takagi (eds) *Punishment and Penal Discipline*, Crime and Social Justice, pp. 146–54.
9. Davis, A. (1971) *If They Come in the Morning*, New American Library, p. 37 (emphasis in the original).
10. Cohn-Bendit, D. (1968) *Obsolete Communism: The Left Wing Alternative*, André Deutsch; Hall, S., Critcher, C., Jefferson, T., Clarke, J. and Roberts, B. (1978) *Policing the Crisis*, Macmillan.
11. Hall, S. and Scraton, P. (1981) 'Law, class and control', in M. Fitzgerald, G. McLennan and J. Pawson (compilers) *Crime and Society: Readings in History and Theory*, Routledge & Kegan Paul, pp. 460–97.
12. Patton, P. (1979) 'Of power and prisons', in M. Morris and P. Patton (eds) *Michel Foucault: Power, Truth and Strategy*, Ferrall Publishers, p. 110.
13. Ibid.
14. Simon, J. (1974) 'Michel Foucault on Attica: an interview', *Telos*, 19, spring, pp. 155–6.
15. Cohen, S. (1985) *Visions of Social Control*, Polity Press, p. 24.
16. Ignatieff, M. (1978) *A Just Measure of Pain*, Macmillan, pp. xi–xii.

17. Ibid., p. XII.
18. Ibid.
19. Cohen, S., op. cit., p. 23.
20. Melossi, D. and Pavarini, M. (1981) *The Prison and the Factory*, Macmillan, p. 1.
21. Cohen, S., op. cit.; Ignatieff, M. (1983) 'State, civil society and total institutions: a critique of recent social histories of punishment', in S. Cohen and A. Scull (eds) *Social Control and the State*, Macmillan, pp. 75–105.
22. Gunn, J., Robertson, G., Dell, S. and Way, C. (1978) *Psychiatric Aspects of Imprisonment*, Academic Press; Topp, D. O. (1977) 'The doctor in prison', *Medicine, Science and the Law*, pp. 261–4; Prewer, R. R. (1974) 'The contribution of prison medicine', in L. Blom-Cooper (ed.) *Progress in Penal Reform*, Oxford University Press, pp. 116–28; Smith, R., op. cit.
23. Smart, B. (1985) *Michel Foucault*, Tavistock, pp. 22–5.
24. Calhoun, C. (1982) *The Question of Class Struggle*, Blackwell; Campbell, B. (1984) *Wigan Pier Revisited*, Virago; Willis, P. (1977) *Learning to Labour*, Gower; Gilroy, P. (1987) *There Ain't No Black in the Union Jack*, Hutchinson.
25. Clarke, J., Hall, S., Jefferson, T. and Roberts, B. (1976) 'Subcultures, cultures and class', in S. Hall and T. Jefferson (eds) *Resistance Through Rituals*, Hutchinson, pp. 44–5 (emphasis in the original).
26. Kaye, H. (1984) *The British Marxist Historians*, Polity Press, pp. 241–2.
27. Humphries, S. (1981) *Hooligans or Rebels? An Oral History of Working-Class Childhood*, Blackwell, p. 239.
28. Piven, F. F. and Cloward, R. (1979) *Poor People's Movements*, Vintage Books, pp. 20–1.
29. Lukes, S. (ed.) (1986) *Power*, Blackwell; Hunt, A. (1978) *The Sociological Movement in Law*, Macmillan; Collins, H. (1984) *Marxism and Law*, Oxford University Press; Taylor, I., Walton, P. and Young, J. (1973) *The New Criminology*, Routledge & Kegan Paul.
30. Sim, J., Scraton, P. and Gordon, P. (1987) 'Crime, the state and critical analysis', in P. Scraton (ed.) *Law, Order and the Authoritarian State*, Open University Press, pp. 1–70.
31. Garland, D. (1985) 'Politics and policy in criminological discourse: a study in tendentious reasoning and rhetoric', *International Journal of the Sociology of Law*, 13, 1, pp. 1–33.
32. Scraton, P. (1985) 'The state vs. the people: an introduction', in P. Scraton and P. Thomas (eds) *The State vs. The People*, Blackwell, pp. 251–66.
33. Hall, S. *et al.*, op. cit.
34. Gilroy, P., op. cit.
35. Brophy, J. and Smart, C. (eds) (1985) *Women in Law*, Routledge & Kegan Paul.
36. Sykes, G. (1958) *The Society of Captives*, Princeton University Press; Irwin, J. and Cressey, D. (1962) 'Thieves, convicts and the inmate culture', *Social Problems*, 10, pp. 142–55.
37. Cohen, S. and Taylor, L. (1972) *Psychological Survival*, Penguin; Fitzgerald, M., op. cit.; Fitzgerald, M. and Sim, J. (1979) *British Prisons*, Blackwell, 1st edn; Carlen, P. (1983) *Women's Imprisonment*, Routledge & Kegan Paul; Carlen, P. Hicks, J., O'Dwyer, J., Christina, D. and Tchaikovsky, C. (1985) *Criminal Women*, Polity Press; Box, S. (1982) *Power, Crime and Mystification*, Tavistock.
38. Ignatieff, M. (1981) op. cit., p. 78.
39. Cousins, M. and Hussain, A. (1984) *Michel Foucault*, Macmillan, p. 146.
40. Rabinow, P. (ed.) (1984) *The Foucault Reader*, Peregrine, pp. 283–4.

41. Ibid., p. 224.
42. Patton, P., op. cit., p. 121.
43. Foucault, M. (1977) *Discipline and Punish*, Allen Lane, p. 250.
44. Smart, B., op. cit., p. 93.
45. Rabinow, P., op. cit., p. 204.
46. Cousins, M. and Hussain, A., op. cit., p. 151.
47. Rabinow, P., op. cit., p. 224.
48. Smart, B., op. cit., p. 135.

2 THE GENESIS OF THE PRISON MEDICAL SERVICE

1. Philips, D. (1980) 'A new Engine of power and authority: the institutionalisation of law enforcement in England', in V. Gatrell, B. Lenman and G. Parker, (eds) *Crime and the Law*, Europa.
2. McConville, S. (1981) *A History of English Prison Administration Vol. 1 1750–1877*, Routledge & Kegan Paul, pp. 76–7.
3. Ibid., p. 15.
4. Ignatieff, M. (1978) *A Just Measure of Pain*, Macmillan, pp. 60–2.
5. Aikin, J. (1772) *A View of the Character and Public Services of the Late John Howard*, J. Johnson, pp. 79–81 (emphasis in the original).
6. Good, J. M. (1795) *A Dissertation on the Diseases of Prisons and Workhouses*, C. Dilly, pp. 118–19.
7. Ibid., p. 133.
8. Ibid., p. 23.
9. Ibid., p. 26.
10. Ibid., pp. 106–7.
11. Ignatieff, M., op. cit., p. 59.
12. Lettsom, J. (1786) *Memoirs of John Fothergill*, C. Dilly, pp. 126–7.
13. Ibid., p. 128.
14. Ibid., pp. 133–7 (emphasis in the original).
15. Fox, R. Hingston (1919) *John Fothergill and his Friends: Chapters in 18th Century Life*, Macmillan, pp. 105–6.
16. Guy, W. (1882) *John Howard's Winter's Journey*, Thos De La Rue.
17. Ibid., p. 13.
18. McConville, S., op. cit., p. 85.
19. Ignatieff, M., op. cit., p. 100.
20. Ibid., p. 101.
21. Ibid.
22. Cited in Whiting, J. S. (1975) *Prison Reform in Gloucestershire 1776–1820*, Philmore, p. 42.
23. Ibid., pp. 42–3.
24. Ibid., p. 44.
25. McConville, S., op. cit., p. 130.
26. *Rules and Regulations of the General Penitentiary at Millbank*, Ordered by the House of Commons to be printed on 4 March 1817, University of Cambridge, Institute of Criminology Blue Books, pp. 11–12.
27. Ignatieff, M., op. cit., p. 171.
28. Griffiths, A. (1875) *Memorials of Millbank and Chapters in Prison History*, 2 volumes, Henry S. King, 1, p. 197.

29. McConville, S., op. cit., p. 142.
30. *Parliamentary Papers*, Session 1823–4, 10, p. 3, Irish University Press, (hereafter *PP*).
31. *The Lancet*, 1823–4, 1, p. 99.
32. Latham, P. (1825) *An Account of the Diseases Lately Prevalent at the General Penitentiary*, Thomas and George Underwood, p. 14.
33. *PP*, Session 1823–4, 1, p. 11.
34. *Parliamentary Debates*, 1814, 28, Cols 93–5, 116–21, 826–7, 746–7 (hereafter *PD*).
35. Ibid., Cols. 839–42.
36. Ibid., Cols. 258.
37. Ibid., Cols. 483–4.
38. Gurney, J. M. (1819) *Notes on a Visit Made to Some of the Prisons in Scotland and the North of England*, Archibald Constable.
39. Ibid., p. 112.
40. Ibid., pp. 112–13.
41. Cited in Henriques, U. (1979) *Before the Welfare State*, Longman, pp. 160–1.
42. Forbes, T. R. (1977) 'A mortality record for Cold Bath Fields', *Bulletin of New York Academy of Medicine*, 53, 7, pp. 668–9.
43. *PD*, 1816, 33, Col. 545.
44. *The Lancet*, 26 July 1828, p. 534.
45. *The Lancet*, 1828–9, 2, p. 754.
46. Cited in Ward, T. (1984) 'Coroners, police and deaths in custody in England: a historical perspective', in B. Rolston (ed.) *The State of Information in 1984: Working Papers in European Criminology No. 6*, European Group for the Study of Deviance and Social Control, p. 191.
47. *The Lancet*, 1830–1, 2, p. 144.
48. Ibid.
49. Atholl, J. (1953) *Prison on the Moor*, John Long, p. 35.
50. Ibid., p. 36.
51. *Parliamentary Reports*, 1812, 3, p. 145 (hereafter *PR*).
52. Ibid., p. 418.
53. *PD*, 1822, 6, Col. 862.
54. Ibid., Col. 1078.
55. Ibid., Col. 1079.
56. Ibid., Cols. 14–15.
57. Ibid., Col. 15.
58. *First Report of the Inspectors of Prisons*, 1836, p. 90.
59. *Second Report of the Inspectors of Prisons*, 1837, p. 38.
60. Fraser, D. (1973) *The Evolution of the British Welfare State*, Macmillan, pp. 82–3.
61. *The Lancet*, 1836, 2, pp. 338–9.
62. *The Lancet*, 1836–7, 2, p. 169.
63. Ibid.
64. *The Lancet*, 1837–8, 2, p. 779.
65. Ibid., p. 780.
66. Ibid., pp. 780–1.
67. *The Lancet*, 1839–40, 2, p. 530.
68. Ibid., p. 428.
69. *The Lancet*, 1831–2, 2, pp. 505–6.

70. Godfrey, C. (1979) 'The Chartist prisoners 1839–41', *International Review of Social History*, 24, 2, p. 217.
71. Ibid., pp. 217–18.
72. *Seventh Report of the Inspectors of Prisons*, 1842, p. 103.
73. Ibid., p. 137.
74. Priestley, P. (1985) *Victorian Prison Lives*, Methuen, p. 151.
75. Ibid., p. 157.
76. Ibid., p. 162.
77. Ibid., p. 158.
78. *The British and Foreign Medico-Chirurgical Review*, 11, July–October 1848, p. 413.
79. Ibid., p. 415.
80. Ibid., p. 421.
81. *The Lancet*, 1843, 2, p. 390 (emphasis in the original).
82. *The Lancet*, 1858, 2, p. 285.
83. McConville, S., op. cit., p. 398.
84. Ibid.
85. P.R.O. Prison Comm. 2–293 *Governors Journal HM Prison Bedford 1852–59* (Kew Gardens).
86. Ibid.
87. *British Medical Journal*, 5 October 1861, p. 365 (hereafter *BMJ*).
88. Ibid.
89. Ibid.
90. *The Lancet*, 1854, 2, p. 107.
91. Cited in Priestley, P., op. cit., p. 130.
92. Ibid., pp. 211–12.
93. Ibid., p. 213.
94. *The Lancet*, 1855, 2, p. 131.
95. Ibid., p. 132.
96. *The Lancet*, 1842–3, 2, p. 305.
97. *The Lancet*, 1845, 1, p. 275.
98. *Cited in Report of the Inspectors of Millbank Prison for the year 1849* (Blue Book, Institute of Criminology, Cambridge) p. 12.
99. Ibid.
100. Baly, W. (1845) 'On the mortality in prisons and the diseases most frequently fated to prisoners', *Medico-Chirurgical Transactions*, 28, Longman, Brown, Green and Longman, p. 234.
101. Ibid.
102. *Further Papers with Reference to the Inquiry Respecting the Treatment of Prisoners in the House of Correction Knutsford 1843* (Blue Book, Institute of Criminology, Cambridge) p. 5.
103. *P.R.O. P. Com. 2354 Portland Governors' Journal*, 24 November 1848 to 9 August 1851 (Kew Gardens).
104. Priestley, P., op. cit., p. 188.
105. Ibid., p. 190.
106. *P.R.O. P. Com. 2165* (Kew Gardens).
107. Priestley, P., op. cit., p. 188.
108. Ibid., p. 190 (emphasis in the original).
109. Pellow, J. (1982) *The Home Office 1848–1914: From Clerks to Bureaucrats*, Heinemann, pp. 132–3.

110. Davis, J. (1980) 'The London garotting panic of 1862; a moral panic and the creation of a criminal class in mid-Victorian England', in V. Gatrell *et al.*, op. cit., pp. 190–213.
111. Tomlinson, M. H. (1981) 'Penal servitude 1846–1865: a system in evolution', in V. Bailey (ed.) *Policing and Punishment in Nineteenth Century Britain*, Croom-Helm, p. 141.
112. *Observations in Parliamentary Debates* 26 Vic 1863, Third Series, 169, Cols 475–93 (Home Office Library).
113. Ibid., Col. 478.
114. *British Parliamentary Papers*, 1863, 6, Select Committee on Prison Discipline, Irish University Press, p. 208.
115. McConville, S., op. cit., p. 418.
116. There are various documents in the Wellcome Institute for the History of Medicine relating to William Guy. See *Aberdeen M-Cs Tracts 8TP 44 A 25; Wellcome Institute T. 508; A Third Contribution to a Knowledge of the Influence of Employment upon Health.*
117. McConville, S., op. cit., p. 357.
118. Ibid., p. 418.
119. Ibid.
120. Guy, W. (1863) 'On sufficient and insufficient dietaries with especial reference to the dietaries of prisoners', *Journal of the Statistical Society*, 26, 3, p. 280.
121. Cited in Priestley, P., op. cit., p. 156.
122. Ibid.
123. *P.R.O. H.O.45 9450/69228* 1877–8 (Kew Gardens).
124. *The Lancet*, 16 July 1864, p. 77.
125. Ibid.
126. Ibid.
127. *BMJ*, 5 September 1863, p. 266.
128. *BMJ*, 14 July 1866, p. 45.
129. *BMJ*, 7 March 1868, p. 223.
130. Ibid.
131. *The Lancet*, 4 April 1868, p. 446.
132. Tomlinson, M. H., op. cit., p. 143.
133. Ibid.
134. Priestley, P., op. cit., p. 164.
135. Ibid., p. 165.
136. *Association Medical Journal*, 16 February 1856, p. 133.
137. Ibid.
138. *Report of the Directors of Convict Prisons for the Year 1857*, Eyre & Spottiswoode (Home Office Library) pp. 30–7.
139. Ibid.
140. Cited in Tomlinson, M. H., op. cit., p. 133.
141. Cited in Priestley, P., op. cit., p. 208 (emphasis in the original).
142. Ibid. (emphasis in the original).
143. Ibid., p. 210.
144. McConville, S., op. cit., p. 440; Report of the Directors of Convict Prisons 1863–66, *Return of Prisoners who have Received Punishment in Millbank Prison in the year 1863*, Eyre & Spottiswoode (Home Office Library).
145. Ibid., *Governor's Report for Dartmoor*, pp. 155–61.

3 CONSOLIDATION AND RESISTANCE 1865–1945

1. Ignatieff, M. (1978) *A Just Measure of Pain*, Macmillan, p. 219.
2. Smith, R. (1981) *Trial by Medicine*, Edinburgh University Press, p. 21.
3. Saunders, J. (1981) 'Magistrates and madmen: segregating the criminally insane in late nineteenth century Warwickshire', in V. Bailey (ed.) *Prisons and Punishment in Nineteenth Century Britain*, Croom Helm, p. 223.
4. Ibid., pp. 223–4. These views were also extended to the question of race and the constitutional inferiority of the people of other lands. As D. A. Lorimar points out, 'by the 1860s many educated mid-Victorians had rejected all hope of alien peoples assimilating English ways, and even doubted if savages, including Africans, could survive the advances of white civilisation': Lorimar, D. A. (1975) *Colour, Class and the Victorians*, Leicester University Press, p. 147.
5. Cited in McConville, S. (1981) *A History of English Prison Administration Vol. 1 1750–1877*, Routledge & Kegan Paul, p. 328.
6. Ibid., pp. 328–9 (emphasis in the original).
7. *BMJ*, 2 December 1871, p. 645.
8. *P.R.O. H.O. 45/9371 382 63* (Kew Gardens).
9. Quinton, R. F. (1910) *Crime and Criminals*, Longman Green, p. 56.
10. Ibid., p. 27.
11. *The Lancet*, 8 February 1873, p. 221.
12. Priestley, P. (1985) *Victorian Prison Lives*, Methuen, p. 129.
13. Cited in Griffiths, A. (1875) *Memorials of Millbank and Chapters in Prison History*, 2 vols, Henry S. King, 1, p. 196.
14. *P.R.O. P. Com. 7351* (Kew Gardens).
15. *The Lancet*, 14 December 1878, p. 859.
16. Ibid. The Justices at Dorchester Prison made a similar complaint in January 1880 about the lack of consultation by the Home Office concerning events in the prison: see *P.R.O. H.O. 144 53 8990 (1879080)* (Kew Gardens).
17. *The Lancet*, 9 August 1879, pp. 209–10.
18. *The Lancet*, 17 January 1880, p. 104.
19. Ibid., p. 105.
20. *BMJ*, 6 October 1866, p. 388.
21. *The Lancet*, 1888, 2, p. 740.
22. *The Lancet*, 1889, 2, p. 1320.
23. Quinton, R. F., op. cit., p. 62.
24. Ibid., p. 256.
25. Merchant, A. (1869) *Six Years in the Convict Prisons of England*, Richard Bentley, p. 46.
26. Ibid., p. 50.
27. Ibid., p. 52.
28. One Who Has Endured It (1877) *Five Years' Penal Servitude*, Richard Bentley.
29. One Who Has Tried Them (1881) *Her Majesty's Prisons, Their Effects and Defects*, 2, Sampson Low, Marston, Searle & Revington.
30. Ibid., pp. 104–5.
31. Ibid., pp. 117–18.
32. Cited in Priestley, P., op. cit., p. 205.
33. *The Lancet*, 10 February 1866, p. 152.
34. *BMJ*, 2 February 1878, pp. 163–4; 6 April 1878, pp. 494–5.
35. *BMJ*, 29 June 1878, p. 936.

36. Quinton, R. F., op. cit., pp. 188–9.
37. *BMJ*, 8 April, 22 April, 27 May, 17 June 1871.
38. *The Lancet*, 6 September 1879, p. 272.
39. *Copy of the Report Made and Evidence Taken by the Commissioner Appointed to Inquire into the Circumstances of the Death of John Nolan in Clerkenwell Prison*, Home Office, 25 February 1879. Matthew White Ridley, p. 3.
40. Press report of the case in *P.R.O. H.O. 45 9471 79161* (Kew Gardens).
41. 'Copy of the Depositions taken before the Coroner at the Inquest on the body of John Nolan', in *Copy of the Report Made*, op. cit., pp. 3–4.
42. Ibid., p. 12.
43. Ibid., p. 36.
44. *The Lancet*, 1879, 2, p. 823.
45. *The Lancet*, 7 February 1880, p. 222.
46. Ibid., p. 223.
47. *The Lancet*, 10 July 1880, p. 62.
48. *The Lancet*, 31 July 1880, p. 182.
49. Ibid.
50. *The Lancet*, 18 June 1881, p. 1003.
51. *The Lancet*, 17 December 1881, p. 1058.
52. *The Lancet*, 21 January 1882, p. 120.
53. *The Lancet*, 15 April 1882, p. 616.
54. *The Lancet*, 29 April 1882, pp. 698–9.
55. *BMJ*, 29 April 1882, p. 587.
56. *BMJ*, 6 May 1882, p. 680.
57. Ibid.
58. *The Lancet*, 20 May 1882, p. 834.
59. *The Lancet*, 10 June 1882, p. 968.
60. *The Lancet*, 17 June 1882, p. 996.
61. *The Lancet*, 24 June 1882, p. 1047.
62. *The Lancet*, 2 December 1882, p. 952.
63. *The Lancet*, 12 March 1887, p. 530.
64. *BMJ*, 7 March 1885.
65. *The Lancet*, 9 March 1895, p. 626.
66. Ibid., p. 634.
67. *The Lancet*, 16 March 1895, p. 708.
68. *The Lancet*, 30 March 1895, p. 839. Serious questions were also being raised about the state of medical care in Duke Street Prison, Glasgow. See *The Lancet*, 1 July 1899, p. 64.
69. *BMJ*, 23 December 1893, p. 1398.
70. Smith, R., op. cit., p. 32.
71. Doyal, L. and Pennell, I. (1979) *The Political Economy of Health*, Pluto, p. 148.
72. R. M. Young, cited in ibid.
73. Rose, S., Kamin, L. and Lewontin, R. (1984) *Not in our Genes*, Penguin, p. 55.
74. Ibid., pp. 50–1.
75. McGrath, R. (1984) 'Medical police', *Ten 8: Quarterly Photographic Journal*, 14, pp. 14–15.
76. Currie, E. P. (no date) *Managing the Minds of Men: The Reformatory Movement 1865–1920*, unpublished Ph.D. Dissertation Department of Sociology University of California, Berkeley, p. 263.
77. Garland, D. (1985) *Punishment and Welfare*, Gower, p. 236.

78. *BMJ*, 31 March 1888, p. 707.
79. Garland, D. (1981) 'The birth of the welfare sanction', *British Journal of Law and Society*, 8, 1, 38.
80. *Medical Times and Gazette*, 17 October 1885, pp. 550–1.
81. *The Lancet*, 8 May 1886, p. 891.
82. *The Lancet*, 9 February 1889, pp. 281–2.
83. Ibid.
84. Garland, D. (1985) op. cit., p. 148.
85. *The Lancet*, 25 January 1890, p. 189.
86. *The Lancet*, 8 February 1890, p. 305.
87. *The Lancet*, 31 May 1890, p. 1173.
88. *The Lancet*, 18 January 1873, p. 102.
89. Ibid.
90. *The Lancet*, 5 June 1875, p. 298.
91. *The Lancet*, 11 March 1876, p. 400.
92. Ibid.
93. *The Lancet*, 7 July 1877, p. 18.
94. *The Lancet*, 21 April 1877, p. 579.
95. *The Lancet*, 8 December 1888, p. 1142.
96. *The Lancet*, 17 August 1889, p. 321.
97. Cited in Watson, S. (1988) *The Moral Imbecile: A Study of the Relations Between Penal Practice and Psychiatric Knowledge of the Habitual Offender*, a dissertation submitted in partial fulfilment of the degree of Ph.D., University of Lancaster, p. 135.
98. Quinton, R. F., op. cit., p. xi.
99. Ibid., pp. 203–28.
100. Jones, G. Stedman (1971) *Outcast London*, Clarendon Press.
101. Quinton, R. F., op. cit., pp. 99–100.
102. Ibid., pp. 18–19.
103. Ibid., p. 15.
104. Ibid., pp. 12–13.
105. Ibid., pp. 21–7.
106. Ibid., pp. 225–7.
107. Campbell, J. (1884) *Thirty Years Experience of a Medical Officer in the English Convict Service*, Nelson & Sons, pp. 130–3.
108. Ibid., pp. 73–4.
109. Ibid., pp. 128–9.
110. *The Lancet*, 4 October 1890, p. 737.
111. *The Lancet*, 1892, 2, pp. 370–1.
112. Morel, J. (1892) 'The psychological examination of prisoners', *Journal of Mental Science*, 39, pp. 13–14.
113. Ibid., p. 15.
114. *The Lancet*, 14 October 1893, p. 940.
115. *The Lancet*, 24 February 1894, p. 487.
116. *The Lancet*, 15 July 1893, p. 146.
117. Ibid., p. 147.
118. *The Lancet*, 19 November 1898, p. 1342.
119. *The Lancet*, 13 March 1897, p. 751.
120. Garland, D. (1988) 'British criminology before 1935', in Rock, P. (ed.) *A History of British Criminology: British Journal of Criminology*, 28, 2, pp. 4–5.

121. *The Lancet*, 12 October 1895, p. 911.
122. The latest in this line is Stern, V. (1987) *Bricks of Shame*, Penguin, p. 60.
123. Young, P. (1983) 'Sociology, the state and penal relations', in D. Garland and P. Young (eds) *The Power to Punish*, Heinemann, p. 97.
124. Gatrell, V. (1980) 'The decline of theft and violence in Victorian and Edwardian England', in V. Gatrell *et. al.* (eds) op. cit., p. 83.
125. *The Lancet*, 11 September 1897, p. 669.
126. *Statement By the Prison Commissioners of the Action which has been taken up to January 1898 to carry out the Recommendations in the Report of the Departmental Committee on Prisons, 1895*, HMSO Blue Book, Institute of Criminology, Cambridge, p. 29.
127. *The Lancet*, 19 March 1898, p. 799.
128. Ibid.
129. Ibid.
130. Cited in Turner, E. S. (1958) *Call the Doctor: A Social History of Medical Men*, Michael Joseph, p. 214.
131. Garland, D. (1988) op. cit., pp. 4–5.
132. Ibid., p. 5.
133. Watson, S., op. cit., p. 132.
134. Ibid.
135. *The Lancet*, 1907, 2, p. 268.
136. Watson, S. op. cit., pp. 258–9.
137. Ibid., pp. 95–6.
138. Ibid., p. 132.
139. Ibid., p. 133.
140. Ibid., p. 157.
141. *P.R.O. Prison Com. 7 326 1922* (Kew Gardens).
142. Watson, S., op. cit., p. 145.
143. Ibid.
144. Smith, M. Hamblin (1934) *Prisons*, John Lane, The Bodley Head, pp. 130–9.
145. Ibid., p. 143.
146. Ibid., p. 146.
147. See recommendations 46 and 47 of the House of Commons *Third Report from the Social Services Committee Session 1985–86*, Prison Medical Service, 1, 25 June 1986, p. 63.
148. *P.R.O. H.O. 45 1110 34 A53933 Document 10* (Kew Gardens).
149. Ibid.
150. Ibid.
151. Ibid.
152. Ibid., File 26.
153. Ibid.
154. Ibid., File 29.
155. *P.R.O. H.O. 45 18366 122929/7*, Letter 10 December 1904 (Kew Gardens).
156. Ibid.
157. Ibid.
158. *The Lancet*, 25 November 1905, p. 1556.
159. Simmons, H. (1978) 'Explaining social policy: the English Mental Deficiency Act of 1913', *Journal of Social History*, 11, p. 391.
160. Garland, D. (1985) op. cit., p. 223.
161. Ibid., p. 224.

162. Ibid., p. 225.
163. *The Lancet*, 25 November 1925, p. 1557.
164. *The Lancet*, 17 October 1908, p. 1156.
165. Mort, F. (1987) *Dangerous Sexualities*, Routledge & Kegan Paul, pp. 171–2.
166. Garland, D. (1985) op. cit., pp. 153–4 (emphasis in the original).
167. Hobhouse, S. and Brockway, F. (1922) *English Prisons Today*, Longman, p. 261.
168. Ibid., p. 290.
169. Ibid.
170. Ibid., p. 291. The state, however, still made distinctions in the punishment for British and foreign prisoners. In August 1917 it was recommended that figure-of-eight handcuffs should be discontinued in British prisons but that colonial governments should retain them as 'negroes, in particular, are apt to be of great muscular power and a very passionate temperament', *P.R.O. H.O. 18366 122929/14* August 1917 (Kew Gardens).
171. Macartney, W. C. (1936) *Walls Have Mouths*, Victor Gollancz, p. 292.
172. Ibid., p. 165.
173. Ibid., pp. 165–6.
174. Ibid., p. 103.
175. Ibid., pp. 123–4.
176. Ibid., pp. 312–13.
177. Red Collar Man (1937) *Chokey*, Victor Gollancz, p. 122.
178. Ibid., p. 155.
179. Ibid., pp. 116–17.
180. Ibid., p. 69.
181. Ibid., pp. 69–70.
182. Clayton, G. F. (1958) *The Wall is Strong*, John Long, p. 164.
183. Ibid., pp. 164–5.
184. Prison Medical Reform Council (1943a) *Prison Medical Service*, PMRC, p. 14.
185. Ibid, pp. 14–15.
186. Prison Medical Reform Council (1943b) *Prisoners' Circle*, PMRC, p. 32.
187. Prison Medical Reform Council (1943a) op. cit., pp. 3–4.
188. Ibid., p. 13.
189. Prison Medical Reform Council (1943c) *Prison For Women: Some Accounts of Life in Holloway*, PMRC, pp. 21–2.
190. Prison Medical Reform Council (1944) *Prisoners Medical Charter*, PMRC, p. 3.
191. Prison Medical Reform Council (1945) *The Case of Prisoner Alpha*, PMRC, p. 4.
192. Ibid., p. 10.

4 DISCIPLINING THE BODY, RECONSTRUCTING THE MIND: MEDICAL POWER AND THE CRIMINAL 1945–64

1. Lloyd, R. and Williamson, S. (1968) *Born to Trouble*, Cassirer, pp. 72–3.
2. Carlen, P. (1986) 'Psychiatry in prisons: promises, premises, practices and politics', in P. Miller and N. Rose (eds) *The Power of Psychiatry*, Polity Press, pp. 265–6.
3. Gilroy, P. (1987) *There Ain't No Black in the Union Jack*, Hutchinson.
4. *Report of the Commissioners of Prisons and Directors of Convict Prisons 1945*, p. 51 (hereafter *RCPDCP*).
5. Fox, L. (1952) *The English Prison and Borstal Systems*, Routledge & Kegan Paul, pp. 154–5; p. 239.

6. Ibid.
7. Ibid., p. 241.
8. Ibid., p. 242.
9. *RCPDCP*, 1945, p. 52.
10. *RCPDCP*, 1947, p. 61.
11. *RCPDCP*, 1949, p. 67.
12. Ibid., p. 68.
13. *BMJ*, 8 September 1951, p. 594.
14. Cited in Elkin, W. (1957) *The English Penal System*, Penguin, p. 18.
15. *Hansard*, 7 February 1946, Cols 1859–60.
16. Home Office Notice 141/1946 *The New Post of Medical Advisor to the Home Office*.
17. Ibid.
18. *The Times*, 3 January 1951.
19. *BMJ*, 16 February 1963, p. 484.
20. Home Office (1950) *Prisons and Borstals*, HMSO, p. 11 (emphasis in the original).
21. Ibid.
22. *BMJ*, 22 November 1947.
23. Gunn, J., Robertson, G., Dell, S. and Way, C. (1978) *Medical Aspects of Imprisonment*, Academic Press, p. 24.
24. Ibid.
25. *RCPDCP*, 1949, p. 69.
26. Ibid.
27. Ibid.
28. *The Times*, 23 October 1953.
29. *RCPDCP*, 1949, p. 120.
30. Ibid.
31. *RCPDCP*, 1950, p. 78.
32. Ibid., p. 113.
33. *The Times*, 10 October 1953.
34. Ibid.
35. *BMJ*, 24 April 1954, p. 981.
36. Ibid.
37. Ibid.
38. Report of the Commissioners of Prisons, 1952, pp. 106–7 (hereafter *RCP*).
39. Ibid., p. 107.
40. *The Lancet*, 5 December 1953, pp. 126–7.
41. *RCP*, 1956, p. 1.
42. Ibid.
43. *RCP*, 1957, p. 2.
44. *RCP*, 1958, p. 2.
45. *The Lancet*, 27 July 1957, p. 200.
46. *BMJ*, 8 November 1958, p. 1154.
47. Ibid.
48. Ibid., p. 1169.
49. *BMJ*, 12 August 1961, p. 436.
50. Ibid., p. 437.
51. Ibid.
52. Ibid.
53. Ibid.

54. *RCP*, 1951, pp. 90–3.
55. *RCP*, 1952, p. 146.
56. *RCP*, 1954, p. 141.
57. *RCP*, 1956, p. 115.
58. Ibid.
59. *RCP*, 1955, p. 148.
60. *RCP*, 1957, p. 24.
61. Snell, H. (1959) 'The Prison Medical Service', *Howard Journal*, 10, 2, pp. 84–5.
62. *RCPDCP*, 1949, p. 122.
63. Ibid.
64. Ibid., p. 92.
65. *RCPDCP*, 1945, p. 52.
66. 'Psychiatry in prisons and corrective institutions', *Proceedings of the Royal Society of Medicine*, 1954, 47, p. 223.
67. Ibid., p. 224.
68. Parker, T. and Allerton, R. (1962) *The Courage of his Convictions*, Hutchinson, pp. 138–9.
69. Calder, W. (1955) 'The sexual offender: a prison medical officer's viewpoint', *British Journal of Delinquency*, July, pp. 28–30.
70. Ibid., pp. 32–9.
71. *RCP*, 1953, p. 139.
72. Wildeblood, P. (1955) *Against the Law*, Penguin, pp. 103–4.
73. Showalter, E. (1987) *The Female Malady*, Virago, pp. 205–6.
74. Ibid., pp. 206–7.
75. *RCP*, 1960, p. 74.
76. Showalter, E., op. cit., p. 253.
77. Ibid., p. 209.
78. Ibid.
79. Ibid., p. 210.
80. Lloyd, R. and Williamson, S., op. cit., p. 144.
81. Ibid., p. 145.
82. Ibid., pp. 145–6.
83. Probyn, W. (1977) *Angel Face: The Making of a Criminal*, Allen & Unwin, p. 43.
84. Ibid., p. 53.
85. Lloyd, R. and Williamson, S., op. cit., p. 82.
86. Probyn, W., op. cit., p. 53.
87. *RCP*, 1958, p. 140.
88. Ibid.
89. *RCP*, 1959, p. 143.
90. Ibid., p. 141.
91. *RCP*, 1958, p. 103.
92. Ibid., p. 138.
93. *RCP*, 1962, p. 86.
94. *The Lancet*, 23 December 1961, p. 1409.
95. *RCP*, 1954, p. 137.
96. Ibid.
97. *RCP*, 1955, p. 149.
98. Ibid.
99. *RCP*, 1956, p. 166.
100. *RCP*, 1959, p. 24.

101. Ibid.
102. *RCP*, 1957, p. 32.
103. Vick, G. R. (1958) *Allegations of Ill Treatment of Prisoners in HM Prison Liverpool*, HMSO, p. 13.
104. Morris, T., Morris, P. and Bìely, B. (1961) *Unpublished Report on the Prison Community Research Project 1958–61*, HM Prison Service Staff College Library, Wakefield, p. 18.
105. *The Lancet*, 31 July 1948, p. 191.
106. Baker, P. (1962) *Time Out of Life*, Quality Book Club, pp. 130–52.
107. Ibid., p. 131.
108. Ibid., p. 138.
109. Prison Reform Council (1962) *Inside Story*, Prison Reform Council, p. 6.
110. Ibid., p. 8.
111. *The Lancet*, 4 August 1945, pp. 145–6.
112. *The Lancet*, 8 February 1947, p. 219.
113. *The Lancet*, 31 January 1948, p. 197.
114. Taken from *RCP*, 1956–60.
115. *RCP*, 1952, p. 102.
116. *RCP*, 1958, p. 95.
117. *RCP*, 1951, p. 82.
118. *RCP*, 1954, p. 99.
119. Ibid., p. 140.
120. *RCP*, 1961, p. 58.
121. Cited in *The Lancet*, 15 October 1955, pp. 830–1.
122. *The Lancet*, 28 April 1956, p. 574.
123. Ibid.
124. *The Lancet*, 29 May 1954, p. 1136.
125. *The Lancet*, 16 March 1957, p. 583.
126. *The Lancet*, 31 December 1960, p. 1455.
127. *The Lancet*, 11 February 1961, p. 346.
128. *BMJ*, 13 May 1961, p. 1393.
129. *The Lancet*, 16 February 1963, p. 396.
130. *Daily Telegraph*, 19 February 1959.
131. *The Lancet*, 4 April 1959, p. 734.
132. Ibid.
133. *The Lancet*, 23 May 1959, p. 1100.
134. Ibid.
135. *The Lancet*, 7 October 1961, p. 810.
136. Ibid.
137. Ibid., p. 810–11.
138. *The Lancet*, 11 November 1961, p. 1097.
139. *The Lancet*, 9 December 1961, p. 1309.
140. *The Lancet*, 23 December 1961, p. 1409.
141. *The Lancet*, 7 April 1962, p. 745.
142. *The Lancet*, 1 September 1962, p. 440.
143. *RCP*, 1961, p. 86.
144. *RCP*, 1962, p. 73.
145. *RCP*, 1961, p. 18.
146. Ibid., p. 20.
147. *RCP*, 1961, p. 13.

148. *RCP*, 1960, p. 15.
149. *RCP*, 1962, p. 12.
150. *BMJ*, 17 November 1962, p. 1337.
151. *The Lancet*, 16 February 1963.
152. Corrigan, P. and Sayer, D. (1985) *The Great Arch*, Blackwell, p. 197.
153. Ibid., p. 6; Sim, J. (1986) 'Watching the prison wheel grind: the 1985 Report of HM Chief Inspector of Prisons', *The Abolitionist*, 21 (1986)1 p. 8.
154. The Medical Directory (1972) *128th Annual Issue Part 1*, Churchill Livingstone, p. 1145.
155. The Medical Directory (1972) *128th Annual Issue Part 2*, Churchill Livingstone, p. 2283.
156. *Report of the Work of the Prison Department 1964*, pp. 2–3 (hereafter *RWPD*).
157. *BMJ*, 2 May 1964, p. 1134.
158. *The Lancet*, 2 May 1964, p. 968.

5 MEDICINE AND REGULATION: FROM THE 1960s TO THE 1980s

1. Jones, H. (1965) *Crime in a Changing Society*, Penguin, pp. 116–17.
2. Ryan, M. (1983) *The Politics of Penal Reform*, Longman, p. 35.
3. Fitzgerald, M. and Sim, J. (1982) *British Prisons*, Blackwell; Wright, M. (1982) *Making Good*, Burnett Books.
4. Cohen, S. and Taylor, L. (1981) *Psychological Survival*, 2nd edn, Penguin, p. 10.
5. King, R. (1985) 'Control in Prisons', in M. Maguire, J. Vagg and R. Morgan (eds) *Accountability and Prisons*, Tavistock, p. 191.
6. Sinn Fein (1980) *Irish Political Prisoners in England*, Sinn Fein, p. 11.
7. *Guardian*, 17 November 1986.
8. Greater London Council Women's Committee (1986) *Breaking the Silence*, London Strategic Policy Unit, p. 165.
9. *Hansard*, 1 February 1980, Cols 821–2.
10. Prison Reform Trust (1984) *Parliamentary All-Party Penal Affairs Group: Working Party on Life Sentence Prisoners*, Submission by the Prison Reform Trust, p. 3.
11. *BBC Radio 4 News*, 19 November 1987.
12. Fitzgerald, M. and Sim, J. op. cit.
13. King, R. and Morgan, R. (1980) *The Future of the Prison System*, Gower, p. 79.
14. Home Office (1984) *Managing the Long-Term Prison System*, HMSO, Annex D.
15. Fitzgerald, M. and Sim, J., op. cit.
16. King, R., op. cit., p. 191.
17. *Draft Memorandum Submitted by Prison Medical Officers to the Royal Commission on the Prison System*, HM Prison Service Staff College Library, Wakefield, p. 4.
18. *The Times*, 20 May 1970.
19. Home Office (1969) *People in Prison: England and Wales*, HMSO, p. 22.
20. Miller, A., op. cit., p. 103.
21. Fitzgerald, M. (1977) *Prisoners in Revolt*, Penguin.
22. Williams, J. E. Hall (1975) *Changing Prisons*, Peter Owen, pp. 119–20.
23. Ibid.
24. Leigh, D. (1980) *The Frontiers of Secrecy*, Junction, p. 121.
25. Ibid.

26. Birkinshaw, P. (1981) 'The control unit regime: law and order in prisons', *Howard Journal* 20, p. 70.
27. Notes from Documents in HM Prison Service Staff College Library, Wakefield.
28. Coggan, G. and Walker, M. (1982) *Frightened for my Life*, Fontana, pp. 137–40.
29. Ryan, M., op. cit., p. 49.
30. Sinn Fein, op. cit., p. 73.
31. MacLaughlin, R. (1987) *Inside an English Jail*, Borderline, p. 87.
32. Cited in Ryan, M., op. cit., p. 58.
33. Thomas, J. E. and Pooley, R. (1980) *The Exploding Prison*, Junction, pp. 104–5.
34. See ibid., pp. 98–118.
35. Thomas, J. E. and Pooley, R., op. cit., p. 107.
36. Alexander, J. (1984) *A Review of Protective Equipment for the Prison Service*, HM Prison Library Wakefield, p. 1.
37. *The Abolitionist*, 1982, 11, p. 5.
38. Ibid.
39. Ibid., p. 6 (emphasis in the original).
40. *World in Action* (1982) *Prisoners' Medicine*, 19 July 1982, 568/603, p. 4.
41. Ibid., p. 5.
42. Ibid., p. 11.
43. Owen, T. and Sim, J. (1984) 'Drugs, discipline and prison medicine: the case of George Wilkinson', in P. Scraton and P. Gordon (eds) *Causes for Concern*, Penguin, p. 243.
44. Read, P. P. (1978) *The Train Robbers*, W. H. Allen, p. 214.
45. Probyn, W. (1977) *Angel Face*, Allen & Unwin, pp. 108–9.
46. Miller, A., op. cit., pp. 132–3.
47. Keeley, F. (1979) 'The Home Office and the liquid cosh', *The Abolitionist*, January 1979, p. 5.
48. Fitzgerald, M. and Sim, J., op. cit., pp. 118–19.
49. Ibid.
50. *Guardian*, 7 December 1979.
51. *Weekly Hansard*, Issue 1156, 14–17 January 1980, Col. 559.
52. *Hansard*, 21 January 1980, Cols 15–16.
53. *Hansard*, 18–24 July 1980, 1181, Col. 131.
54. *Probe*, May 1979, p. 8.
55. 'Unpleasant but not painful: medical treatment of sex offenders', *The Abolitionist*, 1981, 9, p. 20.
56. Owen, T. (1980) *The Use of Behaviour Modifying Drugs in British Prisons: An Analysis of the Medical Statistics Published in the 1979 Report on the Work of the Prison Department*, RAP Briefing, p. 4.
57. Ibid., p. 5.
58. Ibid.
59. Ibid., p. 6.
60. Ibid., p. 8.
61. *Daily Mirror*, 8 December 1982.
62. *Guardian*, 1 August 1980.
63. *Guardian*, 28 February 1986.
64. *Guardian*, 10 October 1984.
65. Cited in Shaw, S. (1985) 'Introduction: the case for change in the Prison Medical Service', in Prison Reform Trust *Prison Medicine: Ideas on Health Care in Penal Establishments*, Prison Reform Trust, p. 5.

66. *Hansard*, 5 July 1984, Col. 224.
67. *Hansard*, 23 July 1984, Cols. 402–3.
68. *The Times*, 23 March 1984.
69. Whitehead, T. (1985) 'The use of psychotropic drugs in prison', in Prison Reform Trust, op. cit., p. 81.
70. *Insiders*, 28 January 1986.
71. Sim, J., Scraton, P. and Gordon, P. (1987) 'Crime, the State and Critical Analysis' in P. Scraton (ed.) *Law, Order and the Authoritarian State*, Open University Press, p. 14.
72. *Guardian*, 16 April 1981.
73. *Coroner's Court Birmingham. Notes of Evidence in the Inquest on Barry Prosser before Dr Richard Michael Whittington, H.M. Coroner*, 7 April 1981, p. 147 (hereafter *CCB*).
74. Ibid., pp. 146–9.
75. Ibid., pp. 306–7.
76. Ibid., p. 307.
77. Ibid., p. 308.
78. Ibid.
79. *Hansard*, 24 February 1989, Cols 835–9.
80. *Inquest Bulletin* 11, p. 1.
81. Ibid.
82. *Guardian*, 28 June 1988.
83. *Guardian*, 1 July 1988.
84. *Liverpool Daily Post*, 1 July 1988.
85. *Independent*, 1 July 1988.
86. Ibid.
87. *Guardian*, 11 May 1988.
88. *Observer*, 28 May 1989.
89. *Independent*, 30 September 1989.
90. Ibid.
91. *Sunday Correspondent*, 22 October 1989.
92. *Sunday Correspondent*, 29 October 1989.
93. *Guardian*, 2 December 1989.
94. Fitzgerald, M. and Sim, J., op. cit.
95. Royal College of Psychiatrists (1979) 'The college's evidence to the prison services inquiry', *Bulletin of the Royal College of Psychiatrists*, May 1979, p. 83.
96. *Howard Journal*, 18, 3, p. 132.
97. *Guardian*, 31 March 1982.
98. *Observer*, 16 October 1983.
99. *Guardian*, 19 August 1985.
100. House of Commons Social Services Committee, 1, op. cit., para. 2.
101. Ibid., para. 5.
102. Ibid., para. 8.
103. Ibid., para. 11.
104. Ibid., para. 12.
105. House of Commons, *Third Report from the Social Services Committee Session 1985–86*, Prison Medical Service, 2, Minutes of Evidence and Appendices, p. 83.
106. Ibid., p. 84.
107. Ibid., p. 83.
108. House of Commons Social Services Committee, 1, op. cit., para. 13.

109. Ibid., para. 16.
110. Ibid.
111. Prison Reform Trust (1985) *House of Commons Social Services Committee: Inquiry into the Prison Medical Services, Submission by the Prison Reform Trust,* July 1985, p. 19.
112. House of Commons Social Services Committee, 2, op. cit., pp. 82–3.
113. Ibid., p. 62.
114. House of Commons Social Services Committee, 1, op. cit., para. 129.
115. *The Government's Reply to the Third Report from the Social Services Committee Session 1985–86,* Prison Medical Service, HMSO.
116. Ibid., pp. 2–4.
117. Ibid., p. 4.
118. Shaw, C. (1987) 'Prison Medicine', *Open Mind,* 26, April/May, p. 15.
119. *Guardian,* 27 February 1988.
120. *Guardian,* 6 May 1988.
121. *Guardian,* 3 May 1988.
122. Ibid.
123. See the overviews by Gordon, P. (1983) *Whitelaw,* Pluto; Scraton, P. (1985) *The State of the Police,* Pluto; Sivanandan, A. (1982) *A Different Hunger,* Pluto.
124. *Guardian,* 19 June 1986.
125. Greater London Council Ethnic Minorities Unit Policy Report (1985) *Local Authorities and Penal Establishments: A Race Dimension,* GLC, pp. 9–17.
126. *Guardian,* 13 June 1988.
127. Ibid.
128. Black Health Workers and Patients Group (1983) 'Psychiatry and the corporate state', *Race and Class,* 25, autumn, pp. 60–1.
129. Ibid., p. 60.
130. Ibid., p. 50.
131. *Observer,* 1 November 1987; *Independent,* 10 November 1987.
132. *Guardian,* 30 September 1987.
133. Ibid.
134. McGovern, D. and Cope, R. (1987) 'The compulsory detention of males of different ethnic groups with special reference to offender patients', *British Journal of Psychiatry* 150, pp. 505–12.
135. Cited in Benn, M. (1983) 'Women in prison: breaking the silence', *Spare Rib* 137, December, pp. 52–3.
136. *Guardian,* 30 March 1988.
137. Rutherford, A. (1983) *Prisons and the Process of Justice,* Heinemann.
138. Box, S. and Hale, C. (1982) 'Economic crisis and the rising prisoner population in England and Wales', *Crime and Social Justice,* 17, September, pp. 20–35.
139. Box, S. (1983) *Power, Crime and Mystification,* Tavistock, p. 22.
140. Poulantzas, N. (1978) *State Power Socialism,* New Left Books; Hall, S. (1985) 'Authoritarian Populism: a reply to Jessop *et al.*', *New Left Review* May/June, pp. 115–24; Hillyard, P. (1983) 'Law and Order', in J. Darby (ed.) *Northern Ireland: Background to Conflict,* Appletree Press, pp. 32–60; Centre for Contemporary Cultural Studies (1982) *The Empire Strikes Back,* Hutchinson.
141. Sim, J. (1987) 'Working for the clampdown: prisons and politics in England and Wales' in P. Scraton op. cit., pp. 190–211.
142. Ignatieff, M. op. cit., p. 220.

6 AT THE CENTRE OF THE PROFESSIONAL GAZE: WOMEN, MEDICINE AND CONFINEMENT

1. *The Times*, 11 July 1966.
2. Carlen, P. and Worrall, A. (1987) 'Introduction: gender, crime and justice', in P. Carlen and A. Worrall (eds) *Gender, Crime and Justice*, Open University Press, p. 2.
3. Ibid., pp. 3–4.
4. Allen, H. (1987) *Justice Unbalanced*, Open University Press, pp. 111–12.
5. Edwards, S. (1984) *Women on Trial*, Manchester University Press, p. 82.
6. Ignatieff, M. (1978) *A Just Measure of Pain*, Macmillan, p. 144.
7. Rose, J. (1980) *Elizabeth Fry*, Macmillan, p. 84.
8. Ibid., pp. 134–5.
9. Dobash, R., Dobash, R. E. and Gutteridge, S. (1986) *The Imprisonment of Women*, Blackwell, p. 79.
10. Ibid.
11. Cited in Whiting, J. (1975) *Prison Reform in Gloucestershire 1776–1820*, Phillimore, p. 44.
12. Ibid.
13. Cited in Priestley, P. (1985) *Victorian Prison Lives*, Methuen, p. 214.
14. Cited in Heidensohn, F. (1985) *Women and Crime*, Macmillan, p. 66.
15. Dobash, R. *et al.*, op. cit., p. 80. When transportation was in use, women were violently repressed. They were in the words of Robert Hughes 'the prisoners of prisoners', where degradation, violence and enforced slavery were part of their everyday lives. See Hughes, R. (1987) *The Fatal Shore*, Guild, pp. 258–64.
16. Ibid., p. 83.
17. Walkowitz, J. (1980) *Prostitution and Victorian Society*, Cambridge University Press, p. 220.
18. Ibid., p. 222.
19. Ibid., p. 221.
20. Ibid., p. 215.
21. Showalter, E. (1987) *The Female Malady*, Virago, p. 17.
22. Ibid., p. 81.
23. Ibid.
24. Griffiths, A. (1905) *Fifty Years of Public Service*, Cassell, p. 205.
25. Ibid., pp. 205–6.
26. Ibid., p. 207.
27. Ibid., p. 208.
28. Ibid., p. 209.
29. Ibid., p. 205.
30. Ibid., pp. 210–12.
31. Griffiths, A. (1884) *Memorials of Millbank and Chapters in Prison History*, Chapman Hall, pp. 117–18; p. 198.
32. Prison Matron (1864) *Female Life in Prison*, Sampson, Low & Son & Marston, p. 26.
33. Ibid., p. 102.
34. Ibid., p. 48.
35. Ibid., p. 79.
36. Ibid., p. 29.
37. Ibid., p. 72.

38. Cited in the Preface to the new edition of Prison Matron, op. cit.
39. Ibid., p. 239.
40. Ibid., p. 185.
41. Ibid., p. 264.
42. Quinton, R. F. (1910) *Crime and Criminals*, Longman Green, p. 42.
43. Ibid., pp. 138–40; p. 239.
44. Ibid., pp. 140–1.
45. Ibid., pp. 141–2.
46. *BMJ*, 7 March 1885.
47. Ibid.
48. Size, M. (1957) *Prisons I Have Known*, Allen & Unwin, pp. 38; 44; 89; 112.
49. Ibid., pp. 90–1.
50. Kelley, J. (1967) *When the Gates Shut*, Longman Green, p. 166.
51. Showalter, E., op. cit., p. 75.
52. Ibid., p. 76.
53. Ibid., p. 107.
54. Ibid.
55. Ibid.
56. Dobash, R. *et al.*, op. cit., p. 114.
57. Showalter, E., op. cit., pp. 107–8.
58. *The Lancet*, 1900, 2, p. 367.
59. Ibid.
60. *The Lancet*, 11 August 1900, p. 446.
61. Ibid.
62. *The Lancet*, 20 January 1900, p. 169.
63. *The Lancet*, 24 May 1904, p. 1477.
64. *The Lancet*, 7 May 1904, p. 1292.
65. 'The proposed sterilization of certain degenerates', *Transactions of the Medico-Legal Society*, 1904/5, 2, pp. 23–4.
66. Ibid., p. 25.
67. Ibid., p. 22 (emphasis in the original).
68. Eastlea, B. (1981) *Science and Sexual Oppression*, Weidenfeld & Nicolson, p. 160.
69. Ibid., pp. 160–1.
70. Ibid., p. 163.
71. Cited in Garland, D. (1985) *Punishment and Welfare*, Gower, p. 277.
72. *Transactions of the Medico-Legal Society*, op. cit., p. 24.
73. Simmons, H. (1978) 'Explaining social policy: the English Mental Deficiency Act of 1913', *Journal of Social History*, 11, pp. 292–4.
74. Ibid., p. 397.
75. MacKenzie, D. (1976) 'Eugenics in Britain', *Social Studies of Science*, 6, pp. 503–18.
76. Ibid., pp. 516–17.
77. Ibid., p. 522.
78. Dobash, R. *et al.*, op. cit., pp. 116–19.
79. Ibid., p. 119.
80. Rose, N. (1985) *The Psychological Complex*, Routledge & Kegan Paul, p. 52.
81. Ibid. p. 85.
82. Ibid., pp. 85–6.
83. *The Lancet*, 15 April 1905, p. 1010.

84. Rose, N., op. cit., p. 103.
85. Ibid., p. 128.
86. Sullivan, W. C. (1912) 'Feeble-mindedness and the measurement of intelligence by the method of Binet and Simon', *The Lancet*, 23 March, p. 778.
87. Sullivan, W. C. (1921) 'Crime and mental deficiency', *The Lancet*, 15 October, p. 789.
88. East, W. N. (1921) 'A case of moral imbecility', *The Lancet*, 19 November, p. 1051.
89. Ibid., p. 1056.
90. See Watson, S. (1988) *The Moral Imbecile: A Study of the Relations Between Penal Practice and Psychiatric Knowledge of the Habitual Offender*, a dissertation submitted to the University of Lancaster, January 1988, pp. 198; 297.
91. Size, M., op. cit., p. 110.
92. Cited in Camp, J. (1974) *Holloway Prison: The Place and the People*, David & Charles, p. 62.
93. Size, M., op. cit., p. 110.
94. *The Lancet*, 20 August 1904, p. 554.
95. Ibid.
96. Size, M., op. cit., pp. 110–11.
97. Ibid., p. 120.
98. *The Liverpool South West Lancashire and Wirral Discharged Prisoners' Aid Society in connection with HM Prison Liverpool*, Annual Report 1913, The Gainsboro Press, 1924, p. 3.
99. Ibid., 1916 Report, pp. 18–19.
100. *The Lancet*, 1908, 1, pp. 42–3.
101. *The Lancet*, 20 August 1904, pp. 553–4.
102. Size, M., op. cit., pp. 76–7.
103. *Public Record Office P Com 7 326* (Kew Gardens).
104. Ibid.
105. Fletcher, S. W. (1884) *Twelve Months in an English Prison*, Lee & Shepard, pp. 322–3.
106. Ibid., p. 388.
107. Maybrick, F. E. (1905) *Mrs. Maybrick's Own Story: My Fifteen Lost Years*, Funk & Wagnalls Company, p. 121.
108. Ibid., pp. 121–2.
109. Ibid., pp. 116–17.
110. Ibid., p. 126.
111. Ibid., p. 189.
112. Lytton, C. (1976) *Prisons and Prisoners: Experiences of a Suffragette*, E. P. Publishing, pp. 268–70.
113. *P.R.O. P Com 7 40 9670* (Kew Gardens).
114. Ibid.
115. Ibid.
116. *P.R.O. P Com 7 40 9670*, op. cit.
117. Ibid.
118. Cited in Heidensohn, F., op. cit., p. 66.
119. *P.R.O. HO 45 11135* (Kew Gardens).
120. Hobhouse, S. and Brockway, A. F. (1922) *English Prisons Today*, Longman, p. 339.
121. Ibid., pp. 351–2.

122. Ibid., p. 345.
123. Ibid., p. 337.
124. Ibid., pp. 345–6.
125. Cited in Camp, J., op. cit., pp. 75–6.
126. Gordon, M. (1922) *Penal Discipline*, Routledge & Kegan Paul, pp. 234–5.
127. Kennedy, L. (1988) 'Review of *Criminal Justice: The True Story of Edith Thompson* by Rene Weis', *Observer*, 17 July.
128. Weis, R. (1988) *Criminal Justice: The True Story of Edith Thompson*, Hamish Hamilton, p. 301.
129. Gordon, M., op. cit., p. 46.
130. Ibid., p. 29.
131. Ibid., p. 236 (emphasis in the original).
132. *The Lancet*, 23 September 1922, p. 664.
133. Cited in Calvert, E. R. and Calvert, T. (1933) *The Lawbreaker*, Routledge, p. 233.
134. Ibid., p. 231.
135. *P.R.O. Prison Commissioners 9 192* (Kew Gardens).
136. Ibid.
137. *P.R.O. Prison Commissioners 9 31* (Kew Gardens).
138. Dobash, R. *et al.*, op. cit., p. 120.
139. Ibid., p. 121.
140. Calvert, E. R. and Calvert, T., op. cit., p. 228.
141. Blacker, C. P. (ed.) (1937) *A Social Problem Group?*, Oxford University Press, p. 4.
142. Cited in ibid., pp. 128–50 (emphasis in the original).
143. *Report of the Commissioners of Prisons and Directors of Convict Prisons*, 1945, p. 73.
144. Ibid.
145. *RCPDCP*, 1946, p. 59.
146. *RCPDCP*, 1949, p. 125.
147. Ibid., p. 28.
148. Ibid., p. 129 (emphasis in the original).
149. *The Times*, 8 March 1952.
150. *Report of the Commissioners of Prisons* 1953, p. 58.
151. Ibid.
152. *RCP*, 1954, p. 144.
153. Ibid., p. 137.
154. *RCP*, 1953, p. 56.
155. Fox, L. (1952) *The English Prison and Borstal Systems*, Routledge & Kegan Paul, pp. 154–5 (emphasis in the original).
156. Size, M., op. cit., pp. 188–9.
157. *RCP*, 1960, p. 58.
158. Kelley, J. (1957) 'Some aspects of the work at Askham Grange Open Prison for Women', *Journal of the Medical Women's Federation*, July, p. 195.
159. *The Times*, 15 February 1947; *The Times*, 9 August 1949; *The Times*, 5 August 1949.
160. Prison Medical Reform Council (1943c) *Prison for Women: Some Accounts of Life in Holloway Prison for Women*, PMRC, pp. 18–19.
161. Ibid.
162. Ibid.
163. Ibid.

164. Henry, J. (1952) *Women in Prison*, Doubleday, pp. 54–5; 84–5.
165. Ibid., p. 86.
166. Epps, P. (1951) 'A preliminary survey of 300 female delinquents in Borstal institutions', *British Journal of Delinquency*, 1, p. 187.
167. Ibid., pp. 187–92.
168. Ibid., pp. 194–7.
169. Epps, P. and Parnell, R. W. (1952) 'Physique and temperament of women delinquents compared with women undergraduates', *British Journal of Medical Psychology*, 25, 4, p. 254.
170. Epps, P. C. (1954) 'A further survey of female delinquents undergoing Borstal training', *British Journal of Delinquency*, 4, 4, pp. 270–1.
171. *BMJ*, 14 December 1946, p. 909.
172. *BMJ*, 11 March 1950; *The Lancet*, 26 May 1951.
173. Jones, H. (1956) *Crime and the Penal System*, University Tutorial Press, p. 277.
174. *The Lancet*, 21 April 1956, pp. 96–8.
175. Marcus, B. (1958) 'A dimensional study of a prison population', *Psychologists Monograph No 2*, Office of the Chief Psychologist Prison Commission, London SW1, December, pp. 4–5.
176. *The Lancet*, 7 January 1961, p. 37.
177. *BMJ*, 30 December 1961, pp. 1752–3. Dalton's argument was supported by a letter in the *BMJ* in March 1962. It was from Nairobi. The writer pointed out that he had performed a number of necropsies on Hindu women who had committed suicide by pouring kerosene over their bodies and and setting it alight. Out of twenty-two cases, nineteen had been menstruating at the time. Additionally the writer also found the same thing in women of different races, four of whom had committed suicide by other means. All had been menstruating (*BMJ*, p. 640).
178. Woodside, M. (1962) 'Instability of women prisoners', *The Lancet*, 3 November, p. 930.
179. *RCP*, 1961, p. 51.
180. Carlen, P. and Worrall, A., op. cit., p. 4.
181. *RCP*, 1963, p. 44.
182. Kelley, J., op. cit., p. 53.
183. Ibid., p. 54.
184. Ibid., p. 125.
185. Ibid., pp. 102–3.
186. Ibid., p. 125.
187. Ibid., p. 135.
188. Ibid., p. 63.
189. Ibid., p. 75.
190. Ibid., p. 79.
191. Ibid., p. 178.
192. Ibid., p. 60.
193. Morgan, A. M. (1964) 'Women in preventive detention', *Prison Service Journal*, 4, 13, October, p. 21.
194. *RCP*, 1961, p. 97.
195. Henry, J., op. cit., pp. 65–6.
196. Buxton, J. and Turner, M. (1962) *Gate Fever*, Cresset Press, p. 58.
197. Field, X. (1963) *Under Lock and Key*, Parrish, pp. 157–62.
198. Kelley, J., op. cit., p. 104.
199. Ibid., p. 106.

200. Field, X., op. cit., p. 164.
201. Ibid., p. 163.
202. *Report of the Work of the Prison Department*, 1964, p. 39.
203. Ibid.
204. Ibid.
205. *Prison Medical Journal*, July 1965, 2, p. 23.
206. *The Times*, 11 July 1966.
207. *Memorandum submitted by Prison Medical Officers to the Royal Commission on the Penal System*, HM Prison Service Staff College Library, Wakefield, p. 1.
208. *RWPD*, 1967, p. 19.
209. Smith, A. (1965) 'Penal policy and the female offender', in P. Halmos (ed.) *Sociological Review Monograph No. 9*, University of Keele, p. 114.
210. Ibid.
211. *Minutes of the Regional Conference of Governors held at Haverigg Prison 10th June 1969*, HM Prison Service Staff College Library, Wakefield, p. 3.
212. Ibid., p. 4.
213. Dobash, R. *et al.*, op. cit., p. 127.
214. Ibid., pp. 127–9.
215. Cited in Morris, A. (1987) *Women, Crime and Criminal Justice*, Blackwell, pp. 109–10.
216. Home Office (1969) *People in Prison, England and Wales*, HMSO, pp. 61–2.
217. Camp, J., op. cit., pp. 149–51.
218. Ibid.
219. Ibid., p. 153.
220. Ibid., p. 154.
221. Smart, C. (1976) *Women, Crime and Criminology*, Routledge & Kegan Paul, pp. 144–5.
222. *BMJ*, 7 October 1972, p. 58.
223. Cited in Heidensohn, F. (1980) *Women and the Penal System*, paper presented at the Cropwood Round-Table Conference on Women and Crime 1980, pp. 6–7.
224. Ibid., p. 7.
225. Matthews, J. (1980) *Women in the Penal System*, NACRO.
226. Ibid., p. 4.
227. *H.M. Prison Holloway: Purpose and Regime PDG/77 184/177/3*, HM Prison Service Staff College Library, Wakefield, p. 2.
228. Ibid.
229. Ibid.
230. Ibid., pp. 2–3.
231. Ibid., p. 3.
232. Ibid., p. 4.
233. Cited in Padel, U. and Stevenson, P. (1988) *Insiders*, Virago, pp. 170–1.
234. *Hansard*, 6 March 1984, Col. 542.
235. *The Abolitionist*, 1984, 17, p. 18.
236. *The Abolitionist*, 1984, 16, p. 16.
237. *The Abolitionist*, 1986, 22, p. 21.
238. *The Abolitionist*, 1984, 17, p. 19.
239. Padel, U. and Stevenson, P., op. cit., p. 10.
240. Ibid., p. 38.
241. Carlen, P. (1982) 'Papa's discipline: an analysis of disciplinary modes in the Scottish women's prison', *Sociological Review*, 30, 1, pp. 119–20.

242. *Guardian*, 14 March 1983.
243. Allen, H., op. cit., p. 59 (emphasis in the original).
244. Carlen, P. (1983) *Women's Imprisonment*, Routledge & Kegan Paul, p. 210. See also Rowett, C. and Vaughan, P. (1981) 'Women and Broadmoor: treatment and control in a special hospital' in B. Hutter and G. Williams (eds) *Controlling Women*, Croom Helm, pp. 131–53.
245. For an analysis of the figures for the early 1980s, see Owen, T. and Sim, J. (1984) 'Drugs, discipline and prison medicine–the case of George Wilkinson' in P. Scraton and P. Gordon (eds) *Causes for Concern*, Penguin, pp. 228–55.
246. Carlen, P. op. cit., pp. 200–1.
247. Mandaraka-Sheppard, A. (1986) *The Dynamics of Aggression in Women's Prisons in England*, Gower, p. 208.
248. Genders, E. and Player, E. (1987) 'Women in prison: the treatment, the control and the experience' in P. Carlen and A. Worrall op. cit., p. 165.
249. See Padel, U. and Stevenson, P. op. cit., p. 58; House of Commons *Third Report from the Social Services Committee Session 1985–6*, Prison Medical Service, 2, Minutes of Evidence and Appendices, p. 93.
250. Benn, M. and Tchaikovsky, C. (1983) 'Women behind bars', *New Statesman*, 9 December 1983, p. 8.
251. Greater London Council Women's Committee (1986) *Breaking the Silence*, London Strategic Policy Unit, p. 154.
252. Ibid., p. 155.
253. *Guardian*, 12 October 1984.
254. Ibid.
255. *Guardian*, 11 November 1985.
256. *Guardian*, 22 May 1985.
257. *Observer*, 23 March 1986.
258. Ibid.
259. *Hansard*, 24 February, Col. 840.
260. Stevenson, P. 'Women in Special Hospitals', *Open Mind*, 41, October/November 1989, p. 16.
261. *Observer*, 28 May 1989.
262. Carlen, P., Hicks, J., O'Dwyer, J., Christina, D. and Tchaikovsky, C. (1985) *Criminal Women*, Polity Press, p. 188.
263. Ibid.
264. Greater London Council Women's Committee, op. cit., pp. 179–80.
265. See *The Abolitionist*, nos 17, 18, 19, 21.
266. *The Abolitionist*, 1986, 22, p. 23.
267. Ibid.
268. Carlen, P. (1985) 'Law psychiatry and women's imprisonment: a sociological view', *British Journal of Psychiatry*, 146, p. 620.

7 CONCLUSION

1. Donnelly, M. (1986) 'Foucault's genealogy of the human sciences', in M. Gane (ed.) *Towards a Critique of Foucault*, Routledge & Kegan Paul, p. 19.
2. Taussing, M. (1987) *Shamanism, Colonialism and the Wild Man: A Study in Terror and Healing*, University of Chicago Press.

3. Mullin, C. (1986) *Error of Judgement*, Chatto & Windus; Kee, R. (1986) *Trial and Error*, Hamish Hamilton; Foot, P. (1986) *Murder at the Farm*, Sidgwick & Jackson.
4. Report of the Independent Committee of Inquiry (1987) *The Roof Comes Off*, Gateway Exchange.
5. Beresford, D. (1987) *Ten Men Dead*, Grafton; Sands, B. (1983) *One Day in My Life*, Pluto.
6. Soyinka, W. (1985) *The Man Died*, Arrow.
7. Steinert, H. (1980) 'The development of "discipline" according to Michel Foucault: discourse analysis vs. social history', *Crime and Social Justice*, 20, p. 96.
8. Ibid.
9. MacKinnon, C. (1987) 'Feminism, Marxism, method and the state: towards feminist jurisprudence', in S. Harding (ed.) *Feminism and Methodology*, Open University Press, p. 136; Connell, R. W. (1987) *Gender and Power*, Polity Press, pp. 125–36.
10. Oakley, A. (1982) *Subject Women*, Fontana; Stacey, M. and Price, M. (1981) *Women, Power and Politics*, Tavistock; Spencer, A. and Podmore, D. (eds) (1987) *In a Man's World: Essays on Women in Male-Dominated Professions*, Tavistock; Sassoon, A. S. (ed.) (1987) *Women and the State*, Hutchinson.
11. Connell, R. W., op. cit., p. 130.
12. De Sousa Santos, B. (1985) 'On modes of production of law and social power', *International Journal of the Sociology of Law*, 13, p. 325.
13. Excum, W. (1986) 'Review of *Crime, Madness and Politics in Modern France: The Medical Concept of National Decline* by Robert A. Nye', *American Journal of Sociology*, 91, 2, p. 468.
14. Report by the Research and Advisory Group on the Long-Term Prison System (no date) *Special Units for Long-Term Prisoners: Regimes, Management and Research*, Home Office; *Guardian*, 14 January 1988; Williams, M. and Longley, D. (1986) *Identifying Control Problem Prisoners in Dispersal Prisons*, paper presented at 18th Cropwood Conference on Long-Term Imprisonment, University of Cambridge, 19–21 March 1986.
15. Donnelly, M., op. cit., p. 20.

Index

prisons and gaols – *cont.*
  Holloway, 55, 138, 143, 147–8, 152,
    154–5, 159, 160, 161, 163, 164-7,
    168–9, 173–4
  Hull, 107–8
  Huntingdon, 36, 51
  Illchester, 21
  Ipswich, 23
  Kirkland, 44
  Lincoln, 21
  Manchester, 48
  Millbank, 17–18, 19, 31, 35, 39, 57, 132,
    136
  New Baly, 28
  Norwich, 121
  Parkhurst, 2, 27, 91, 94–5, 105, 108, 110
  Pentonville, 38, 193
  Perth, 37
  Peterhead, 2
  Portland, 31, 39
  Portsmouth, 144
  Reading, 27, 82
  Risley, 117
  Stirling Castle, 38
  Wakefield, 35, 76, 88, 94
  Walton, 92–3, 144, 147
  Wandsworth, 28, 51, 70, 71, 124
  Wormwood Scrubs, 75–6, 88, 107, 108,
    122
Prosser, Barry, 115–16

Quinton, R. F., 42, 44, 51, 57–9, 63, 137,
  179

Radical Alternatives to Prison (RAP), 109,
  110, 112–13, 174, 175
Rampton, 88
resistance to domination, 5–7
Rich, John, 159
Roper, Dr, 76, 84
Rose, Nikolas, 142
Rose, Steven, 52
Rowbotham, Sheila, 6
Royal Portsmouth Hospital, 133
Rusche, George, 2

San Quentin, 2
Santos, Bouventura De Sousa, 181
Scott, Dr Peter, 84, 100, 101
Select Committee on Gaols (1835), 22,
  33–4
sex offenders, 111–12
Shaw, Chris, 123
Simon, John, 3
Size, Mary, 144, 155
Smalley, Dr, 66–7

Smart, Carol, 166
Smith, Ann, 164
Smith, Dr Edward, 28, 36
Smith, Roger, 41, 52
Snell, Dr Harvie, 76, 83, 101
Staker, A., 78
Steinert, Heinz, 179
sterilization, 54, 140–1
Stevenson, Prue, 170
Sullivan, Dr W. C., 143
Sutherland, Dr, 179

Taylor, Dr Charity, 138
Taylor, Laurie, 103
Tchaikovsky, Chris, 173
Thomas, J. E., 107
Thompson, Edward, 6
Thompson, Dr James, 41
Thornton, Dr, 52
Toynbee, Polly, 171, 173

Vicks, Sir Geoffrey, 92

Watson, Stephen, 63
Whitehead, Dr Tony, 114
Wilkins, Leslie, 80–1
Women in Prison (WIP), 174–5
women prisoners
  black, 125, 127
  breaking out, 134, 136
  control, 39, 43
  deaths, 48, 147–8, 173
  domesticity, 130–2, 151–2, 153–5, 161
  drugs, 113, 151, 172
  feeble-mindedness, 140
  individualization, 143, 177–8
  infantilization, 161
  medical care, 145, 149, 156–7, 162,
    169–70
  medical control, 150–1
  nature, 132–4, 137, 139
  psychiatry, 157–60, 166, 171–2, 178
  psychology, 139, 152–3, 154, 164–7
  resistance, 39, 132–5, 146, 160, 174–5
  rule infraction, 170–1
  security, 162–4, 169
  self mutilation, 136, 174
  sexuality, 130, 138, 143
  solitary confinement, 134, 136
  special hospitals, 157, 175
  strip searching, 146, 170
  surveillance, 130, 136, 143–5, 166,
    170–1
Woodside, Moya, 159

Young, Dr, 76